# Expressive Arts Therapy for T Children and Adolescents

*Expressive Arts Therapy for Traumatized Children and Adolescents* is the book so many expressive arts and trauma therapists have been waiting for. Not only does it lay out an organized, thorough framework for applying varied expressive arts modalities, but it also provides clear directions for the application of these modalities at different phases of treatment. Both beginning and experienced clinicians and students will appreciate the thoughtful analyses of ways for introducing expressive arts to clients, engaging clients with their art, being present to the art that is created, and working within a particular session structure that guides the treatment process. Readers will also receive more specific learning regarding the process of using body-focused and sensory-based language and skills in the process of trauma treatment over time. Readers will pick up more than 60 priceless expressive arts assessment and treatment interventions that are sure to serve them well for years to come. The appendices feature these interventions as photocopiable handouts that will guide the therapist working with youth through each phase of treatment.

**Carmen Richardson, MSW, RSW, RCAT, REAT,** is a registered clinician spanning three professions: clinical social work, art therapy, and expressive arts therapy. She is the founder and director of the Prairie Institute of Expressive Arts Therapy (PIEAT), where she develops professional trainings for facilitators and therapists in the field of expressive arts. She has maintained a full time private practice in Calgary for over 19 years, and she provides clinical supervision for social workers, art therapists, and expressive arts therapists.

# Expressive Arts Therapy for Traumatized Children and Adolescents

## A Four-Phase Model

Carmen Richardson,
MSW, RSW, RCAT, REAT

Routledge
Taylor & Francis Group

NEW YORK AND LONDON

First published 2016
by Routledge
711 Third Avenue, New York, NY 10017

and by Routledge
27 Church Road, Hove, East Sussex BN3 2FA

*Routledge is an imprint of the Taylor & Francis Group, an informa business*

*Library of Congress Cataloging-in-Publication Data*
Richardson, Carmen.
  Expressive arts therapy for traumatized children and adolescents : a four-phase model / by Carmen Richardson. — 1 Edition.
    pages cm
  Includes bibliographical references and index.
  1. Art therapy for children.   2. Psychic trauma in children—Treatment.   I. Title.
  RJ505.A7R53 2016
  618.92′891656—dc23
  2015007082

ISBN: 978-0-415-73377-9 (hbk)
ISBN: 978-0-415-73378-6 (pbk)
ISBN: 978-1-315-81785-9 (ebk)

Typeset in Galliard
by Apex CoVantage, LLC

To each child who taught me what it means to do brave therapy

## Tell Me, She Said

Tell me, she said:
What is the story you are telling?
What wild song is singing itself through you?

Listen:
In the silence between there is music;
In the spaces between there is story.

It is the song you are living now.
It is the story of the place where you are.
It contains the shapes of these old mountains
The green of the rhododendron leaves,
It is happening right now in your breath,
In the heartbeat still drumming the deeper
rhythm
Beneath your cracking words.

It matters what you did this morning and last
Saturday night and last year,
Not because you are important
But because you are in it and it is still moving,
We are all in this story together.

Listen:
In the silence between there is music;
In the spaces between there is story.

Pay attention:
We are listening each other into being.

*Sally Atkins*[1]


## NOTE

1. Appalachian Expressive Arts Collective. (2003). *Expressive arts therapy: Creative process in art and life.* Boone, NC: Parkway Publishers. Reprinted with permission.

# Contents

x   *Contents*

# Foreword

What I most appreciate about Carmen Richardson's presentation of this four-phase expressive arts intervention model is that it is not only a presentation of case studies to support the value of the model, but also the story of the author and her clients' journeys on untraveled paths, as unknowing individuals, never quite sure what they might discover while learning along the way how best to manage those discoveries, no matter the challenge.

*Expressive Arts Therapy for Traumatized Children: A Four-Phase Model* represents a consilience of the author's experiences with action therapies—dance, music, creative writing, poetry, drawing, play, and art—and her years of training in the use of the arts and varied modalities, including Inner Relationship Focusing, Sensorimotor Psychotherapy, and Integrative Body Psychotherapy. Her use of an intermodal approach to treatment establishes her appreciation for the reality that there is no one intervention that fits every child and the reality that at any given time, in any one session, children may need several different modalities to communicate verbally and nonverbally what matters most at that moment in time.

Although rich with creative activities, the author quickly establishes that these are not to be approached as a "recipe" of activities to pick and choose from, but as strategically placed activities to support the larger picture of helping children develop the resilience needed to experience posttraumatic growth. The structured framework helps to ensure a process that is safe, but it also provides the flexibility necessary for following the child's creative processing and use of varied activities at a pace that is safe and tolerable. Under each intervention/activity we're given the rationale for its use and the process for engaging the child in the activity. The author also provides us with several starting points based upon the number of sessions available. For example, if there are only five sessions available, safety and stabilization, including regulation, become the focus of the intervention.

What is refreshing is that prior to introducing the model, the author spends much needed time discussing the "persona" of the therapist and the many hats that need to be worn in order to bring forward aspects and dimensions of the therapist and the therapy to benefit the child. She identifies six different personas. There is the scientist, who acquires knowledge by observing responses following the exploration of different art forms with clients. The explorer has a courageous spirit for going where he has not been before. The detective is curious minded and allows children to go deeper into their subjective worlds. The magician is skilled at being playful and creative in her use of varied modalities. The curious cat is an observer first and only jumps into action when the time is right. The clown brings the element of laughter to the therapeutic process—a reminder that life is more than just the "hard stuff." The model is as much about therapists working within themselves and their relationships with art as it is about guiding the ways they assist children through the use of art.

The four phases are assessment; cultivating safety and resources; trauma processing; and reclaiming, reframing, repairing, and reorienting. The assessment phase is not about making assumptions about children based solely on their behaviors and symptoms, which are often misleading, but on using action activities and the arts to discover how they are subjectively experiencing the varied environments that they struggle daily to navigate and survive. The assessment process guides the practitioner beyond the administering of tools to the processes necessary to become deeply curious about how children see themselves, others, and the world as a result of their traumatic experiences.

Positioning the therapist as "non-knowing" is an excellent beginning, as it demands that the therapist becomes immediately curious. Hughes (2009) wrote, "When curiosity is directed toward the child's experience rather than toward the factual events in his life and when it is conveyed with both affective and reflective features, the child is likely to go with the therapist very deeply into his or her life story and experience a co-regulating of emotions related to what is being explored and the meaning given those events" (p. 169). In essence, curiosity is the cornerstone of empathy, and as such, it is essential for establishing a trauma-informed relationship.

What is so important about Phase Two is that it is not only about helping children ready themselves to safely process their trauma, but also to empower them to regulate their reactions to daily worries, fears, threats, or ongoing trauma that may yet be enduring. In this effort, the author has masterfully integrated the arts with working with the body as a wise resource. Teaching children to be attuned to their bodies and to respond to their bodies' assessments of what is or is not helping empowers children and develops the resilience needed to process their traumas in the next phase.

The author's emphasis on the body as a resource took me back to my personal experience with Dr. Alexander Lowen, the founder of Bioenergetics. My body had tightly locked away the sensations and memories of earlier traumas that cognitive processes simply could not reach or release. In one session, Dr. Lowen analyzed my body through its language—body posture, breathing, movement, rigidity, shape, and so on. He prescribed a series of body positions and activities to use to release, reveal, and then refocus my view of self and life. That process became the major turning point in my life. The body holds the key to healing, to regulating unwanted reactions, and to bringing energy and vitality to one's life. The author's incorporation of the use of the body through developmentally appropriate activities is not only essential for safely processing trauma, but also for experiencing a renewed confidence about the future. Every child deserves this gift.

One of the primary goals of trauma processing is helping survivors discover, through the wisdom of their bodies that, despite the many triggers in their environment that can remind them of their traumatic experiences, they need no longer be trapped or held hostage by those memories. In Phase Three, activities such as Surfing the Waves, My Iceberg, Pieces of My Story: Putting It All Together, Time Lines and Road Maps, and Honor and Transformation help children master their trauma memories by organizing them in meaningful ways. This helps children put the trauma in the past so they can focus on the future.

Too often, trauma processing becomes the goal of treatment rather than children learning to flourish as thrivers. In Phase Four, the author has developed a process that prepares children to go beyond processing the trauma to rediscovering the many parts that make them who they are and can become. This helps them reclaim what was lost and repair the "who" and "what" that emerge as important in their efforts to now thrive and reframe the larger picture to reorient themselves to the future.

The final activity is a celebration of the child's courage, tenacity, trust, creativity, empowerment, and mastery. It is designed as a co-celebration because both the therapist and the child have traveled an amazing journey. It is a journey Carmen Richardson has made safe, creatively inviting, and empowering for any new or seasoned therapists interested in using expressive interventions within an intermodal framework to assist traumatized children in their efforts to flourish.

William Steele, PsyD, MSW
*Founder, The National
Institute for Trauma and Loss
in Children (TLC)*

# REFERENCE

Hughes, R. (2009). Attachment focused treatment for children. In M. Kerman (Ed.), *Clinical pearls of wisdom* (pp. 169–181). New York: W. W. Norton.

# Preface

## TURTLE STORY

It was an early morning run on a beach in Mexico. There in front of me was a wee turtle struggling on her back. I stopped running and, in a moment of panic, thought, "What do I do?" In my body, I noticed such a strong pull to protect this vulnerable little creature. My instinct was to try to put her in the water. In the next moment, a woman wandered by and said, "Oh you found one!" She went on to inform me that there was a protection program for the local turtles. She told me that the best practice was to first wet your hands, then rub them with sand, and then to take the turtle to the security guard at the hotel. The hotel staff then pass them on to the protection program, which releases the turtles at night when they have the best chance for survival. During the day, the struggling infant turtles are vulnerable to the hungry birds circling above.

The following morning began with another encounter with a baby turtle flailing on its back. That morning, there was no question. I knew what to do. As I rubbed sand on my wet hands and picked it up, another woman went by and said that she had tried to put the turtle back in the water but it kept being washed back on the beach by the waves, stating, "I thought I had left it for dead." Equipped with new knowledge of the right thing to do, I eagerly shared, "You begin by wetting your hands in the water. . . ."

That morning, I began to recognize a familiarity in the strong pull in my body, the desire and natural instinct to protect, because it is a similar experience I follow every day when I engage in therapeutic work with clients. This is why I do what I do. Doing this work is not a job; rather, it is a calling from somewhere deep inside my body that invites me to follow the impulse in me to journey with others in a therapeutic way. It is a full body, mind, and heart calling.

## FOUR THINGS

These vulnerable turtles taught me four things about my work with trauma: knowing the "right thing" to do (being trauma informed) can increase confidence and passion when helping others; passing this information on to colleagues and clients can empower others; the body is a powerful informer, and the impulse in the body is a great guide; and being open to unexpected teachers enriches our learning and widens our field of knowledge.

## WHY THIS BOOK WAS WRITTEN

Having worked in the fields of social work, art therapy, and expressive arts therapy for 28 years, I felt a need for a more guided approach to working with the creative arts and trauma. I had many resources that offered creative arts interventions, but few offered guidelines on how to incorporate the creative arts in an overall framework to trauma work with children. This book was written in an effort to provide an expressive arts structured approach to trauma treatment with children.

Providing safe trauma treatment means we are trauma informed. This book is embedded in trauma-informed practices. As in the turtle story, when we know what to do, we can help others with more confidence. Being trauma informed helps guide us as therapists to know how to provide the best interventions for clients with increased assuredness. Whether we are part of a larger organization or are in private practice, we can provide trauma-informed care. Being trauma informed means understanding the impact of trauma experiences on the brain, memory, and body. It means being guided and educated on current literature to provide structured, sensory-based interventions. It also means understanding best practices for our particular client population. Educating our therapist selves by being trauma informed is one of the most empowering things we can do in our practice and to pass that learning on to our clients and colleagues. This learning can help keep our passion alive in the work.

This book was also written to contribute to the literature by providing therapists with a way of working with children that included the wisdom of the body. For me, there has always been a knowing that the body has an essential role in treating injuries of the heart, mind, and body. While talking is a part of the process, I believed that somehow the body needed to be included in this work. I just didn't know how. My first in-depth body psychotherapy training experience was a 4-year journey learning Integrative Body Psychotherapy (IBP). Core elements of body, breath, and boundary exercises provided me with a framework in which to understand how to incorporate the body in the therapy experience.

My training in art therapy and then in expressive arts therapy contributed to understanding the body's role in therapy. These creative arts experiences are body-born experiences, and every impulse to write the story, paint the image, or speak the poem has origins from deep within. We smell, taste, touch, see, and hear through the body. These sensory experiences are central to expressive arts therapy and key to healing trauma in the body. My training with the National Institute for Trauma and Loss in Children (TLC) provided a critical foundation for my work with the sensory experience of trauma and the need to provide sensory interventions to children.

Inner Relationship Focusing training has been pivotal in teaching me about mindfulness, patience, and the deep practice of learning to listen to the different parts of myself and then my clients. Focusing has been a great guide to the inner terrain of sensations and allowing the inner body experiences time to form and become known.

My most recent training in Sensorimotor Psychotherapy for trauma treatment has given me further language to explain what I often witness when working with the expressive arts, children, and trauma. It has expanded the process of how to work, in a sensory way, with the body and trauma. It has also shaped how I choose to incorporate the creative arts in trauma treatment. Each training I have taken has been a following of my own impulse within, which comes from the same impulse to want to protect the turtle, work as a therapist, expand my learning, provide responsible treatment, and, above all, to do the right thing.

## UNEXPECTED TEACHERS

As a therapist with prior trauma, I have often silently considered my personal healing journey to be a gift, a resource, to what I bring to the therapeutic relationship. Yet, there was always something seemingly taboo about discussing this topic with colleagues. It is as though we must somehow separate from, bracket out that experience, and be neutral and somewhat distant from our personal stories. Yet, inside my own body, I knew that this experience is what brings a certain depth of understanding of personal suffering that cannot be learned in books or school. Even if we do not have significant traumas in our lives, the fact of being human on this earth brings us our fair share of grief and loss. These personal experiences and stories are what bridge our lives to the lives of our clients. In this way, we can sit with others with a shared knowing of the trials we face on this journey. We are not so different. It does not mean we get tangled up in unclear boundaries or that we feel as though we know our client because we have "been there." In fact, our own stories and experiences can tell us that we need to listen first and listen last, and that we are attentive and nonjudgmental. It is how we listen, the way we are with others, the dropping into safe, silent spaces with others. We create a safe enough space for this child to bring forward her unique story so that we may come to see, from her point of view, how she has been shaped by her story.

Through training at TLC, my understanding about resilience and posttraumatic growth (PTG), in particular, deepened. I began to identify that what I was doing now, in my everyday life, with passion, was an act of PTG. It was because of my own trauma as a child and youth that I have a clear vision of moving toward working with young people. It was choosing to live in a connected way and my desire to give back and to walk alongside those who also experienced body, heart, and mind injuries as young people. While I did not have the resources to support me as a young person, it was as a young adult that I found a way to heal and truly transform my own traumas so that I was able to be with and offer clear presence to others. I love this gift. I would have it no other way. This book was born from posttraumatic growth. My own experience of trauma has, in many ways, been an unexpected teacher.

# Acknowledgments

I have a Grateful Heart for . . .

The little ones (and not-so-little ones) who have offered opportunities to help me cultivate a deeper knowing and understanding of how to be present, to listen, and to learn what worked and what didn't.

Teri Brannen Gallagher for singing "You Gotta Have Pep" whenever I needed that little push of encouragement to keep moving forward, giving perspective when I lost it, and being available to review the work as needed.

Lori Boyko for your helpful feedback, your very caring and tender heart, and our focusing partnership that nourishes me.

Lenore Mulvaney for our shared journey of doing our best, your encouragements to keep believing, and, most important, your playfulness and laughter. You inspire always.

Dan Pasley for your daily ear of the heart listening. Your feedback and support were invaluable.

Ralph, my precious husband, for your infinite presence, steadfastness, and constant, gentle care and taking care of "everything else." And I do mean everything else. You are my rock.

# Introduction

This book describes a four-phase model for using expressive arts therapy for the treatment of trauma. It was written for professionals who are working with school-age children aged 6 to 18 years. It is based on my 28 years of clinical experience with children, adolescents, and their families both in private practice and in providing assessment and treatment of child sexual abuse for Calgary and Area Child and Family Services. For simplicity's sake, I use the words *child* or *client* as inclusive of this age range. Although the interventions were designed for this age range, the language of some of the interventions will need to be modified to meet the developmental age of each child. I have also chosen to alternate the use of male and female pronouns throughout the book.

There are many examples of children's art throughout the book that the children and their guardians have graciously given permission for me to use. All names and identifying information have been changed to protect clients' identities. These children, and all the children I have journeyed with over the past 28 years, have inspired and challenged me to continue to learn from them as teachers, to listen with the ear of my heart, and to remain a playful ally in the therapeutic work.

There are three parts to this book. Part One begins with a general exploration of the field of expressive arts therapy, highlighting many of the shapers of the field as well as my own approach to an expressive arts practice. This part also explores the action and process of an expressive arts therapy framework. Part Two highlights how the experience of trauma and the practice of expressive arts fit well together. It begins with an overview of a child's experience of trauma, followed by a detailed look at how expressive arts is a resource-oriented approach to trauma. Part Three introduces the therapist to the four-phase model that includes both assessment and treatment of trauma. The four-phases are: Phase One: Understanding the Child's World; Phase Two: Cultivating Safety and Resources; Phase Three: Trauma Processing; Phase Four: Reclaiming, Reframing, Repairing, and Reorienting. The appendices include the handouts for each intervention within each phase.

This book is by no means an exhaustive exploration of body-centered psychotherapy, trauma and neurobiology, or expressive arts. If one is to truly enter into the work of the expressive arts or work from a body-centered approach, experiential training is required. Further reading into the philosophy and theory is encouraged to deepen the understanding of the work of expressive arts. The interventions that make up the four-phase model are not simply recipe-like activities to pick and choose from. They are each part of an overall process embedded in a particular way of working with the body and the arts. It is imperative that the whole book is read to have an appreciation for the intricacies of the process of this work. Readers are encouraged to take what piques their interest and delve further into these amazing fields of study.

This is a book about many things. It is about expressive arts therapy. It is about trauma and children. It is about providing sensory interventions through a structured four-phase model. Most of all, it is about working from a resource-oriented perspective. From this perspective,

I believe it should be called "Brave Therapy." My experience with young people tells me that every child who engages in this four-phase model steps into the therapeutic space with tremendous courage. Returning to the scene of the crime is no easy feat. Going there can trigger a trembling of body and mind. However, when we work with the resources that are inherent in the expressive arts process and product, and when we develop a resource-oriented attitude, we can offer a safe, structured, and thorough approach to trauma treatment. Right now, I can envision so many of the faces of these young people who have ventured on this healing path with the bravest of hearts. I have been inspired by their ability to teach me what worked for them and what didn't and showing me their forgiveness by allowing me to try again. This is humbling work. We do our best as therapists to do no harm. There are successes and challenges, and we learn from both.

Part 1

# The Expressive Arts
# Therapy Way

# 1 Expressive Arts Therapy

## THE EXPRESSIVE ARTS WAY

> Expressive arts therapy . . . is the practice of using imagery, storytelling, dance, music, drama, poetry, movement, horticulture, dreamwork, and visual arts together, in an integrated way, to foster human growth, development, and healing.
>
> Appalachian Expressive Arts Collective (2003, pp. 3–4)

Six-year-old Kali stepped into the room with art boards, paints, drums, and puppets. She looked around attentively and said, "This is a magical place." Over time, she found her own way with creative expression, following her senses; she found her unique way of demonstrating all that she needed to express. She loved to dance and knew exactly which song she wanted me to play. One day, Kali sat with the bin of puppets and, one by one, she held them and looked them deep in the eyes and asked if they needed a friend. She would turn her head, then listen to the answer the puppet would whisper in her ear. She then turned to me and shared the suffering and story of each puppet and how each needed a friend. She developed a special connection to Licorice, the stuffed kitty. Licorice helped Kali tell her story of suffering by sitting with her while she told me the details. I wrote out her story in the form of a play that Kali and Licorice later acted out. Kali painted small backdrops to each scene in her four-part play. She was engaged in full creative expression through storytelling, creative writing, visual art, and play.

Imagination was at the heart of Kali's expression. In this book "art form" and "modality" are used interchangeably. When the various art forms are used sequentially or simultaneously, full life expression and healing occur. Each art form has a unique sensory expression, such as sound, movement, or sight. They are not separate; in fact, they come to life when one art form enhances another through the imagination of the child—in this case, Kali, as actor, storyteller, and artist.

The arts have been, and continue to be, the way of life for many indigenous cultures. Rituals of dance, music, and poetry celebrate and honor traditions of burial, marriages, and other life transitions. These action therapies bring us into active involvement with the "stuff of life," including the hurts, pains, joys, and celebrations that are part of the therapeutic landscape. We may well be returning to the source of our own ancient roots as the arts are invited into the center of the psychotherapy room.

There are a variety of names to describe this work, including *expressive therapies, creative therapies, integrative therapies,* and *intermodal expressive arts.* The expressive therapies are also known as *action therapies.* Each art form, such as music, dance/movement, or drama, is a profession in its own right, and many forms have their own regulatory bodies, codes of ethics, and standards of practice. Expressive arts therapy is based upon the interrelatedness of the arts—that common ground of imagination, play, and self-expression. These self-expressions through movement, writing, and visual arts are more related than they are different. All art forms are available to the client to express himself for whatever purpose, be it to simply play, to heal, or to maintain health and vibrancy on life's journey.

The client learns to listen to the creative impulse within that may be wanting to tell her life story through music and images. This impulse asks to be known through a modality that best expresses its intention, such as the woman who grew up in silence and never knew she could speak her mind who finds her voice through spoken poetry and dramatic enactment of her own story. The expressive arts therapist guides and witnesses this process of expression and offers simple frames that may bring this seed of self-expression, this impulse, to life. This seed may blossom and grow into fruit through the use of many art forms. If we were flies on the wall of an expressive arts therapist's office, we might see some of the following: The making of masks with gypsona, dancing or moving in response to a picture painted, drumming as the client speaks a poem he just created, a group making clay fantasy creatures, family members wearing hats as they act out their family dynamics, writing stories, telling stories with puppets, listening or drawing to music, creating images in a sand tray . . . and so many more possibilities.

Although we may not produce what some would deem as gallery- or stage-worthy art or acting, we all have within us the capacity to use our voices, to create images with paint, to sound the xylophone, and to string words together to make poems. We have the ability to use language not only for meaning making, but also for creative self-expression. The arts are not available only for the gifted; they belong to all of us as individuals and communities as a means to unite, celebrate, grieve, and express all elements of human existence.

My own training in intermodal expressive arts therapy influences and guides the therapeutic model described in this book. Intermodal expressive arts is the movement from one art form to another in a single session (Knill, Barba, & Fuchs, 2004). A client may begin by painting an image, then move to writing a poem about the image, then finally, he may speak or sing the poem. As he stays in the creative world, moving from art form, to art form, transformation can be experienced. As creator of the art, the client is encouraged to be open to learning from what becomes visible, tangible, or known before him in this process. The client's art is not simply an extension of his inner world; it can be that and more. From the art expression itself, he may learn new ways of being in the world. For example, if a client has drawn an image of his memory of a traumatic event, his relationship with the memory can begin to change as he works imaginatively with the art. The expressive arts process is active and alive. There is movement and a growing relationship between the creator of the art and the art that is emerging. The client is often surprised by some element of his creation, something new and fresh that he had not recognized before. Herein lies the gift of transformation that the arts offer.

## THE PROFESSION OF EXPRESSIVE ARTS THERAPY

Expressive arts therapy is a nascent therapeutic field. The registering body, the International Expressive Arts Therapy Association (IEATA), was formed in 1994. There are many training programs internationally that offer various master's or doctoral degrees or certificates in expressive arts. IEATA's website has a list of expressive arts training programs around the world (www.ieata.ca). The IEATA code of ethics can also be found on their website.

There are two streams of expressive arts professionals as outlined by IEATA. IEATA recognizes therapists who, with the proper credentials, may register as registered expressive arts therapists (REATs) or artists/facilitators who may register as registered expressive arts consultants/educators (REACEs). How REATs and REACEs utilize the expressive arts in their work is different. The REAT utilizes the expressive arts therapy process for individual, family, or group healing that is part of the REAT's overall therapeutic work. The REACE is not necessarily a trained therapist, but may be a teacher, nurse, educator, or coach who uses the expressive arts processes for health and well-being, social action, teaching purposes, and community events or projects. IEATA acknowledges the professionalism of both streams.

## THE SHAPERS OF THE FIELD

One of the exciting elements of this profession is the unique approaches that various leaders in the field have developed in expressive arts. While there are too many to acknowledge, some key contributors to the field will be highlighted. Anna and Daria Halprin developed an approach they call the Life/Art Process that emphasizes drawing, movement, and writing (Halprin, 2003). This movement-based approach to expressive arts works with "body stories" through movement metaphors. Halprin (1999) states,

> Movement is the body's mother tongue, a powerful and universal language. Made conscious and creative, movement is a language for the body and soul to speak through, a bridge to the interior world of self and between self and the world; it is a way to build bridges and begin dialogues between the separated parts.
>
> (p. 134)

Natalie Rogers developed a person-centered process she calls the Creative Connection®, which is moving from one art form to another for healing, self-exploration, and personal growth (Rogers, 1993). The Creative Connection approach specifies that the role of the therapist is one of "being empathic, open, honest, congruent, and caring as she listens in depth and facilitates the growth of an individual or a group. This philosophy incorporates the belief that each individual has worth, dignity, and the capacity for self-direction" (Rogers, 1993, p. 3). Rogers combines her own love of the arts, influenced by her mother, who was a gifted artist, with the person-centered philosophy developed by her father, Carl Rogers. The Creative Connection philosophy is also used in groups for personal healing and social action; she has written about this extensively in her book, *The Creative Connection for Groups* (2011).

Intermodal expressive arts therapy, developed by Paolo Knill, articulates a theory drawing upon principles of polyaesthetics and crystallization theory (Knill et al., 2004). The theory of polyaesthetics is a way of understanding how all art forms are interconnected: "Roscher's theory of polyaesthetics was premised on the observation that all the art disciplines engage, to some extent, in all the sensory and communicative modalities" (Knill et al., 2004, p. 28). Crystallization theory, when applied to an expressive arts process, elucidates the unfolding of meaning and clarity that occurs as one engages in art making through the use of layering of art modalities and/or the moving from one art form to another. Imagination, ritual, and play are key elements in this approach.

Ellen and Stephen Levine have contributed significantly to the teaching and practice of expressive arts therapy and the written documentation of the practice of intermodal expressive arts in their works *Foundations of Expressive Arts Therapy* (Levine & Levine, 1999) and *Principles and Practice of Expressive Arts Therapy* (Knill, Levine, & Levine, 2005). Stephen Levine has been a primary contributor to the development of the philosophical underpinnings of expressive arts by grounding the work in the philosophies of Heidegger and Kant. Levine identifies that suffering, while part of the human condition, can be reshaped and transformed through the imagination and creativity (Levine, 1992, 2009).

Shaun McNiff has developed his own therapy of imagination, proposing that art itself is the medicine (McNiff, 1992). In this seminal work, McNiff encourages the active engagement with the imagination through whatever artistic means necessary to express and heal. McNiff advocates using multimodal approaches to engage meaningfully with what has been expressed. He emphasizes developing a relationship with the *image,* a term that not only refers to visual art images, but that is also inclusive of poems, movement, and enactments. Rather than analyzing and interpreting images, he suggests

> we meditate on them, tell stories about how we created them, speak to them, listen to what they have to say, dramatize them through our bodily movement, and dream about them. All of these methods are dedicated to the ongoing release of art's expressive medicine.

> (1992, p. 3)

McNiff further distinguishes between telling stories about the art and creating stories with the art, the latter meaning we enter into dialogues with the art. McNiff suggests that "the painting might have something to say to me, and so I take on the role of listener rather than explainer" (1992, p. 105). We are encouraged to ask the art questions about what it is feeling or needing. When we enter a relationship with art that is personified, a multitude of possibilities open before us, such as soulful connections within ourselves and between self and the art.

Another approach was developed through the collaborative work of a variety of faculty members at Appalachian State University. From this collaboration, two primary pieces of written work have evolved and contributed to the expressive arts world (Appalachian Expressive Arts Collective, 2003; Atkins & Duggins Williams, 2007). The unique perspectives emerging from this approach include an emphasis on the practitioner becoming "a theory maker as well as a toolmaker" (Atkins & Duggins Williams, 2007, p. 4). The idea is to encourage the deepening experience of the practitioner by finding his own voice, perspective, and knowing in this work. Another feature that distinguishes the Appalachian philosophy from other philosophies is the importance of the natural world as it informs and guides the creative process. Learning from the cyclical nature of the natural world teaches us about the interconnectedness of all life forms. Two other features that are specific to this expressive arts philosophy are the resources found by working with the material of dreams and the emphasis on community building.

## EXPRESSIVE ARTS THERAPY: THE PRAIRIE APPROACH

At the Prairie Institute of Expressive Arts Therapy, we work therapeutically with clients and we train students and professionals. Expressive arts therapy embraces all modalities of creativity that can be imagined by an individual or group, including movement, rhythm, writing, enactments, sound, or visual images. It is the body, mind, and soul in harmony or chaos finding a way to be witnessed, heard, healed, changed, challenged, deepened, discovered, or surrendered through a relationship between self, the arts, and the therapist/facilitator. It is active engagement with the arts incorporating the senses, the body, and intellect. Creating art is not simply a reflection of our inner states. What emerges in the artistic work has the potential to tell a new story, offer resources, or identify a fresh way of viewing an old struggle. It is this transforming potential, along with the curious attitude of the therapist/facilitator, that creates space for something new to unfold and expand.

### Body-Centered Approach

The body is comprised of complex relationships between the senses, movement, thoughts, images, behaviors, sensations, and emotions. Whether we paint, move, or create sound or music, the body is central to the experience. We begin with breath and take time to tune into and connect with the client's inside world where creativity waits to be uniquely expressed. The therapist/ facilitator consults and collaborates with the client about her inner knowing to determine if we are moving in the right direction. There is a back and forth flow between body, art, and client. We co-create an expressive arts experience that meets the goals of the client.

## Resource-Oriented Perspective

Expressive arts are natural resources for people who use, for example, dancing, painting, or writing as forms of self-expression and avenues for managing life's challenges. Further, both the process and product in expressive arts carry with them specific resources. The process of creating offers resources such as self-exploration, inspiration, and connection with the body through the imagination and senses. In turn, such resources create fresh perspectives and new ways of viewing oneself and develop new self stories. The product created in the art process can be a symbolic reminder of newfound strength or meaning that the client can integrate into his world as a resource. Finally, the therapist/facilitator is trained to adopt a mindful, resource-oriented attitude of working with expressive arts. This means we slow the process and become curious about what is unfolding in the art and body of the client, allowing integration of new information in the process. This mindful, resource-oriented perspective suggests that we pay attention to and highlight resources already used by clients and those resources that are newly unfolding in the expressive arts process.

## The Relationship With Art

The Prairie Approach promotes the notion of developing a relationship with what emerges in the art forms, to be with them as you would a friend, to pull up a chair and listen with compassionate interest to what the art is expressing or teaching. For example, if the client has written a story, she is encouraged to be curious about the story, to listen to the words and the rhythm. We invite the client to respond to the story through another art form: telling the story aloud, moving to the story, or finding the story's rhythm with the drum. Often there is something different, fresh, or new that is experienced by the client; this is described as the "surprise" or the unexpected experience of being assisted by the developing relationship with the art.

## Imagination

Our imaginations are embodied through creative expression. Imagination brings possibilities. As we engage with the arts through, for example, writing a poem, imagination expands our thinking and takes us on a journey beyond our fixed reality. This imaginative expansion assists the client in discovering creative impulses and potential resources in both the process and product of writing the poem.

## A Collaboration

The expertise of our clients is paramount. We invite their wisdom, encourage their consultation with their inner knowing, and reflect back to them how they are the expert regarding their lives. The therapist/facilitator also brings wisdom, knowing, and expertise of lived experience and professional training. The powerful worlds of both client and therapist/facilitator come together in a collaborative dance, taking turns leading and following.

## Seeds Become Blossoms, Blossoms Become Fruit

A single seed of creative expression is all that is required to begin. The simplest act of creative expression can have a very deep and profound meaning to a client. Transformation is possible from this very seed, which contains the healing properties required to blossom and ultimately transform into fruit.

## Practice Wisdom

Often, training programs ask that students leave behind what they know or suspend it for a time as they learn a new way of therapy. The Prairie Approach encourages students to bring their own wisdom and expand it by integrating the new with the old. Learning with the arts is a lifelong journey as each therapist/facilitator continues to integrate the arts with a cohesive and sound approach to assist clients. At the very core, expressive arts commands that we articulate our particular way of being an arts therapist/facilitator as we continue to discover and deepen our relationship with the arts both personally and professionally. It is in the integrative process of bringing new knowledge into one's current framework that the unique work emerges.

## REFERENCES

Appalachian Expressive Arts Collective. (2003). *Expressive arts therapy: Creative process in art and life.* Boone, NC: Parkway Publishers.

Atkins, S., & Duggins Williams, L. (2007). *Sourcebook in expressive arts therapy.* Boone, NC: Parkway Publishers.

Halprin, D. (1999). Living artfully: Movement as an integrative process. In S. Levine & E. Levine (Eds.), *Foundations of expressive arts therapy: Theoretical and clinical perspectives* (pp. 133–149). London: Jessica Kingsley.

Halprin, D. (2003). *The expressive body in life, art and therapy: Working with movement, metaphor and meaning.* London: Jessica Kingsley.

Knill, P. J., Barba, H. N., & Fuchs, M. N. (2004). *Minstrels of soul: Intermodal expressive therapy* (2nd ed.). Toronto: EGS Press.

Knill, P. J., Levine, E. G., & Levine, S. K. (2005). *Principles and practice of expressive arts therapy: Towards a therapeutic aesthetics.* London: Jessica Kingsley.

Levine, S. K. (1992). *Poiesis: The language of psychology and the speech of the soul.* London: Jessica Kingsley.

Levine, S. K. (2009). *Trauma, tragedy, therapy: The arts and human suffering.* London: Jessica Kingsley.

Levine, S. K., & Levine, E. G. (Eds.). (1999). *Foundations of expressive arts therapy: Theoretical and clinical perspectives.* London: Jessica Kingsley.

McNiff, S. (1992). *Art as medicine: Creating a therapy of the imagination.* Boston: Shambhala Publishers.

Rogers, N. (1993). *The creative connection: Expressive arts as healing.* Palo Alto, CA: Science & Behavior Books.

Rogers, N. (2011). *The creative connection for groups: Person-centered expressive arts for healing and social change.* Palo Alto, CA: Science & Behavior Books.

# 2 The Action of Expressive Arts Therapy

## AN EXPRESSIVE ARTS THERAPY FRAMEWORK

For many clients there is beauty and freedom in the creative process, while for others there can be chaos and fear. Therapists are faced with numerous decisions and questions as they invite clients to expressive arts therapy. Where do you start? What do you do with the art when it is created? What kinds of questions are appropriate? Having a clear framework to work from can provide a safe structure to work within. Once the therapist is familiar with the framework, there is room for flexibility.

## THE PERSONA OF THE THERAPIST: THE MANY HATS WE WEAR

Described in this section are six different hats therapists might wear at any given time in the therapeutic process with our clients. There are likely many more, as every therapist might identify with her own unique persona; however, these are some of the personas that frequently emerge in my work with young people. Sometimes we may wear three different hats at different times and for various reasons during a single session.

Having an awareness of the various personas can support the therapist in bringing forward aspects and dimensions of self to benefit the therapeutic work with clients. There may be particular times to call on the detective persona, when we really need to be curious and search for clues, whereas with other clients, the need for the clown is highly appropriate when play would be good therapeutic medicine.

### The Scientist

The quest of a scientist is to acquire knowledge through many means, including observation of reality. Scientists are curious and hungry for new knowledge and often desire to prove theories. Like scientists, we are interested observers, inviting our clients to experiment with new behaviors, with the arts, and with expressing themselves. Experiments are a significant part of the overall expressive arts process.

Taking on the role of the scientist can invite inquisitiveness in our young clients. Are they willing to experiment with movement or with paints? Can a client give a voice to the dinosaur he just drew? Approaching our work with a desire to discover something new can increase client motivation to experiment or try something different. There is no pressure to succeed, because it is only an experiment and the outcome is unknown. Clients are invited to do experiments at home, sometimes with the support of a caregiver, and sometimes with the intention of observing who in the family notices what they are doing.

### The Detective

Detectives are also of curious mind, asking questions and trying to find things out. They inquire, investigate, and solve crimes. As therapists, we inquire, try to find things out, and problem solve. Why are things the way they are? What contributes to this behavior or that? The hat of the detective signifies curiosity without threat.

We can be playful in these roles and invite our clients to also take on the nature of the detective: "Why don't we both put on our detective hats and see what we can find out here?" The detective hat can be useful when the therapist detects the presence of a wall (a protective defense) in the therapy process: "Hmmm, did you just notice that when we brought up the topic of divorce, you changed the subject? Let's be curious about this together. Notice what happens in your body as we even approach this subject."

### The Explorer

Explorers are often known for their courageous spirits, discovering new lands, and going where others have not gone before. Explorers are prepared to face fears and difficulties as they enter the unknown. Together with our clients, we explore what is before us in any given session. We can speak about how brave it is of our clients to move into the inner world of feelings and sensations that they perhaps know little about. They require courageous hearts to express what has not been expressed before through voice, body, and the arts. We may not know what lies ahead or what will be unearthed within, but we are prepared to take that journey together.

An aspect of the explorer is that she can see things as though for the first time and with fresh eyes. Viewing the world of our clients in this way is invaluable. Each client has a unique inner world and distinct experience of the problem. Even though we may have worked with trauma for many years, through the eyes of the explorer, we bring ever-opening minds and hearts to what is freshly before us.

### The Magician

The spirit of a magician is a person with exceptional talent and skills in a particular area. The persona of the magician is playful, mysterious, and powerful. We can adopt some of the qualities of the magician in our work, which, from time to time, comes in handy along with the magic wand that has a special place on my table in the therapy room. The energy of the magician can support the therapist by inviting clients to think about their goals and dreams and how they might bring them to fruition.

Like the magician, expressive arts therapists work in the realm of the imagination, where vision, inspiration, and creativity are alive and abundant. These qualities bring a special energy to the therapeutic work. We help to bring vision in sometimes the most tangible of ways and see possibilities of new ways of being. Inspiration is contagious, and when it is alive in the therapy room, it can invigorate both therapist and client. Creativity abounds in the world of the imagination. While we also teach skills and strategies, true transformation happens as clients engage their imagination to create art and discover resources and strategies while in the flow of the creative process. There are times when transformation happens and artistic acts of victory unfold. There are no other words but to say that something magical is transpiring right here, right now.

### The Curious Cat

One of the things I have learned from living most of my life with precious and beautiful felines is that they are observers first, until the right time arrives to take action. Therapists are also observers. We take in, notice, and pay attention, and when the time is right, we take action.

The curious cat can teach us about the importance of patience and establishing safe, committed relationships. The cat also has a way of charming itself into the lives of those around it. Like the feline, therapists do well to endear ourselves to those we work with to create safe and stable therapeutic relationships.

The energy of the curious cat makes us experts of inquisition without being intrusive or leaving our clients feeling interrogated. We find our way around sensitive matters and tough issues with an interested stance that says, "You are important. I want to understand your world but I won't push." It is with this intention that the therapist, with the assistance of the curious cat persona, moves around safely in the therapy world.

### The Clown

In life, incorporating both times of pleasure and times of work is an important balance. This combination is also required in therapy. Embracing the persona of the clown can bring play, fun, and even silliness to the therapy. Our own unique clown personas will have the opportunity to grow as we explore together with our clients ways to be playful and have fun. The energy of the clown brings much needed relief from the demanding trauma work. Laughter is as much a part of healing as crying, as it brings a discharge of energy in the body that can ground and balance both ourselves and clients in the process. Laughter can improve mood and bring a more positive attitude to the experience of trauma therapy. It is an important reminder that we are more than the trauma, and there is more to life than just the hard stuff.

## INTRODUCING THE ARTS TO CLIENTS

> *I saw myself not as an authority in expressive arts, but as a companion in the process of the client's self-discovery.* . . . . I saw my role as one of creating a trusting environment in which the client would be heard at the deepest level, and where various means of self-exploration would be available.
>
> (Rogers, 1993, p. 106)

Exploring the creative interests of our clients is as important as knowing their histories and the experiences that brought them to therapy. With younger children, there tends to be unbounded enthusiasm that leads them into the creative process. With adolescents, there is more to explore about their ideas and beliefs about creativity. Many adolescents can't wait to express through the arts, while others have come to see themselves as having no sense of creativity.

My experience with introducing expressive arts to adolescents typically goes one of three ways. One way is that they enter the therapeutic space with excitement, wholeheartedness, and a sense of relief at finally having found someone who "gets" their language. These teens can't wait to move into the action of the arts where they can express themselves in a way that feels safe, fun, and meaningful. The second way is that they stare at me blankly and say they are not creative in any way, nor are they interested. The third way is that some teens are curious about the arts but have no idea how they might use them in a therapy setting. Any way it goes, there are possibilities and openings.

### Invitations

While the four phases to treatment in this book are a sequential series of interventions, they are really "invitations" that guide the healing within an expressive arts framework. We can say, "You are invited to. . . ." or "The invitation is. . . ." Invitations imply that there is room and possibility for the client's own desired direction. While it is often difficult for children or adolescents to speak up to adults, if we use the word "invitation" and the attitude of the therapist is truly one of invitation, over time, as the therapeutic relationship develops, there is an increased chance that our clients will follow their own creative impulses.

It may seem contradictory to promote a structured approach that also invites the client to follow his own needs and impulses. It can be both. We can stay within the framework of the intervention *and* allow freedom for clients to follow their own impulses within that framework. When a client is invited to create something that shows how she has been affected by trauma, we can offer many options. She can create a dance with a specific song, write her own song, create a poem, paint an image, or act it out. There is plenty of room for client self-determination within a structured, trauma-informed, expressive arts framework.

### Personal Stories of Creativity

Each client carries within him his story about himself as a creative being. I have heard many variations of the following stories:

> I am not an artist (or poet, musician, dancer, or actor).
> My grade 4 teacher told me I couldn't draw trees the right way.
> I am not creative. My sister was the artsy one.
> What is the point? I can bang on a drum at home by myself.

These stories are met with respect and an attentive ear, but this does not mean we align with the story. We now know an aspect of the client's story, how the client has come to see herself in this creative capacity, and the perceived blocks that stand in the way of her possibly engaging therapeutically with the arts. It is now up to the therapist to find a way in, as well as to create meaningful and accessible experiences with the arts.

### Finding the Portal

It is not our work to convince our clients of their birthrights to live a creative life, or to tell them we believe all people have capacity for creativity within them. First, we hear the story with compassionate ears and heart and empathize with the client's experience. As with any aspect of therapy, our clients must feel understood as the stories of their experiences are acknowledged. Second, we can don the hat of the explorer and even the clown, and ask clients if they might be open to playfully exploring the different art modalities. Usually there is a yes to this invitation, and clients can begin to explore, with playful spirits, the different art forms. Third, clients can complete the handout, Exploring Art Modalities and Creativity Beliefs (Appendix E), which may provide hints about their potential interests that are sometimes hidden in areas of art that they don't know much about or have never had the opportunity to explore.

I have rarely met a teen who was not interested in music. Often, this is the way in. We can ask about the music he has on his phone or music he currently listens to. At this early stage it is about finding the portal, no matter how small or narrow. I am always amazed that once I find a way in, there is a relaxation that happens between myself and the client. He starts to realize and know in his body that this experience is somehow different from what he may have expected. We can do different *and* meaningful things. We can be both serious *and* invite a playful spirit.

We can also explore the various modalities together. At this stage, the goal is to build a safe therapeutic container, so we might finger paint, doodle together, or play scribble tag. Whatever the outcome, we are always assessing what is happening for our clients and looking for that spark of interest. Often clients have not had opportunities to even explore what the various modalities might be like. As we do these very important tasks of introducing our playful therapist selves along with introducing the arts, our clients may also be discovering unknown sides of themselves. This exploration and playfulness also gives the message that although clients are there because of trauma, play can be part of our work. Our clients can start to feel in their bodies that perhaps this work is tolerable, and perhaps parts of the work will even be enjoyable.

## Creating Meaningful Art Frames

Art frames are the experiences offered to our clients in the expressive arts process. Meaningful art frames meet the client where she is concerning her interests, art making ability, and connection to relevant therapeutic themes. This means that the art experiences offered meet the client in ways that are not too simple or unnecessarily complex. We run the risk of losing the client's interest if the experiences are not meaningful enough or if they are so simple that there is little to no connection with the art. Offering frames that are too difficult is often met with a feeling of overwhelm.

How do we know what frames might be too simple or too difficult? We can start with the handout Exploring Art Modalities. We can suggest to the client that we are explorers together and that our work is to find meaningful experiences with the arts. This way, we are in it together, and his opinions and ideas are important. The client will show us what he is most comfortable with. We follow his lead, and as the therapeutic relationship develops, we can invite, suggest, and challenge our client to take safe enough risks exploring various art modalities. We must also be willing to engage with the arts as we model the explorer persona that brings adventure and wonder to the process of art making.

Creating meaningful frames also means our clients will have an experience of how the arts can assist in the healing process. This reminds me of 17-year-old Natalie. She loved the arts, but she really didn't know how it could be useful therapeutically. The invitation was to create, in whatever art form she loved, something that could tell the story about why she was coming to therapy at this point in her life. She enjoyed drawing with chalk pastels, and she created a large picture in response to the invitation. As she shared her image, she spoke of the reasons why she was here. I asked if there was anything she would like to do with the image and she sat with it for a few minutes. Slowly she began to cut out pieces, asked for another paper, and began creating a new image with some of the old pieces while creating new ones as well. When she was done, I invited her to write a written response or use another modality in response to this new image. She wrote a poem. This new image and poem deepened what she knew she wanted from therapy and identified the parts of her that were already strong and powerful. These parts became newly identified resources. She was moved by this whole experience.

This experience was simple, yet meaningful, to Natalie. Now there was no question for her how the arts might assist her on her therapeutic journey, as well as how the arts could be transforming. Engaging with this art experience clarified her therapy goals and highlighted personal resources that were important to identify and claim as she began her therapeutic journey.

The expressive arts experience does not always unfold in such meaningful ways for clients, and for some, there is little interest in the creative process. However, for the interventions in this model that are designed to treat trauma, clients are encouraged to do the best they can with using the arts in some form. Engagement with the arts varies greatly for clients. For clients with less interest in the arts, there is flexibility about how frequently they engage with the arts, and there are alternatives that can be inviting. For example, using therapeutic storytelling cards (see Further Resources in Appendix J) is a very basic intervention that has the potential to bring forward personal and meaningful stories while being accessible to all ages. The gathering drum or hand drum are some of the more approachable, versatile instruments, and they have great potential to create powerful energy, to assist with telling a story, or to simply have fun with.

### Experience, Beliefs, and Permission Statements

We will inevitably hear our clients tell stories about their creative abilities. Some are stories of freedom and liberation, while others are stories of restriction and limitations. Younger children tend to be much more willing, curious, and ready to explore with the arts. While some adolescents can't wait to express through their preferred mediums, others need more meaningful invitations to play with the arts, as previously highlighted. In the beginning phase of therapy, when required, we can offer some beliefs about expressive arts and healing, some of our own experiences with the arts, and gentle permission statements that may help teens connect with their willingness to explore with the arts. We share according to need and developmental age of the client. Each of us will have our own authentic beliefs and specific experiences from which to draw.

Permission statements can be important messages to be shared with our clients. We can never know for sure what particular statement might be just the right message needed at any given point. However, for some clients, being given permission is like an invitation to explore. We can also remember to lead by example rather than only by words. Permission statements can be a portal into exploring one's creativity. The following are some examples of permission statements:

- We don't need to be artists, dancers, musicians, or actors to enjoy the benefits of playing with the arts.
- Have fun.
- Let yourself explore with things you have never even tried before.
- There is no right, wrong, or perfect way.

### Making Meaning of an Expressive Arts Work

While many art therapy educational programs have emphasized the interpretation of images, I am convinced that our nature is more about being interested and curious about imagery. This is very different from interpretation, because being interested and curious generates questions and engagement. Being an interpreter generates statements.

(Moon, 2000, p. 61)

One of the most personal and meaningful experiences we can have is expressing ourselves with the arts. Art making has the potential to be a vulnerable, raw, exquisite, heart wrenching, and playful experience. It is important to exercise caution when making meaning of a client's work. We can't assume to know what an image represents to our client. Whether it is a gesture or a visual image, we look to the creator of the art to share the meaning it holds. One youth was expressing the anger she felt related to the sexual abuse she experienced as a child. She drew an image of a rainbow. This was not a typical symbol of anger that I had witnessed over the years, and I was curious. She explained that as a child, when there was a rainbow, her parents would point it out but she couldn't see it and would feel really angry. "It is the same as the sexual abuse, it was right there in front of me but I didn't see it. No one saw it." The personal meaning of a symbol is unique to each client. I couldn't imagine what this meant to her until she shared her story of the rainbow.

In my work with adolescents in particular, I find it important to say a few things about the process of finding meaning in the expressive arts work. One teen created a clay sculpture and then turned to me and said, "Okay, now tell me what this means about me." This teen gave up her power by asking me to tell her the meaning of her art work and of her life. Another teen refused to do any art in front of me for fear that I would know things about her that she didn't want me to know. This young person felt highly vulnerable with no sense that there could be boundaries and safety in the process. Both adolescents needed information about the process of meaning making in our expressive arts work together and needed to know that boundaries are part of the process. The following are some of the statements we can use:

> I don't interpret or analyze your work. You are the creator of your work. I won't know until you tell me about your image/song/poem.
>
> We both might have ideas about what other art forms you could use to deepen or expand your experience with your art, but we always come back to what your knowing or impulse is in your body.

Younger children are typically less concerned about these issues and are more spontaneous in their creating. When talking about their art, we might say something like, "Let's explore, play with, and be curious about what you have created, like being detectives or curious cats!" However, we can also invite an intermodal movement, asking, "Is there a story that goes with that picture?"

Seven-year-old Sky lost her grandfather whom she was very close to. She had been coming to therapy for other reasons, but her grandfather died suddenly. By this time, we had a strong therapeutic connection and she loved to create art about the various things that were happening in her life as a way to express her feelings. I saw her some weeks after the funeral, acknowledged her loss, and asked if there was anything she wanted to do in her art about her grandfather. She said no, though she did want to draw. She drew a bunny in a garden (Figure 2.1). She didn't say much about it, so I asked if there was a story that went with this picture and she quite happily announced that there was.

*Figure 2.1* Sky's drawing of a bunny. Used with permission.

She wrote the following story:

> One summer day a bunny named Fluffy was hopping in a pretty garden. She saw a very beautiful flower and she wanted to pick it. Fluffy bent over to pick the flower but then the flower shouted, "Hey do not pick me!"
>
> Fluffy said, "But I would like to take you home and you could be the shiniest flower in my garden."
>
> "Okay," said the flower, "I will go home with you and I will be the shiniest flower in your garden!"
>
> One day, winter came and the flower became frozen. Fluffy went outside and saw that the flower was frozen. She felt lonely, sad, mad, and disappointed. So she went in the house and grabbed the phone and she called the flower doctor and said, "Hurry, get over here because my new flower is frozen."
>
> So, the doctor raced over to her house and the doctor said, "I will take your flower back to my house where it is nice and warm. I will bring your flower back to you in three days."
>
> Fluffy said, "Hurry," and the doctor drove off with her flower. After three days, Fluffy looked out her window and saw her flower in her pretty garden. The flower was not frozen anymore and spring came and they happily lived together in their home.
>
> The end!

Sky's experience illustrates three points about making meaning of an expressive arts work. First, moving to another art form can further the expression of the emerging story and deepen the meaning of the art to the client. I didn't need to ask about the bunny and the bunny's feelings. Rather, it was the giving of space and offering alternatives to stay in the artistic process that allowed Sky to do what she needed to do. Dealing directly with the death of her grandfather was too painful at this time. Yet, she was indirectly and metaphorically working with her grief through drawing and writing. There was a definite shift in Sky's body as she gave an enthusiastic "yes" to the invitation to write. It was like her own inner knowing was inviting her to do more art to assist her with her grieving. There appeared to be relief as she finished her story, read it aloud, and enthusiastically asked to share it with her mother.

Second, art *is* the medicine. There is little benefit to interpreting the art in this example. The process of creating the image, followed by her writing the story, supported her grief process. The act of creating can sooth the hurting heart.

Third, instead of trying to make meaning of the art, we can track the energy and movements in the body while the art is being created. Often, small shifts and changes can be observed in the client. I witnessed a sense of excitement as Sky transitioned to writing the story, followed by relief, a full bodily sigh, then a sense of completion, and a genuine liking of her own story. She seemed proud of her work. The energetic shifts and movements that are experienced in the body are another level of meaning for the client. There are times when those shifts can be worked with directly and times when they are simply allowed to be.

## ENGAGING CLIENTS WITH THEIR ART

### The First Modality: Where Do We Start?

How do we know what art form to begin with? Again, we can return to the handout, Exploring Art Modalities and Creativity Beliefs (Appendix E), to guide these early decisions. In the beginning, it is most important that safety is established in the therapeutic relationship and in the process of creating. Clients are encouraged to express themselves in ways that are most meaningful, beginning with whatever art form they choose, as this is likely the safest choice.

As safety is established, felt, and experienced in the bodies of our clients, other less familiar art modalities can be explored by forming simple frames that can be easily experienced. Experimenting with unfamiliar modalities has the potential to bring unknown material to the surface or can identify and develop new personal resources that can be of assistance to our clients.

## The Rite of Passage

What do we do now that we are present with our client and his art? We can check in with the client and invite him to express what he is experiencing or knowing at this point in terms of sensations, thoughts, or feelings. As we stay with what is happening within, we might ask, "How was that?" This open, simple question takes us to the process of the experience. If the client has a hard time articulating a response after space is given to explore within himself, tentative observations can be offered. We might say, "I noticed you seemed to be rather quiet after you drummed. What did you notice?" Often, clients will share very quickly whether our observations fit or not.

Typically, after completing the first art modality, the creator of the art has a need to share about the process of creating this piece or the meaning it has with very little prompting. He may need to share why he chose this color or the surprise that happened in the process. This process is what McNiff calls *creation stories*. He further explains, "Telling creation stories is the *rite de passage* that initiates outsiders into the inner context of the image" (1992, p. 100). Leaving space for the creation story can be an important step before moving on to the next modality. The creation story further establishes the relationship between client and his art and invites the therapist into the inner world of the client's art.

## The Second Modality

We have now crossed the rite of passage and our client has shared what she wanted and needed to about the process of creating her first work of art. We may have also explored questions that helped our client connect to particular aspects of creating. We are ready to invite engagement in a second art experience.

First, the most respectful path is to check in with our client. Have her consult with what she might already know or have an impulse or curiosity to do. Inviting our client first to check in with herself and her inner world supports her developing relationship with self, as well as her art. We want to know her thoughts, feelings, and sensations that can act as guides to help her move into a second modality assisted by some of the questions in Appendix I. She is encouraged to stay close to what she notices inside; nothing is too small to follow.

We can say some variation of the following: "You might check in with yourself and see if there is any impulse to do something with or to your poem (image, etc.)." We wait to see what happens with this invitation. If there is a genuine impulse, we have allowed the space for it to arrive. Sometimes, it is beneficial to offer a menu of options that also give permission: "You might want to cut out parts, add to the image, play the drum, or give the sculpture a voice." This menu is offered based on knowing the client, his therapeutic needs, and being curious about what this art piece is "asking" for. For example, if the art piece is a head with an open mouth, we might be curious about that and offer alternatives for the art piece to speak or have a voice.

Impulse is often associated with being impulsive, which tends to have a negative connotation with words like reckless, careless, or hasty. However, the impulse that is associated with creativity is a bodily knowing, urge, or desire to act on what arises from instinct rather than cognition. *Impetus* is another word that closely connects with this urge to move forward to create something new and perhaps unknown. If we work with the body and slow the process down, we will more likely connect with what the body already knows it needs to do.

Eva had completed many paintings, poems, and other art expressions during our 8 months together. When we had all her creations displayed, I asked if there was something she would like to do with them. Without hesitation she said yes, and she began ripping small pieces out of certain images. She then made a mobile out of these pieces and wrote a poem in response to her new mobile. Eva followed her own creative impulse, and almost without thinking, she began creating.

In the creative work, it seems that impulse and imagination are sisters. Imagination is the part of the mind that can envision things. Impulse is the body's drive to act with creative intention. If we encourage, acknowledge, and create space for the impulse, we allow imagination and impulse to take form in a creative act.

Second, if the client is uncertain about what to do next, look to the client's art that is already telling a story. Staying present with the art, which also means staying present to the client, we take the time to listen to what this art work is potentially asking for. Our client is guided back to his art and together we become detectives, curious about the work and what might be needed to further articulate this unfolding story.

This happened with 14-year-old Meagan. She had taken much time to paint the image of the impact that abuse had on her world. When asked if there was any impulse or desire to move to a second modality, nothing was coming to her. So together, we became curious about her painting. As we wondered out loud about her story, I asked what she was noticing in her body as she looked at her painting. Right away she said she felt a tightening in her throat and suddenly noticed how silent her image felt to her. In that moment, she scanned the room and saw several drums on the floor. She immediately went over and selected the hand drum, sounded it, and smiled as she heard the deep resonant tone. Then, walking very slowly toward her image, her eyes lowered, and she played the drum, first softly, then loudly, then softly again. She stood in quiet stillness for some time, then whispered, "That tells the story. That is the voice."

Third, the therapist may have an inkling about how moving to a particular modality might further the client's therapeutic goal or strengthen his relationship with the art. There are times when we can wonder out loud with our client about various possibilities when he is asking for guidance. This wondering aloud is not a demand; rather, it is an invitation that the client either connects with or leaves. These invitations are quite simple and basic, as noted earlier with Sky when I wondered if there is a story that went with her picture. I could also have wondered if she would like to act out her story with puppets, hats, and props.

Moving to a second modality is also known as *working intermodally*. Intermodal movement encourages a deepening relationship between the client and her art. In this way, as our client stays in the creative process, the meaning of the work or play becomes clearer. The refining process or clarity of meaning that is experienced is referred to as the *crystallization* process (Knill, Levine, & Levine, 2005, p. 123). This metaphor is used as a way of understanding what happens in the expressive arts process. The longer we stay in the process of creating using various modalities, the meaning of the art work becomes clearer and we have the potential to learn something new from the experience. Moving from one art form to another gives the meaning more opportunity to be crystallized. Therapists encourage clients to move to other art modalities to expand their range of experiences and knowing with their art.

## THE ART OF QUESTIONS

Questions are part of most therapeutic methods. The kind of questions, the timing, and the purpose of the questions are determined, in part, by the theoretical foundation of the therapist. There are a wide range of approaches to art therapy, including psychodynamic, humanistic, systemic, psychoeducational, and integrative approaches (Rubin, 2001). Each approach has varying ideas and beliefs about the manner in which questions are utilized in the therapeutic process. Regardless of what theory guides our work, it is important to be mindful about the questions themselves. Cornell (2013) writes,

> Many of us are used to asking questions to invite the other person to say more. But questions are not necessarily the most facilitative way to do this, and their use in some circumstances can block avenues that would otherwise open. Asking questions can be helpful, so we are not against all questions, but they need to be used consciously, with awareness of their impact.

(p. 77)

Cornell advises to use what she calls "cushioned suggestions" (p. 79). Instead of asking directly how something feels in the body, she suggests inviting the client to take some time to stay with what he is sensing or knowing in his body. Cornell offers a variety of suggestions or prompts that can guide the therapist with being more mindful about the kinds of questions that open one up to the inner world and the kinds of questions that bring clients out of their bodily experiences. Keeping in mind the developmental age of the client, our goal is to ask questions that open children to their art and to the inner worlds experienced of their bodies.

**Questions for Further Exploration**

Once the client has shared her "creation story," that is, the story about the process of creating and about the meaning of her work (if she chooses to), we might explore the art in a way that helps the client discover what is not yet known. To do this, we can ask questions that contact different aspects of the poem, the song, or the collage. First, we can begin by being curious about the process of creating. Although the client may have already shared about some aspects of the process, there may be other parts of the process that we have taken note of and are curious about. We can ask, "What part of the process was most difficult, emotional, or fun for you?" Second, we can ask questions directly about the art: "What are you most drawn to or curious about? If you could step inside the world of your image, what might you hear, see, or touch?" Third, we can ask questions that contact the experience in the body as the client is present with his art work: "What are you noticing right now in your body as you look at your image, or as you read your words, or as you play the drum?"

Fourth, we can contact feelings about the client's art: "Is there a feeling that goes with the song?" Fifth, we can contact the relationship between the art and the client and/or the therapist: "How is it for you that I am witnessing your dance, your poem, your painting?"

Asking these kind of questions can potentially open up places for further exploration. Clients often hear and sense their own knowing of what to do next if we slow the process and ask curious questions. See Appendix I for further questions for exploration.

## EXPERIMENTS

When it is not clear what modality might be useful, we can call upon the energy of the scientist persona. Engaging in experiments can be an interesting process without attaching meaning to the outcome or product. These experiments tend to spring up spontaneously, often in response to what is happening in the body of the client, in the art, and in the relationship between the two. Experiments are as many and varied as the clients and therapists themselves. We might say to the client, "I have an idea that we could experiment with. I am not sure what will happen, but just check inside to see if it is something you would be willing to try."

One particular type of experiment is with magnification. There are times when the client is sharing that something in particular stands out in her art. This can happen with most modalities including visual art, creative writing, dramatic enactment, music, or movement. We could use a mat for a frame or a picture frame that could be held up to the art or used symbolically depending on the fit with the modality. We can wonder out loud about framing or magnifying a certain section of the image, the poem, or the dance and invite the client to become curious about it as well.

I recall 9-year-old Jennifer, who came to therapy due to physically not feeling well. Even though she had been to her family physician and several specialists, nothing was found to be wrong. Her family physician suspected there may be an emotional component to her feeling sick. One of the first images Jennifer painted was of a stomach with all the complexities of feeling sick in her belly. I took out the picture frame and became curious about what we might find if we went deep into the stomach to really see what was going on inside that was making her sick. Jennifer magnified the framed section of her image by creating a second image that showed all these little people inside fighting and doing damage to her body. She started to cry as she shared the stress of going between two homes because her parents divorced, and she discussed how very sad she felt when each parent spoke poorly of the other. Jennifer identified feeling extremely trapped and unable to tell either parent how she felt.

Experiments can be shaped for any modality. We can experiment with voice by having clients speak their poems or stories, or we can experiment with making larger movements in the dance, using more or less space in the movement or gesture. There are no limits to what can be experimented with using the various art forms and sensory modalities.

## ARTISTIC ACTS OF VICTORY

Sensorimotor psychotherapy (Ogden, Minton, & Pain, 2006) is founded partly on the early work of French psychologist Pierre Janet, who used a somatic approach for the treatment of dissociation and trauma. One aspect of his work highlights an innate body process he called an "act of triumph" (p. 187). At the time of trauma, the body can become frozen and unable to engage in effective defensive actions. The act of triumph is when a person completes a physical body defensive action that couldn't be completed at the time of trauma but is experienced in the present as empowering. There is a noted shift in energy in the person who completes the act of triumph.

There is a similar body/art process that can be witnessed in the creative work of our clients. While it is not a physical defensive action, it is an energetic transformation directly related to the movement from being stuck in some part of the trauma experience to finding some freedom. For example, when a client completes a work of art that illustrates some aspect of the trauma, there is often a sense of heaviness or even dread that is experienced in the body as he speaks about the art. What happens next is sometimes spontaneous, or it follows from the invitation to check in with his body. The invitation is to first notice and explore what is happening in the inside world of feelings and sensations. Next, the client is asked if he has any impulse to do something to the art (e.g., add to or change the art in some form). Often the client will notice the impulse—the body wanting to do something different and change the art. The energy shifts as the client changes and works with the art or follows it with another form of art. This is like a releasing of energy that was not released at the time of trauma but is used now in an energizing and empowering way through the client's art. The client discovers a new strength or rediscovers a resource that he had forgotten existed within himself. Crenshaw (2006) described this well: "These are empowering and corrective actions that the child can enact in a symbolic realm, thereby overcoming the physiologically frozen state that has persisted long after the events have passed" (p. 34).

Van der Kolk (2002) wrote, "performing the actions that would have overcome one's sense of helplessness at the time of the experience that became traumatic and expressing the sensations associated with the memory of trauma effectively helps people overcome their traumas"

(p. 62). This is, in essence, what happens as a client initially senses the helplessness, then takes action in the art that moves him into a state of empowerment.

These artistic acts could be described as acts of victory, mastery, or joy because they bring out a newfound energy, strength, and cognitive awareness in the client. The client's energy visibly shifts. When the energy shift occurs, take the time to experience what has just happened. We might slow things down, acknowledge the behavior or act we have just witnessed, and stay with what has just happened—in a sense, frame the experience. First, we notice this change and what it means to both of us to witness this in the art. Clients are encouraged to pay attention to what it is like for them to notice the victory, and then what it is like to have another person witness and acknowledge their victory. We might amplify the experience by encouraging our clients to notice the sensations associated with the victory, then expand the sensations by staying with them. Clients are taught to delight in the positive experience and allow it space and time to really be felt to its fullest extent. These skills will be more fully explored in Chapter 4 and are highlighted in the example below.

**Example of an Artistic Act of Victory**

Fourteen-year-old Conor created an image by painting his fear about working through the sexual abuse he experienced throughout his young life by a family member (Figure 2.2). He appeared both sullen and agitated as he painted. He was then invited to create a written response to the image.

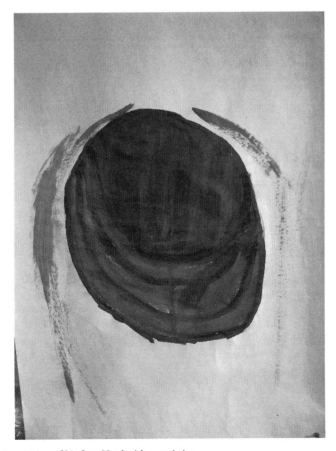

*Figure 2.2* Conor's painting of his fear. Used with permission.

The following poem was written in response to his painting:

> The Hole: This is the hole that has taken his toll, eating everything possible. He is dark and scary with no bottom, an endless pit is what he is. When you see him your vision starts to fizz. Nervousness is what you feel, will you be his next meal? He is hungry and drooling, a sign oh so grueling. You hope he passes by not looking at your eyes. Just go away is what you want to say, but you can't, you just sit there and pant, hoping he will miss you on his evil rant. He is as dark as night, he causes a fright. He has no soul, his heart is heavy and thick as coal.

As we checked in about his inner world experience following the completion of the painting and the poem, Conor noted his heart rate had increased, he was sweating, and his hands trembled. He stayed with the trembling, giving it space until it dissipated. At that point, I asked him, "Is there something you would like to do with this image, like add to it, cut parts, or redo aspects?" He checked in with himself and immediately responded with "yes!" He went back to his image, but this time with a very different energy, one of determination and certainty. He added a flashlight and mouse to the picture (Figure 2.3), then added the following lines to his poem:

> But his scariness has gone away, you found a flashlight and threw it inside and it is just a rodent not an opponent. So don't be scared for the endless pit is just a little hole.

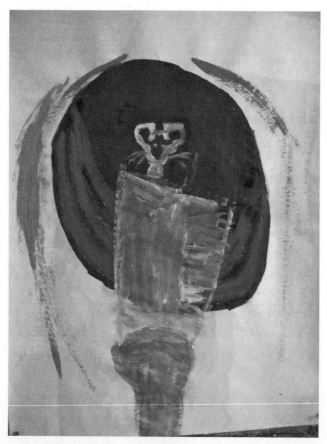

*Figure 2.3* Conor's altered painting. Used with permission.

Checking again with his inside world, Conor noted that not only had the shaking and fear gone away, but he felt his body posture shift. He was sitting taller, he had a smile on his face, and he reported feeling empowered by his ability to write and speak this poem. After the session, this young fellow literally skipped down the stairs, singing, "I am a poet and didn't know it!"

Initially, Conor felt immobilized by his fear of dealing with the sexual abuse trauma, similar to the fear he felt while the abuse was happening. As he found the courage to face his fear of the unknown—addressing the sexual abuse in therapy—Conor learned to tolerate, in small doses, his inner sensations of fear. He began to recognize his ability to stand up to fear, transform it in the art, and then experience the inner body sensations shift from fear to empowerment. This was a beautiful act of victory and mastery. I found it particularly moving to witness this 14-year-old boy experiencing his own power and his body's natural ability to shift from a frozen state of fear to taking action from his place of power. Conor reconnected with his self-confidence and reported feeling tremendous satisfaction while engaging with the arts. At the time of trauma, Conor experienced a complete sense of helplessness and immobilization. He described being unable to ask for help and unable to stop what was happening. In working with the art, Conor experienced sensations, feelings, and behaviors that both mobilized the energy and power he needed to keep himself safe in the world, and he helped himself heal from the effects of the sexual abuse.

Prior to closing this session, Conor and I reviewed what we both witnessed in the session and identified what he could take with him to manage the fears he sometimes experienced in his day-to-day life. What he identified as most valuable was his need to keep perspective, and he identified his "take away" was his ability "to look fear in the eye and see it for what it is." Conor wrote these words on paper and was encouraged to read these words and practice this kind of perspective-taking when needed.

Two processes supported Conor in experiencing this artistic act of victory. First, the intermodal process, moving from painting to writing, helped him stay in the art, allowing something new to emerge. The second process was inviting Conor to check in with his own impulse to do something with the image. As he did, Conor discovered his own resources, which ultimately assisted him with learning strategies to solve problems. His ability to face his fears was now anchored in his body in a sensory way. He was now in a more empowered position to deal with the next phase of therapy, which was processing the trauma story.

The handout Acts of Victory and Mastery (Appendix B) can be used to track these inspiring acts of empowerment. As we keep track of these acts, our clients start to see and build on tangible and concrete evidence of their strengths and resources.

## THE VOICE: BREATHING LIFE INTO WORDS

At the very heart of relational trauma is the lack of regard for the child's being. A client being seen and being heard are part of the healing experiences offered in therapeutic relationships. The voice is literally our way of being heard in the world, and it carries so many meanings on so many levels. Our voice connects us to relationships; it is the vehicle through which we know and are known by others. The voice can be soft, loud, tentative, confident. It is a special instrument of the body, and like the body, it is often not acknowledged or worked with in therapy. From a body-centered expressive arts approach to therapy, paying attention to the voice has the potential to offer meaningful directions and areas of exploration. We have opportunities to invite our clients to work with their voices when it comes to reading their written works. It is one thing for a client to write a response, and it is another experience to invite her to read her work. The invitation to use the voice is part of intermodal work, moving from writing to speaking. Using the voice is an opportunity to bring the written work to life. It is also an opportunity to be heard.

When a youth responds in writing, he is typically less eager to read it aloud and the invitation to speak can be met with hesitation. The word *hesitation* rather than *resistance* is used because the latter implies refusal. What is often witnessed is more of a hesitation to move forward, like a twinge of something in the client that is stopping the process of speaking. Hesitation implies a pausing, with the possibility and likelihood of moving forward with action. If we view the experience as hesitation, we don't have to agree that the client not read his work or take over and read it for him. Rather, we slow down, become curious, and create space to explore the experience around the hesitation.

There is a therapeutic decision to now make: either stay with the hesitation and the experience in the body, or explore alternatives to reading the work. It is difficult to predict what direction to take because each situation is unique. Often, simply naming the hesitation provides enough acknowledgment and permission for the client to speak the written work. If it is a strong hesitation, it may be important to work with the experience in the body, leaving aside the reading for now and tending to the sensations, thoughts, and feelings of the client surrounding the hesitation. The process may unfold something like this:

1.  Invite mindful presence of what the client is noticing as she thinks about trying to speak her words.
2.  If she is having difficulty sensing or noticing, give sensation options (e.g., it might feel tight, like butterflies, or tingly) or offer feeling or thought options.
3.  Ask what happens if we just hang out with this tightness (or whatever sensation the client describes).
4.  Invite being curious about what happens when we are just present with the sensation. If it is too activating, we work to reground; if it is more curious and playful, we can explore until it has shifted and we return to the possibility of speaking.
5.  Once the hesitation is fully explored, we can return to the invitation to read the work. If it continues to be difficult, we can experiment with alternatives, asking:
    *   What if you just start with the first line?
    *   What if I turn away and you read, even just the first line?
    *   What if we alternate speaking lines?
    *   What if I read it first and then you read it?

In my mind's eye, I carry so many poignant stories of young people struggling to find the breath to bring their words forward—the moments of hesitation that finally give way to the freedom of breathing out the words so in need of being spoken and heard. I will share the story of 14-year-old Nicole, who was sexually abused by two males in her family, including her stepfather. She was also betrayed by her mother who did not believe it happened. This story is less about the hesitations and more about a distillation process of continuing to find just the right words to capture the essence of her story, followed by experimenting with speaking her words and how the therapist can join in to support the process.

We were working on acknowledging the impact that the multiple betrayals and perpetrators had on her life. Nicole began by painting an image that captured the "rage" of her betrayals. She then wrote a poem in response to her picture with the prompt "I hate. . . ." Next, she circled the words or phrases in her poem that really captured her rage. She took those words and wrote another poem. She again highlighted the main words, some of which included "anger inside of me," "second best," "loneliness," "tears," and "afraid of you." From these words she chose the line that captured the essence of her rage: "second best." We then played with speaking her words. She would read a line and I would repeat the phrase "second best" at the end of the line until we were done with the poem. Next, I read the poem and she spoke the words "second best" after each line. It was here that the intensity rose; she found the place inside her where she was able to express—through the distillation of her words, speaking her voice, sensing in her body—the deep feeling of "second best." Tears were now streaming down both our cheeks, acknowledging, without words, the experience of the multiple betrayals by those closest in her life. After a few minutes of silence, Nicole looked me directly in the eyes and said, "That was the first time I have ever felt this heard."

## WISE WITNESS

In the field of expressive therapies, the therapist is in the role of witness by virtue of being in the presence of clients, their art, and their process of creating art. The therapist is witness to this person, his particular way of creating, his form of expression, and that which he is bringing into the world through his art. Then there is the action of being witness—that is, how the therapist embodies the role of witness. This is the way of the wise witness. One is not typically born a wise witness, but rather is shaped. We are shaped by our experiences on both personal and professional journeys. We are taught along the way through books and trainings, but most importantly, we learn from those we journey with in a therapeutic way. We may not have a map or plan because each person and situation is unique, but over the years, as we walk a broader terrain with our clients, we learn also to be the guide. Being the guide is an aspect of the wise witness that can, when needed, show the way when our client is stuck or is needing direction.

Many years ago, as I was learning about this embodiment of therapist as witness, I learned an important lesson. I was witnessing my 16-year-old client finish her first painting. As she slipped her last paintbrush into the bucket of water, we both stood before her image. Trying to do the right thing by being a good witness, I began checking in with her about her painting, being curious about different aspects of her image. I noticed a reticence about her as my words were coming out of my mouth. I stopped speaking. She then let me know that talking about her image disrupted her inner experience with her art. She taught me that what she needed was for the two of us to sit in chairs in front of her work and offer a time of silence. This became our practice. After each painting, we would sit together and offer respect through silence. This was a key learning experience for me. Although this does not mean all clients need silence, it means that I check in with each person about what might be the most respectful way of being with them and their art.

The action of being a wise witness to art making of any kind is a full body experience on the part of the therapist. The therapist is fully present and ready to support, engage, and listen in whatever way the client needs. It is a way of knowing when to step in, when to wait, when to speak, or when to remain silent. It is not unlike other therapeutic approaches of paying attention and being ready to intervene as needed. What makes the expressive arts experience unique is the relationship we have of being witness not only to the client but to the art that is emerging and unfolding right before our eyes.

Being wise witness means we have a responsibility to create meaningful experiences for our clients. Levine (2009) suggests that it is the therapist's responsibility

> to help shape the session so that the client herself has the experience of something that affects her. . . . The therapist's role is to make sure that the client has a "poetic" experience, one in which she has a sense of her own formative powers.

> (p. 167)

In addition to shaping the session, there are times when we are invited to be actively involved in the art making with our client. At other times, we model what we are asking of our client by offering a gesture or movement in response to his painting or showing what we mean by modeling the use of our bodies in the session. We offer to shadow the dance or movement or identify what kind of support the client would find helpful. Being a wise witness is a full body, mind, and heart experience.

As wise witnesses, we pay attention to the relationships that are forming between self and client, between client and his art, and between self and the art. We adopt the attitude of curiosity, paying attention to body, emotions, and thoughts within self and client, and finally, we form statements and questions that may further the therapy process, or we simply offer presence through silence. We create a holding space for all of this as we aim to embody the role of wise witness.

We respond in kind to the art making experience of our client. Creating art responses is a powerful way to witness and is discussed further below.

## ART RESPONSES

### Aesthetics at the Heart

Over the years, I have witnessed many images, dances, and spoken or written poems that I have felt personally connected to and deeply moved by. It is from this place of being moved that an art response is created (Atkins & Duggins Williams, 2007; Knill, Barba, & Fuchs, 2004; Knill et al., 2005), or as stated by Levine, "my own experience of your story is given imaginative elaboration." (Knill et al., 2005, p. 68). The art response or "aesthetic response," as described in detail in Knill et al. (2004), is created from a whole-body experience of being present with our clients, their works of art, and the unfolding process of healing. It is also from this compassionate place of witnessing, this unfolding, that the therapist creates a heartfelt artistic response in whatever art form the therapist chooses.

In more traditional therapies, we are often taught to be neutral observers and to remain emotionally distant from our clients. In all therapeutic relationships there are ethical guidelines that are in place to ensure boundaries are maintained in the client–therapist relationship. The expressive arts field is no different concerning the need to be guided by ethical and professional boundaries. To be clear, an art response is not an interpretation of what the client has created or is trying to convey, nor is it motivated by a need for the therapist to have a cathartic experience or to share what she thinks the client needs to hear. The art response serves as a way to strengthen the client–therapist relationship through an authentic artistic response by the therapist to her client. This is an artistic offering to the client that speaks through the connection between therapist and client. When an art response is done well, there is potential for the client and therapist to sense increased attunement in the therapeutic relationship. The client can experience a true sense of being seen and heard, increasing feelings of connection.

When creating an art response, we are mindful about what we are offering and why. The art response has the potential to be a profound offering of affirmation that says, "I see you and I hear you."

### Crafting an Art Response

Our responses are as unique as we are. We might use parallel art with our client. For example, if the client has brought to life and given voice to a puppet he has just created, I, too, may use improvisation with a puppet as my art response. The essential ingredient to creating a meaningful art response is authenticity. Trusting the impulse and the process helps the therapist stay true to the meaning and purpose of the art response.

Simplicity is key not only due to time considerations, but also to model that art responses need not be big productions, but rather are simple acts of acknowledgment. One of my favorite art responses is the collecting of my client's words as he speaks about his art or the things he is learning or noticing throughout the session. I then take these words and offer them back in some poetic spoken and/or written form toward the end of the session.

## WHEN TO USE AN ART RESPONSE

There are times in the therapeutic process when something out of the ordinary captures the attention of the therapist. It might be in response to an emotionally charged experience in therapy or at a time when the therapist feels the need to acknowledge something the client has done or accomplished. Other occasions may also call for an art response, such as the closing of the therapy relationship.

There is careful consideration regarding the timing for the creating and sharing of the art response. The therapist is always mindful about putting the client's needs first. If timing is appropriate, when the impulse to create an art response is present, the therapist might let the client know that she needs a few minutes to respond. The therapist can create the art while the client is working on his own art. There are times when completing the art response in the moment will have the most impact on the client. Alternately, the therapist may complete the art response after the session and offer it at the following meeting.

### When the Therapist Is Moved

Working therapeutically with children and adolescents is one of the most meaningful, fulfilling, and rewarding professions. Working authentically with young people means that we will be moved by their experiences. We are affected by their actions and their abilities to heal and grow from some very devastating experiences. Sometimes the art response can be a way of showing the client how she has influenced me, the therapist. Figure 2.4 is an art response that focuses on the power of the client's voice and the inspiration she can be to others.

### As a Symbol of Hope

Hope is an important message, especially when working with trauma. Yet how it is delivered takes much thought and care and a high degree of sensitivity. Crenshaw (2006) acknowledges that "one of the most delicate of all therapeutic operations is facilitating hope without leaving the person feeling that you have trivialized his despair, hopelessness, pain, sorrow, or trauma" (p. 36). This delicate balance of honoring the suffering while instilling hope and possibilities

*Figure 2.4* My drawing of an art response.

*Figure 2.5* My drawing of an art response reflecting the hope I carry for my client.

for change is essential. There are times when it is difficult for a client to maintain her own hope during the process of therapy. It can be useful to share an art response that is a symbol of the hope that healing is possible while still acknowledging the depth of the suffering. This kind of art response (Figure 2.5) demonstrates how the therapist carries the hope until the client is able to hold or discover it for herself. The therapist is guided by the belief that "hope is a powerful antidote to the helplessness and despair associated with many major traumas and losses . . . the installation of hope is a powerful therapeutic action" (Briere & Scott, 2006, p. 70).

### A Show of Empathy: I See You. I Hear You. I Am With You.

Empathy is our ability as therapists to show we understand the feelings that our clients are experiencing. Showing empathy through art can speak volumes. Even a small gesture of the therapist touching his heart with his hand can convey the meaning that "I am feeling something of what you are feeling. I see you and your pain. I am with you in this." This offering of an art response through gesture can have the powerful effect of mirroring the client's inner experience, and it creates within the therapeutic relationship a true sense of attunement, "feeling felt" (Siegel, 2010, p. 10), seen, heard, and/or known.

### Closing Rituals

An art response can be a meaningful way to honor the therapeutic relationship when closing. The therapist can create art that symbolizes gratitude for the relationship with the client, acknowledgment of therapy closing, and well wishes for the future. Another way the art response could be used at the end of the therapy process is to display all the client's art work in the room and have both the therapist and the client create an art response to the process of therapy over time. This is called an *art review,* and it is further described in Chapter 9.

   The following is my written art response to a young person's closure art:

#### She Sees

She sees hearts in full bloom
she sees her bold movement reaching for life

she weaves trust and confidence throughout the pages of her life
she plays, she dreams, she laughs
she is prosperity, full and rich and alive
she is health and balanced and wise
she is. . . .

A review of client art at the end of therapy supports the termination process and can help synthesize the therapeutic experience. There are many prompts that could be useful to guide the client and therapist with creating art in the termination process, such as:

Using any art modality, create a response of the impact that therapy has had on you.
As you lay out all your art, what strikes you most about this whole process?

For younger children, the following prompts could be used:

Create art that shows how coming here has helped you.
If you could do anything with all the art you have created, what would you like to do?

## INVITING OTHERS TO CREATE AN ART RESPONSE

Family members, group members, or other supportive people in the client's life can create art responses. Clients themselves can create art responses as identified above under Closing Rituals. It is important that others, if invited, understand the purpose and meaning of the art response. Many family members have been invited to respond to their children's art through art rather than through only verbal responses. In group therapy, group members are taught and encouraged to create art responses.

### Caregivers

When working with both caregiver and child, the caregiver can be invited to be present to the story of their child by creating an art response about what the child is sharing rather than responding by talking. This kind of art response tends to slow down the exchange between caregiver and child. The slowing down can be particularly useful when it is emotionally charged material that the child is sharing, thus allowing the caregiver time for her art response to be presented in a mindful and meaningful manner. It also allows the child to be seen and heard in his own artistic language. When a caregiver creates an art response, it is typically a more unusual experience than talking. The art response creates an atmosphere of curiosity because child and caregiver may see one another in a different light, which can create new possibilities for how they communicate.

Fifteen-year-old John communicated primarily and preferably through his visual art. He loved permanent markers, and he sketched his way through many sessions. When the time was right, he invited both his parents and their new partners to a session so that they could witness his therapeutic journey. I asked that they not respond verbally, but that they allow themselves to listen to the sharing of his art and then respond by sketching how they were impacted by witnessing his journey. This invitation created a powerful silence as each parent first listened to John, sketched, and then shared their thoughtful accounts of how they were impacted by witnessing their son's art and his therapeutic journey. By the time the last parent was sharing, we all had tears, including John.

When caregivers use an art response, they are responding in a language that is meaningful to their child, potentially creating a powerful experience for the child. Further, when caregivers put their thoughts and feelings in symbolic form, the process alone slows down the sharing and has the potential to create very meaningful responses. When we slow down, we start to really listen. Often, there is a sense of truly being in the moment, expanding and experiencing the good feelings by all involved, particularly the child.

### Group Members

Art responses can effectively be used in group settings. Group members are coached on how to create art responses that demonstrate how they have been moved by witnessing someone else's process, rather than the response being an interpretation of what they have witnessed. Art responses can relate to how they are moved or inspired by the story of another, or they can offer encouragement. The following is an example of how an art response was used in a therapy group for adolescent girls.

Warrior Girl Spirit Group is a 12-week group for adolescent girls who have been sexually abused. I have been offering this group at various times over the past 18 years. Each girl works toward preparing and sharing her expressive arts story of the abuse. They use whatever art modalities best help them share their stories. While each girl shares her story, the other group members and therapists witness her story. Once the story is told, danced, read, or sung, those who witnessed it make art in silence with the materials provided. They are encouraged to create responses to show how they were moved or inspired by the girl and her story. Each art response in turn becomes a gift to the person who shared her story, and she leaves with small mementos of how her story has impacted her peers and group facilitators. One girl created and offered a warrior shield (Figure 2.6) because she was moved by another girl's story about safety and protection.

*Figure 2.6* A warrior shield as an art response. Used with permission.

# REFERENCES

Atkins, S., & Duggins Williams, L. (2007). *Sourcebook in expressive arts therapy*. Boone, NC: Parkway Publishers.

Briere, J., & Scott, C. (2006). *Principles of trauma therapy: A guide to symptoms, evaluation and treatment*. Thousand Oaks, CA: SAGE.

Cornell, A.W. (2013). *Focusing in clinical practice: The essence of change*. New York: W.W. Norton.

Crenshaw, D. (2006). Neuroscience and trauma treatment: Implications for creative arts therapists. In L. Carey (Ed.), *Expressive and creative arts methods for trauma survivors* (pp. 21–38). London: Jessica Kingsley.

Knill, P. J., Barba, H. N., & Fuchs, M. N. (2004). *Minstrels of soul: Intermodal expressive therapy* (2nd ed.). Toronto: EGS Press.

Knill, P. J., Levine, E. G., & Levine, S. K. (2005). *Principles and practice of expressive arts therapy: Towards a therapeutic aesthetics*. London: Jessica Kingsley.

Levine, S. K. (2009). *Trauma, tragedy, therapy: The arts and human suffering*. London: Jessica Kingsley.

McNiff, S. (1992). *Art as medicine: Creating a therapy of the imagination*. Boston, MA: Shambhala Publishers.

Moon, B. (2000). *Ethical issues in art therapy*. Springfield, IL: Charles Thomas.

Ogden, P., Minton, K., & Pain, C. (2006). *Trauma and the body: A sensorimotor approach to psychotherapy*. New York: W.W. Norton.

Rogers, N. (1993). *The creative connection: Expressive arts as healing*. Palo Alto, CA: Science & Behavior Books.

Rubin, J. (Ed.). (2001). *Approaches to art therapy: Theory & technique*. New York: Routledge.

Siegel, D. (2010). *Mindsight: The new science of personal transformation*. New York: Bantam Books.

van der Kolk, B. (2002). Beyond the talking cure: Somatic experience and subcortical imprints in the treatment of trauma. In F. Shapiro (Ed.), *EMDR as an integrative psychotherapy approach: Experts of diverse orientations explore the paradigm prism* (pp. 57–83). New York: APA Press.

# Part 2

# Trauma and Expressive Arts Therapy

# 3 Children's Experience of Trauma

## THE SENSORY EXPERIENCE OF TRAUMA: HONORING THE INTERNAL WORLD OF THE CHILD

Almost 20 years ago, when I began private practice specializing in the assessment and treatment of child sexual abuse, I would ask children to draw a picture of how they were hurt by the abuse. I witnessed images of bodies that were hurting, screaming out "Help," and bellies with words such as gross, yuck, or puke written in them. These images exemplified the somatic, sensory experience of trauma. It was as if the children's bodies were literally screaming out, needing to be witnessed, saying, "Someone please see what I am feeling!"

Since then, I have witnessed hundreds of similar images and stories. These young people are in the forefront of my mind as I wander into the more technical worlds of brain science and psychophysiology that are currently informing and changing the treatment of trauma in significant ways. Some of these ways will be explored in this chapter; however, we will begin by framing trauma as a sensory experience. As William Steele, founder and past director of the National Institute for Trauma and Loss in Children, says clearly in his training sessions, "Trauma is a sensory experience, not a disorder." Steele has long been providing sensory-based interventions for the treatment of trauma in children and adolescents through the development of many programs, such as Structured Interventions for Traumatized Children, Adolescents, and Parents (SITCAP), that treat trauma themes such as terror and anger rather than treating the symptoms of trauma (Steele & Raider, 2009). The premise that trauma is a sensory experience guides the four-phase treatment process outlined in this book. This means that we pay attention to sensations as they are experienced in the body through what we see, hear, taste, touch, and smell. From this perspective, trauma treatment requires treatment modalities that address trauma exposure on these sensory levels (Levine & Kline, 2007; Malchiodi, 2008; Steele & Raider, 2009). Sensory interventions and a sensory awareness attitude adopted by the therapist are some of the basics of treating trauma within this expressive arts framework.

This chapter explores in further detail how trauma impacts the memory, brain, and body of a child. Each section is followed with a discussion of the meaning this information has on treatment for children exposed to trauma.

## TRAUMA AND THE BRAIN, MEMORY, AND BODY

Trauma is experienced in the body, mind, and spirit of a child through direct or indirect exposure to events such as natural disasters, accidents, maltreatment, or illness. The following sections highlight some key areas that help us understand how exposure impacts the child's functioning. Understanding how trauma alters the body and brain of a child, including how memory is stored and recalled, informs how the treatment interventions in this book can best support the child's healing.

Trauma and its sequela is well described in many texts (American Psychiatric Association, 2013; Briere, 1992; Gil, 2006; Greenwald, 2005; Perry, Pollard, Blakley, Barker, & Vigilante, 1995; Steele & Raider, 2009; Terr, 1990, 1991; van der Kolk, 2003, 2005). Simply put, my personal experiences with trauma and over 25 years of professional work with children and teens tell me that trauma is an experience that has the potential to shock and overwhelm a child, altering his view of self, his relationship with his body, and his relationship with his world, potentially leaving him feeling disconnected and alone. *Relational trauma,* as it is primarily referred to in this text, is trauma that has happened in the context of interpersonal relationships. Often referred to as *developmental trauma* (Heller & LaPierre, 2012; van der Kolk, 2005), it includes physical, emotional, and sexual abuse; neglect; witnessing domestic violence; and loss of or abandonment by primary caregivers. How developmental trauma impacts cognitive, neurological, psychological, and attachment development in children is briefly described next.

Cognitive functioning is how we think, reason, remember, process, and understand self, relationships, and the world around us. In trauma, the main goal is survival; thus, children respond to threat through adaptive responses, including varying degrees of hyperarousal or hypoarousal (Ogden, Minton, & Pain, 2006). This arousal continuum ranges from states of high nervous system activation, creating symptoms of chaos such as anxiety, aggression, or agitation (Siegel, 2010), to the other end of the continuum of hypoarousal or dissociation (Levine & Kline, 2007). On this end of the continuum, we may observe apathy, inattention, lethargy, and an overall slowing or shutting down that Levine and Kline (2007) refer to as "constriction, freeze, and immobility" (p. 78). When in a highly aroused state, it is difficult to process information that is coming in through the senses, and both concentration and focus are impaired (Levine & Kline, 2007; Perry & Szalavitz, 2006; Pynoos, Steinberg, & Piacentini, 1999; Steele & Raider, 2009). Learning can be compromised when a child is triggered into either ends of the continuum. Children often struggle academically as they try to navigate the negative influences of trauma on their cognitive functioning along with the demands of peer, family, and other social relationships.

When in survival mode, children do not have full access to their cognitive resources, primarily located in the prefontal cortex, because survival is primarily a mid-brain dominant experience. However, it is encouraging to know that "once the mid-brain is no longer the predominant processor of daily life, children can often learn at three times the rate compared to when engulfed in trying to survive" (Steele & Raider, 2009, p. 25). Interventions that reduce arousal are required to restore cognitive functioning. Children need support to first address the sensory experience of the trauma, and then to challenge their altered, negative views of self and relationships because "the dominant processes of the traumatized brain is sensory, not cognitive so understanding, logic, reasoning are difficult to access" (p. 24).

From a neurological perspective, trauma triggers create ongoing stress responses in the child's body through hyper- or hypoarousal (Ogden et al., 2006). Over time, if the nervous system remains in a highly activated state, it can complicate the child's world (Levine, 1997; Levine & Kline, 2007). Even if no real threat is evident, the child's nervous system can be easily activated, drawing on daily energy to deal with perceived threat and managing feelings of anxiety and fear. Even though the original trauma is long past, "the stress-response apparatus of the child's brain is activated again and again" (Perry et al., 1995, p. 278).

Interventions need to be aimed at lowering arousal and discharging the stored energy in the child's nervous system that was activated at the time of the trauma. The survival energy that was mobilized at the time of trauma continues to wreak havoc in the world of the traumatized child (Levine & Kline, 2007; Perry et al., 1995).

Psychological impairment due to trauma affects how a child deals with her thoughts and emotions, which are at risk of becoming dysregulated. The experience of trauma can leave children feeling helpless, hopeless, and disempowered (Steele & Raider, 2009). Thinking errors (referred to in this four-phase treatment model as *trauma-influenced thinking*), along with overwhelming feelings, can immobilize children to the point where they withdraw and become depressed or, on the other extreme, act out their overwhelming emotions.

Managing arousal is one of the primary tasks of Phases One and Two of the treatment model outlined in this book. Interventions aimed at working with the instinctual, reactive stress responses are essential. Children learn how their bodies are their resource by noticing how they can move from calm body to activated body. Through repetition of this learning, encouraged by their network of helpers and caregivers, increased self-regulation can be established. Children can then learn to negotiate more cognitive aspects of therapy, such as addressing trauma-influenced thoughts and feelings.

Attachment relationships form the foundation for healthy brain development in children. While connection to others is a basic primary need throughout our lives, infants rely on their caregivers to provide for their every need, including emotional and physical safety, regulation, and material needs. The "attachment system" (Blaustein & Kinniburgh, 2010, p. 49) is this relationship between infant and caregivers that is the blueprint for understanding relationships with self and others. This is the arena in which children learn emotional expression while they are within a safe environment for successful negotiation of developmental tasks.

When children are distressed, caregivers are the external regulators providing calming, nurturing, and soothing sensory touch and words. Children come to learn these self-soothing skills when they are experienced on a repetitive, consistent basis. The attachment bond typically serves to mitigate trauma-related fear (Streeck-Fischer & van der Kolk, 2000). However, if the caregiver is the one maltreating the child, or the caregivers are unable to regulate themselves, the child reverts to more extreme regulating, such as shutdown or overcontrol, and attachment impairment ensues (Perry, 2009; van der Kolk, 2005).

When a child experiences his attachment relationships as unsafe and unpredictable, a range of possible effects can occur. First, his ability to trust others becomes impaired. It becomes difficult to know who he can go to or rely on, and the younger the child, the fewer options he has. Second, because a child relies on his caregivers for external regulation but this does not happen, his inability to regulate his own sensations and emotions can create a mistrust with and a lack of safety in his own body. Third, his young world becomes an unsafe place to navigate and explore.

Interventions that include safe, predictable caregivers in the treatment process are vital for healing attachment trauma. It is essential that caregivers address their own untreated traumas in order to develop the capacity for appropriately responding to the child's stress responses to trauma. The caregiver's calm, regulated nervous system provides a safe emotional container for her child to drop into and be cared for.

## TRAUMA AND THE BRAIN: WIRED TO SURVIVE

The deer catch my eye as I look out my living room window. There is a mother, her young one, and another female feasting on shrubs, while at the same time, their eyes, ears, and heads orient to any sound that may suggest danger. Something catches their attention. Ears tweak, heads lift, and then absolute stillness, until they all break out running and jumping. Then, the perceived threat, a coyote, prances by with a muskrat limp in its jaws.

We too can be on guard and alert with all senses engaged, ready to do what we have to do to be safe. With no history of trauma, we may hear a loud noise, orient ourselves, assess for safety, and then return to what we were doing if no threat exists. If we are not safe or have prior history of untreated trauma, the brain does something very different. The old reptilian brain kicks into fight, flight (mobilization), or freeze (immobilization) response (Levine & Kline, 2007; Ogden et al., 2006; Perry et al., 1995).

Fight, flight, or freeze is a psychophysiological experience (Levine, 1997; Rothschild, 2000). Levine (1997) references his work with observing wild animals in their natural habitat.

Simply put, if the prey is being stalked, they will fight if possible; if assessed as unsafe and there is time and space, they will run; otherwise they default to freezing. The freeze is an altered reality where time slows down, there is no fear, and pain is not felt as intensely. As I watched the deer from the window, I witnessed this incredible survival energy of the deer fleeing from the potential threat of the coyote.

The brain structure develops sequentially from the lower, oldest, less complex part that is known as the *brain stem* (reptilian brain) to the mid-brain, often called the *limbic area* (mammalian brain), to the more highly developed part called the *neo-cortex* (Perry, 2006). When exposed to trauma, we are wired so that our thinking brain (neo-cortex) shuts down or goes "offline," and the mid-brain dominates the experience (Perry et al., 1995; van der Kolk, 1994). What this means is that the amygdala, which is located in the mid-brain, goes on high alert, and it signals the sympathetic nervous system to engage and release chemicals to prepare for fight or flight. If it is not possible to fight or escape, the limbic system then engages the parasympathetic nervous system that creates the freeze response in the body. It is important to understand that the limbic system and autonomic nervous system (sympathetic and para-sympathetic) responses are survival responses, which means they are automatic and instinctual responses to perceived threat (Rothschild, 2000).

Further, the amygdala also plays another important role in survival, which is to assign emotional meaning to experience:

> A part of the limbic system, the amygdala, serves as the "smoke detector" that interprets whether incoming sensory information is a threat. . . . The challenge of any effective psychotherapy, therefore, is to decondition the amygdala from interpreting innocuous reminders as a return of the trauma.

> (van der Kolk, 2002a, pp. 64–65)

For infants and young children, fight and flight behaviors are not real options when the threat is in the relationships that they are dependent on simply because of their limited abilities. Freezing can become the automatic survival response. If children are threatened or there is perceived threat, their alarm reactions are activated and the sympathetic nervous system kicks in by way of increased heart rate and blood pressure, respiration, release of stored sugars, increase in muscle tone, hypervigilance, and screening out all noncritical information. The child may cry out in efforts to bring the caregiver in to protect her. If safety is not established, the child may move to dissociation, particularly when the child is younger, is female, experiences helplessness, and there is physical injury, pain, or torture (Perry et al., 1995). This survival mechanism of dissociation, when repeatedly experienced, can become the child's way of dealing with perceived threat throughout life.

## What This Means for Treatment

Children need support to understand that their bodies did what they were meant to do in order to survive: fight, run away, or freeze. They also need to understand that during a traumatic event, their emotions are stronger than their thinking due to mid-brain dominance. This can help children know how amazing their bodies are and help them understand that their reactions are normal under the circumstances and there is nothing wrong with their bodies or brains. Reframing their experiences at the appropriate time in therapy can support children in feeling empowered by increasing or restoring confidence in their bodies.

Perry (2006) developed a neurosequential model for treating maltreated and traumatized children based on experiences that are "relevant, relational, repetitive, and rewarding" (p. 49) to the child. One of the primary principles of this approach "is that successful treatment with traumatized children must first regulate the brainstem's sensitized and dysregulated stress-response systems" (p. 50). He further suggests that "dance, drumming, music, massage—patterned repetitive sensory input will begin to provide the kinds of experiences that may influence brainstem neurobiology to re-organize in ways that will lead to smoother functional regulation" (p. 38).

Phase One and Two interventions of this expressive arts four-phase model are designed with the understanding of the need for sensory interventions that aim to decrease arousal originating in the reptilian brain. To support the regulation of the stress-response system, expressive arts offers the kind of repetitive and sensory experiences necessary in the early phases of treatment. Some examples include finger painting, coloring mandalas, drumming, and dance/movement, each offering elements of repetitive, calming, and soothing experiences.

## TRAUMA AND MEMORY: THE JOURNEY FROM IMPLICIT TO EXPLICIT MEMORY

> Trauma is essentially the inability to transform sensory memories of distressing events into explicit (cognitive) memory, where these memories could be reframed and managed and where what is happening now (no danger or threat) is distinguished from what happened then (traumatic event).
>
> (Steele & Malchiodi, 2012, p. 152)

When traumatized, it can be difficult for anyone, child or adult, to express their experiences solely with words. They are often said to experience "speechless terror" (van der Kolk, 2002b, p. 35). Young children in particular are challenged to find a vocabulary to express trauma. I often hear from children and teens, "I don't remember what happened." This is not framed as resistance because it can be difficult for children to access the cognitive part of the memory. When asked to draw what happened, typically more of the memory is expressed and aspects that didn't have words are shown through images. Implicit and explicit memory systems help us understand what happens to traumatic memory that makes the trauma difficult to put into words.

The explicit memory system is expressed through language, reason, and logic. When we are using explicit (declarative) memory, words are used to express what we are thinking or feeling and to make sense of our experiences both past and present. The cognitive processes associated with explicit memory help children deal with traumatic experiences through expression of their stories and the feelings related to what happened to them.

Implicit memory is associated with the subcortical parts of the brain, "the primitive parts that are not under conscious control and have no linguistic representation, have a different way of remembering than the higher levels of the brain, located in the prefrontal cortex" (van der Kolk, 2002a, p. 60). Implicit (nondeclarative) memory is experienced unconsciously. For example, as I type these words I am not recalling how to do so or even what letter is what key; it is unconsciously accessed. Similar to riding a bicycle, I just get on the bike and ride, rather than consciously thinking about each step required. There are no words associated with implicit memory, only sensations and images.

The implicit memory system is where trauma is experienced in the mid-brain. When a child experiences trauma-related arousal, he is living in the mid-brain (limbic region), with little access to words or language to express what is experienced. He experiences his world through images and sensations. In studying the brains of individuals with posttraumatic stress, van der Kolk (1996) found that what is known as Broca's area, which is the language center in the limbic region, does not work in trauma. He writes:

> Perhaps most significantly, Broca's area "turned off." We believe that this reflects the tendency in PTSD to experience emotions as physical states rather than as verbally encoded

experiences. Our findings suggest that PTSD patients' difficulties with putting feelings into words are mirrored in actual changes in brain activity.

(p. 233)

Trauma memory is more easily recorded in implicit memory because the amygdala, which is located in the limbic region and plays a primary role in the processing and memory of emotional reactions, is not effected by stress hormones. The hippocampus, which helps consolidate information from short- to long-term memory, is suppressed by stress hormones (Rothschild, 2000). Trauma is the inability to move the sensory memories of those traumatic experiences from implicit to explicit memory.

## What This Means for Treatment

When processing the trauma in Phase Three, the therapeutic work involves assisting the child by accessing the implicit trauma memory so it can be encoded, given a language, and then integrated into conscious, explicit memory. Here the child can reframe the memory in ways he can now manage and use as a resource, and she can now look at his life with new meaning (Steele & Raider, 2009). To further expand on our understanding of trauma processing, it is useful to learn about another implicit memory process called "iconic symbolization" (Michaesu and Baettig, as cited in Steele & Raider, 2009, p. 17) which is referred to by Steele and Raider as "a process of giving our experience a visual identity" (p. 17). The process involves retrieving and externalizing the trauma memory by creating images of the experience that include elements from the senses, details of what happened, and the emotions experienced. Steele and Raider (2009) advise using questions that are trauma specific and sensory oriented to guide the telling of the story. As a child's story unfolds through the drawing of images, we become witness to all aspects of his experience, including how he views self, others, and his environment.

Understanding the basics of these memory processes helps to make sense of how the expressive arts can be utilized as a means to bring life to implicit trauma memories held in symbolic form. Expressive arts have the ability to access implicit memory, which is coded in sensation and imagery, and offer nonverbal processes to express these iconic portrayals through dance, drawing, sculpture, or the sound of the drum. There is no need for words or cognitive processes. We come to further understand the child's world through everything we see, feel, and hear as we witness the child's representation of the trauma memory through the art.

The playful spirit is engaged in both verbal and nonverbal expressive arts processes. Although addressing trauma memory tends to be stressful, the ability of the arts to offer containment and distance, along with playful elements, can assist children with accessing the memory without creating too much arousal. Levine and Kline (2007) discuss the role of playful curiosity in the healing of trauma, stating,

> the trick is to awaken the sleeping primitive brain while tiptoeing around the neocortical "higher" brain to avoid stimulating its favorite pre-occupations: rationalization, denial, judgement, and blame. How do we engage this smaller, deeper, ancient, wiser brain without disturbing the giant? Healing instincts can easily be enticed either through play or a sense of playful curiosity.

(pp. 105–106)

Playful curiosity is invited at every phase of this trauma treatment model. This is done with the hopes that the child will experience a balance of enjoyment along with the more stressful components of trauma treatment. It is the job of the therapist to remember and ensure that healing and play go hand in hand.

## TRAUMA AND THE BODY: NERVOUS SYSTEM AROUSAL

> The key to healing traumatic symptoms in humans is in our physiology. When faced with what is perceived as inescapable or overwhelming threat, humans and animals both use the immobility response. The important thing to understand about this function is that it is involuntary. This simply means that the physiological mechanism governing this response resides in the primitive, instinctual parts of our brains and nervous systems, and is not under our conscious control.
>
> (Levine, 1997, p. 17)

Our bodies are made up of highly complex, finely tuned systems that are geared for survival because we have a basic biological and psychological need to be safe in the world. The body has the capacity to survive and adapt to most of what comes our way through mobilization responses or "human danger responses" (Blaustein & Kinniburgh, 2010, p. 27) described previously as the fight, flight, or freeze behaviors. When something threatens the well-being of a child, many complex mechanisms take over with the goal of increasing the child's chances of survival. When threatened, children don't choose their responses; their bodies do what they are meant to do. Children cannot escape the relational trauma scenario, so the response of fight or flight is often not viable. Typically, when threatened, children use the hyperarousal response, which is designed to call their attachment figures to assist them. When the threat is caused by the attachment figure, freeze is the most likely body response, rendering the child immobile or compliant.

Blaustein and Kinniburgh (2010) identify a range of behaviors particular to each danger response system. When a child perceives a threat and he fights, there will be increased physiological arousal and he may engage in aggressive, angry, or irritable behaviors. If the child engages in the flight response, he may actively avoid others, isolate himself, or run away from others. In the freeze response, the child may have limited expression of affect, deny his own needs, and be overly compliant. These behaviors are considered adaptive survival responses (van der Kolk, 1996) or instinctual survival responses (Perry et al., 1995; Perry & Szalavitz, 2006). All of these reactions are efforts to survive the threat of danger.

In the face of threat, we typically use one of two primary adaptive response patterns: the dissociative pattern or the hyperarousal response (Perry et al., 1995). Adult males more often engage in the fight or flight response, and children (in particular young children) more often use the "freeze and surrender" response (Blaustein & Kinniburgh, 2010; Perry et al., 1995). As the body prepares to protect itself through these adaptive responses, energy is mobilized in the nervous system. If the child is not able to successfully run away or fight off the threat, the energy gets stored in the nervous system and can remain there for years to come (Levine, 1997), making the child vulnerable to easy startle or further freeze at a later time. Prolonged arousal or activation in children can lead to cognitive, emotional, and behavioral issues (Perry et al., 1995).

The arousal energy that resides in the nervous system as a result of trauma can become problematic because it does not automatically dissipate; rather, "it persists in the body, and often forces the formation of a wide variety of symptoms e.g., anxiety, depression, and psychosomatic and behavioral problems. These symptoms are the organism's way of containing (or corralling) the undischarged residual energy" (Levine, 1997, p. 20). We must be prepared to address the excess energy in the treatment process.

### What This Means for Treatment

We often work with children whose nervous systems are easily triggered into high arousal or hypoarousal, leaving them vulnerable to negative experiences such as preoccupation with worry, inability to focus/concentrate, and/or difficulty with establishing meaningful relationships.

As therapists, we monitor a child's experience by tracking any nervous system activation and possible triggers, noting her ability to stay present to the therapeutic work. We also become acutely aware of the impact of our own presence on the child. We take note of how we may trigger the child, paying attention to her ability to tolerate relational closeness or distance, what is potentially activating, and when/if she tunes out.

One of our therapeutic goals is assisting children with developing a more resilient nervous system. Pendulation (Levine & Kline, 2007), which is movement from arousal to calm body, is one way we can work with the energy in the child's nervous system. We do this each time a child experiences some arousal in his body that is triggered by the trauma material he is working on. We support the child by noticing and acknowledging the arousal, then, through the use of personal resources and mindfulness skills, we help the child return to calm body. We become curious observers of the movement between stress and relaxation states in the body. The child learns, through much repetition, to manage his arousal response. Increased body awareness and working to safely discharge arousal further supports self-regulation, lowering mid-brain dominance. The therapist ensures that each therapy session closes with the child experiencing a calm, relaxed nervous system. These safe, controlled experiences strengthen new neuronal connections, and the repetition of safe experiences replaces unsafe sensory memories.

## REFERENCES

American Psychiatric Association. (2013). *Diagnostic and statistical manual of mental disorders* (5th ed.). Washington, DC: Author.

Blaustein, M., & Kinniburgh, K. (2010). *Treating traumatic stress in children and adolescents: How to foster resilience through attachment, self-regulation, and competency.* New York: Guilford Press.

Briere, J. (1992). *Child abuse trauma, theory and treatment of the lasting effects.* Thousand Oaks, CA: SAGE.

Gil, E. (2006). *Helping abused and traumatized children: Integrating directive and nondirective approaches.* New York: Guilford Press.

Greenwald, R. (2005). *Child trauma handbook: A guide for helping trauma-exposed children and adolescents.* New York: The Haworth Reference Press.

Heller, L., & LaPierre, A. (2012). *Healing developmental trauma: How early trauma affects self-regulation, self-image, and the capacity for relationship.* Berkeley, CA: North Atlantic Books.

Levine, P. (1997). *Waking the tiger: Healing trauma.* Berkeley, CA: North Atlantic Books.

Levine, P., & Kline, M. (2007). *Trauma through a child's eyes: Awakening the ordinary miracle of healing.* Berkeley, CA: North Atlantic Books.

Malchiodi, C. (Ed.). (2008). *Creative interventions with traumatized children.* New York: Guilford Press.

Ogden, P., Minton, K., & Pain, C. (2006). *Trauma and the body: A sensorimotor approach to psychotherapy.* New York: W.W. Norton.

Perry, B.D. (2006). Applying principles of neurodevelopment to clinical work with maltreated and traumatized children: The neurosequential model of therapeutics. In N. Boyd Webb (Ed.), *Working with traumatized youth in child welfare* (pp. 27–52). New York: Guilford Press.

Perry, B.D. (2009). Examining child maltreatment through a neurodevelopmental lens: Clinical application of the Neurosequential Model of Therapeutics. *Journal of Loss and Trauma 14*, 240–255.

Perry, B.D., Pollard, R.A., Blakley, T.L., Barker, W.L., & Vigilante, D. (1995). Childhood trauma, the neurobiology of adaptation, and "use-dependent" development of the brain: How "states become "traits." *Infant Mental Health Journal, 16*(4), 271–291.

Perry, B.D., & Szalavitz, M. (2006). *The boy who was raised as a dog and other stories from a child psychiatrist's notebook: What traumatized children can teach us about loss, love and healing.* New York: Basic Books.

Pynoos, R., Steinberg, A., & Piacentini, J. (1999). A developmental psychopathology model of childhood traumatic stress and intersection with anxiety disorders. *Society of Biological Psychiatry, 46,* 1542–1554.

Rothschild, B. (2000). *The body remembers: The psychophysiology of trauma and trauma treatment.* New York: W. W. Norton.

Siegel, D. (2010). *Mindsight: The new science of personal transformation.* New York: Bantam Books.

Steele, W., & Malchiodi, C. (2012). *Trauma-informed practices with children and adolescents.* New York: Routledge.

Steele, W., & Raider, M. (2009). *Structured sensory intervention for traumatized children, adolescents and parents* (SITCAP™) (3rd ed.). New York: Edwin Mellen Press.

Streeck-Fischer, A., & van der Kolk, B. (2000). Down will come baby, cradle and all: Diagnostic and therapeutic implications of chronic trauma on child development. *Australian and New Zealand Journal of Psychiatry, 34,* 903–918.

Terr, L. (1990). *Too scared to cry.* New York: Harper & Row.

Terr, L. C. (1991). Childhood traumas: An outline and overview. *American Journal of Psychiatry, 148,* 10–20.

van der Kolk, B.A. (1994). The body keeps the score: Memory and the evolving psychobiology of post-traumatic stress. *Harvard Review of Psychiatry, 1*(5), 253–265.

van der Kolk, B.A. (1996). The body keeps the score: Approaches to the psychobiology of posttraumatic stress disorder. In B. van der Kolk, A. McFarlane, & L. Weisaeth (Eds.), *Traumatic stress: The effects of overwhelming experience on mind, body, and society* (pp. 214–241). New York: Guilford Press.

van der Kolk, B.A. (2002a). Beyond the talking cure: Somatic experience and subcortical imprints in the treatment of trauma. In F. Shapiro (Ed.), *EMDR as an integrative psychotherapy approach: Experts of diverse orientations explore the paradigm prism* (pp. 57–83). New York: APA Press.

van der Kolk, B.A. (2002b). In terror's grip: Healing the ravages of trauma. *Cerebrum, 4,* 34–50.

van der Kolk, B.A. (2003). The neurobiology of childhood trauma and abuse. *Child and Adolescent Psychiatric Clinics of North America, 12,* 193–317.

van der Kolk, B.A. (2005). Developmental trauma disorder: Towards a rational diagnosis for children with complex trauma histories. *Psychiatric Annals, 35*(5), 401–408.

# 4 A Resource-Oriented Lens

## RESOURCING AS THE FOUNDATION

Identifying, developing, and engaging with resources are some of the first building blocks for creating safety and stability in trauma therapy (Heller & Heller, 2001; Heller & LaPierre, 2012; Levine & Kline, 2007; Rothschild, 2000). In Phase Two of this treatment model, there is a strong emphasis on resource building through creating art around the resources clients have and/or need to develop and learn to incorporate in their daily lives. Resources can be inner qualities that we possess or the things we do that bring us feelings of comfort, connection, peace, or joy and help us feel grounded and present (Levine & Kline, 2007). What brings a smile to my face, warmth in my heart, and an overall feeling of well-being in my skin?

Identifying resources is central to trauma work. Children need to feel secure and able to identify and use their resources before they engage in the trauma processing in Phase Three. Some children may need assistance with developing resources that are either underdeveloped or lacking. We can assess the child's world of resources by asking the child what helps her feel calm or good inside. By identifying and intentionally using these resources, children can learn to more effectively regulate their feelings, experience increased inner stability, and become more grounded and present.

There are many kinds of resources that offer assistance to children in the context of trauma treatment. Inside resources can include qualities the child has, talents, or other personal traits that make the child unique. Outside resources include particular people in the child's life, animals, or places that bring up positive feelings in the child. Other resources that are important to identify and develop are the body and the client's own knowing.

### Inside and Outside Resources

Resources are abundant, varied, and unique to each child. We can help our clients identify resources when they are organized in various categories. One category is inside resources, such as qualities about themselves that are useful, such as enthusiasm, ability to focus, or sense of humor. Identifying hobbies or physical activities can also contribute to developing a healthy sense of self. Some children are good at or enjoy activities such as soccer, knitting, or reading. Talismans and other objects that hold personal significance can be resources, such as a cross necklace that reminds the child of his spiritual beliefs or a stone with a meaningful word written on it.

Another category is outside resources, which includes such things as the people and animals in the child's life who are healthy and who positively support the child, including caregivers, siblings, friends, or adult community members such as coaches, teachers, or clergy. Pets, or a general love of animals, can be a valuable resource for children. Simply asking a child about a pet she loves typically brings a sense of joy and has the power to help the child shift to positive energy in the moment. Places is another category of resources worthy of exploring. Places may include a holiday the child went on, his own bedroom, his church, somewhere in nature, or a sports arena. Resources can also be memories of any of these things that continue to bring the child a positive response.

It can be useful to incorporate resources at any time in the therapy process. Fifteen-year-old Vera had been coming to therapy for many months. On one particular day, Vera was experiencing significant stress and anxiety as she was preparing to go to court to testify against her stepfather for sexually abusing her. She drew an image about how she was experiencing the thought of going to court (Figure 4.1). She shared that the image is of her on the right and her friend on the left who is trying to tell her everything will be okay. "But I am not okay. My eyes are closed because I don't want to hear it," she exclaimed loudly. I knew that one of Vera's biggest supporters and resources was her sister. I asked her to imagine her sister being with her right now. Vera's face softened. She smiled. I asked if remembering the support of her sister would change anything in her image. She answered yes, and she returned to work on her image (Figure 4.2). Vera said, "The flower represents my sister. When I think of her I open my eyes. It makes me feel like there is more light in the darkness, that I can hear the support from others and that I will be okay." Vera asked if she could take this picture home to help her as she prepared to go to court in the coming month. Reminding children of their resources strengthens their internal senses of power and their abilities to deal with the difficult scenarios in their worlds. Vera's images are evidence of the power that resources can have not only in therapeutic work, but also in day-to-day life.

*Figure 4.1* Vera's drawing of her fear about going to court. Used with permission.

*Figure 4.2* Vera's altered image. Used with permission.

### The Body as a Resource

From the first meeting with a young client, we are interested in supporting him to develop a healthy relationship with his body and nervous system. We begin gathering information about his relationship with his body from the first session, noticing what activates our client and what calms him. Children need to be guided to acknowledge and to have a language for the activation in the nervous system (e.g., butterflies in my stomach, increased heart rate, or sweaty palms) and then learn to bring awareness to the resources that restore calm in their bodies (Levine & Kline, 2007). Children are taught to pay attention to the differences between activated and calm body, and how quickly this shift can happen in a session. The more they experience the movement from calm, to activated, back to calm body, the more confident they become with navigating the stressful nervous system response to trauma triggers.

Initially, as we are teaching about body/nervous system activation, we work with minor, non-trauma-related activation. Once the child learns the language for the sensations and activation, we expose her to small bits of activating trauma material in order to create a titrated experience that is managed and mastered by the child little bits at a time (Rothschild, 2000). Just a little activation in the body is required to work with the sensations, stay within a tolerable level, and then return to calm body (Ogden, Minton, & Pain, 2006). This titrated experience, when managed well, strengthens the child's relationship with the resource of her body. We emphasize how it is *her* body that calmed itself and how powerful *her* body is because of this ability. The belief that her body is a resource is acknowledged throughout all phases of treatment.

As in the example of Conor in Chapter 2, he was able to acknowledge his fear of doing the trauma work and at the same time experience the power of facing his fears. As I paid attention to Conor's body and tracked what was happening, I witnessed the movement between fear/distress and empowerment/excitement. This back-and-forth movement between activated and calm body is what Peter Levine calls *pendulation* in his work with Somatic Experiencing. Pendulation is a normal day-to-day process in our nervous systems. "It is this ability to move or 'pendulate' between bodily sensations of helplessness and sensations of empowerment that builds resourcefulness. This pleasurable rhythm of expansion and contraction instead of shutdown and overwhelm is our birthright" (Levine & Kline, 2007, p. 137). This movement back and forth is at the heart of resource building.

### The Client's Own Knowing as a Resource

The sense of helplessness and powerlessness can be deeply ingrained in the mind and body of a child who has experienced trauma. Children who experience relational trauma often have had few experiences with safe and protective adults in their lives. Children need direct relational healing experiences to assist them in knowing who they are and that they can trust themselves. We take any opportunity to highlight their sense of powerfulness and inner knowing. The fact that their bodies survived the trauma and they are here today are evidence of inherent power. When we witness clients making positive choices, we can highlight this as inner knowing. Even with seemingly benign decisions, I point out that children know what they need and/or want.

For example, I ask my clients how they want the paper to be tacked to the wall for painting: portrait or landscape? Often they say they don't care. I stop and ask them to really have a look and notice which direction appeals most to them. When they realize that their opinions do matter and they check in with themselves, they *do* know which they prefer. We continue to build on this knowing throughout the therapy process.

Our clients' own knowing is supported when we frame an experience that highlights what they know, such as what art form they want to engage with, and as we adopt a resource attitude of mindfulness when we slow down the therapy process. The therapist's attitude provides children with the opportunity to really experience their own bodies and their sensations, feelings, and thoughts in more integrated ways.

### Imagination as a Resource

Although trauma can diminish the child's world, the imagination can expand his world. The therapist holds the power of the imagination as the backdrop to the therapeutic work, bringing it to the foreground whenever needed. Children can imagine and create protective figures that come to assist them as they prepare to create the trauma story. They can be encouraged to imagine formidable superheroes (or to imagine themselves as superheroes) with special powers to find relief from distressing memories. Imagination doesn't change the fact that they experienced trauma, but the imagination as a resource can empower children to move and act in ways that assist with shifting out of the trauma freeze.

### Owning the Bravery Resource

Each child that comes through the therapy door brings immense courage. It is there within her, sometimes needing a little encouragement or acknowledgment to truly be seen and felt. It is our job as therapists to authentically highlight moments when we see bravery. There is immense power in the therapeutic connection when the child sees that you believe in him and you see his bravery. The child comes alive, and his belief in himself grows. When a child's belief in himself grows, he becomes more brave in addressing the hard stuff of the trauma. The child begins to trust our trusting of his bravery. Yes, there is natural avoidance of the pain *and* there exits the natural abundance of bravery. As therapists, we make choices about where we focus our own and our client's attention. We don't ignore the suffering, but we do give attention and time to the child's experience of his own bravery. It is in this way that the child may start to own his own experience and knowing of his bravery.

Bravery is not some ethereal quality. It is built into the fabric of our being. It exists right there alongside the trauma experience. Although the trauma can be experienced as very loud and overpowering through posttrauma symptoms, we need to train ourselves to highlight the sometimes quiet, yet profound, voice of bravery. This means we view each session through the brave lens. We pay attention to the moments when we witness bravery. We celebrate bravery through small rituals of creativity, making brave badges, brave flags, or brave stones. Owning the energy of bravery balances out the heaviness of trauma work. Helping children own their bravery is one of the best resources we can cultivate.

After 6-year-old Kali completed her trauma story, she created a large bravery badge. Together we danced to a song about being brave. I invited her to write her own bravery poem by giving her the prompt "I am. . . ." Kali wrote:

> I am a brave little girl
> I speak when I am afraid
> I draw feelings
> I feel good when I speak.

She was so thrilled with her badge and poem, and she could hardly wait to share them with her caregiver. Her caregiver was invited into the session, and Kali proudly shared all the work she had done. The session ended with all three of us "dancing the brave" and celebrating Kali's strengths.

### Spontaneous Resources

There is delight and surprise when a resource suddenly shows up in the art without the client consciously creating a resource. These spontaneously created resources need to be highlighted by the therapist to enlist the resource as an asset to the child's therapeutic work.

Nine-year-old David, had experienced a life of neglect and physical, emotional, and sexual abuse by his biological parents. In spite of the tragedies, his nature was one of optimism and gratitude. As he was illustrating his trauma story, he was explaining a major incident of physical abuse by his father. David drew the house and yard where the incident occurred. After he described what happened, I asked him to tell me about what was in the rest of the picture. He explained that he drew a water sprinkler in the yard. I was curious about that, and he shared further: "The water sprinkler reminds me of what I love about summer. Whenever I draw something bad, I also draw something good. The sprinkler reminds me of the fun times." David inherently knew how to regulate the intensity of his emotions by balancing the hurt with memories of fun experiences. We fully acknowledged his ability to naturally regulate his emotions and how this ability was an important resource to him.

## RESOURCES INHERENT IN THE EXPRESSIVE ARTS PROCESS AND PRODUCT

Expressive arts is an inherently resource-oriented approach to therapy. When practiced in an intentional, mindful, body-focused way, expressive arts offer children resources in the art forms created as well as in the process of creating and the products created. One is not necessarily more important than the other (Atkins & Duggins Williams, 2007; Halprin, 2003; McNiff, 1992); each offers its particular gift to the maker of the art.

### Art Forms as Resources

Some children come to therapy already using the arts, such as dance, journaling, painting, or playing a musical instrument, as a healthy outlet for self-expression. Often, adolescents have music playlists that they listen to in times of need. Others come to realize a love for one art form or another through the expressive arts therapy process, and they learn to integrate the arts more intentionally as resources in their day-to-day lives. Buchanan (2012) writes in detail about the power of music when used intentionally, suggesting, "Music can allow people to feel freedom or connected to others. Music can help us feel balanced and confident or soothed and relaxed. Music, the right music for the right moment, can make us feel better" (p. 9). It is this intentional use of art forms that we support and develop throughout the therapy process.

## Process of Creating

Expressive arts therapy is an inherently resourceful process due to the experience of creating. Creating itself involves resources such as the use of our senses, the imagination, self-exploration, play, inspiration, creation energy, and possibilities of creating new stories. Creating art involves the collaboration of the imagination and the various senses as they entice one another to bring something new into the world and within the creator of the art. Imagination has no bounds; it is as big as the world, with endless possibilities including what we see, hear, taste, touch, and smell. Imagination as a resource in the creative process helps us work with children by inviting them to imagine healing and healthy outcomes. Self-exploration with the arts invites children to find undiscovered parts of themselves that are less restrictive than the trauma experience would like them to see. Play with the arts brings aliveness and energy to the therapy process that balances out the more difficult, stress-related trauma work. Inspiration is at the heart of creating with the arts. When we are inspired, we start to see the world differently. We can learn to believe in and open to the power of the beauty that surrounds us.

Finally, the process of creating releases a powerful creation energy in the creator. This energy has potential to change the client by shifting mood as it brings feelings of inner power, strength, calm, inspiration, and confidence, all of which are resources derived naturally from being in the creative flow. All of these resources together assist children with creating new stories of strength, renewal, and resourcefulness that go beyond the victim/survivor identity (Steele & Malchiodi, 2012). They can begin to imagine themselves as thrivers who are destined to bring to reality the very things they dream of becoming.

## Creation Product as Resource

What emerges as a product of creating can also be of value as a tangible resource that develops organically from the expressive arts process. This resource could be a song, a poem, or a story, or the voice speaking the poem or story or singing the song. The artifact derived from creating can be integrated into the child's daily life or be called upon as a reminder of her power.

It is both the process and the product of the expressive arts experience that offer invaluable resources to clients as they move forward in their healing journeys, as illustrated in the following example.

Five-year-old Tara developed a growing and intense fear of fires destroying her family. In the session, I invited Tara to draw a picture of her fear. She drew the image, but she couldn't speak about it. She was next invited to draw a picture of herself standing up to her fear. Tara drew a picture of herself with a fire in her belly. She then took the blue marker and started covering up the fire; she told me she was putting water on the fire inside her belly. She vigorously moved the blue marker over and over the fire. I noticed her breathing was rapid and that she was fully engaged and very purposeful in what she was doing. After a few minutes, I wondered out loud if she might like to take what she was drawing and use a bigger paper and paint on the wall board. Her smile grew wide at the invitation. She helped put up the large paper on the wall, and she looked closely at the various colors of paints. Just as she dipped her brush into the blue paint, she said, "I think I will paint a happy picture," and she began painting a blue sky. What came next moved me deeply. Humming now, she carefully painted a long row of 12 green stems across the width of the paper. She then took a fresh brush, dipped it in red, turned to look at me and said, "Red can be used for more than just fire you know," as she continued to paint 12 red tulips.

When given the space to create, this little 5-year-old found her own resources. She literally danced her way out of the office with her pictures of courage and belief in herself tucked safely under her arm.

The process and product were essential in this example with Tara. The process of creating included using her body and her imagination, and at the same time she was making her own choices and was in charge of the process. The physical act of moving her arm to cover the red fire with blue marker seemed to activate some of the energy of her fears. Yet, here she was, in charge, choosing the colors that would help the "jam" she reported feeling in her head and in her tummy. As she got up from the table after drawing her fears, and drawing herself with courage to stand up to her fears, something had shifted in her. The process of creating was very important as it engaged the memory of her fear, brought forward the image of the fire, and allowed her to experience herself doing something active to stand up to her fear. The product she created was equally important. She gave form to her fears and worked with them courageously. She wanted to keep two of these images. The image of herself being brave, standing up to her fears by putting out the fire in her belly with buckets of water, and the final "happy" picture with 12 red tulips. As she completed the final large painting, she wondered, "How will we get this big picture in the car?" She could see it up in her room already.

## RESOURCE-ORIENTED ATTITUDE OF THE THERAPIST

The attitude the therapist brings to trauma treatment guides what happens in the process of therapy, including what themes are emphasized, how the sessions unfold, and what behaviors are attended to and framed as important. While the difficult aspects of trauma are safely addressed in treatment, a resource-oriented attitude permeates all aspects of therapy, increasing opportunities for children see all that is going well and all that is good in their world. The therapist cultivates this resource-oriented attitude through mindful awareness, tuning into positive resources, and intentionally slowing the pace of therapy.

### Adopting an Attitude of Mindfulness

Key to this resource orientation is taking a mindful approach to expressive arts therapy. In essence, mindfulness is "the awareness that arises by paying attention on purpose, in the present moment, and non-judgmentally" (Kabat-Zinn, 2013, p. xxxv). It is a distinct way of paying attention to the present moment experience, including awareness of thoughts, feelings, behaviors, and sensations. As we develop the skill of mindful awareness, we can invite our clients to be present in a mindful way.

From the beginning of the work with our young clients, we invite noticing and paying attention to what is happening right now in their bodies. This mindful attitude is embedded throughout all aspects of this work. In Phase Two, we more purposefully teach clients how to develop sensory awareness skills along with teaching a vocabulary for the language of sensations and feelings. These are skills that can maintain a mindful approach. It is the job of the therapist to invite the client to notice resources, to highlight the shifts and changes that occur, to frame particular experiences in the art, and to invite a slower pace when needed to support this integration. The mindful awareness of the therapist supports bringing the child's awareness to his experience in the therapeutic relationship, his experience in his body, and his relationship with the expressive arts experience.

Mindful questions invite the awareness of the client to the present moment experience as she is creating art. Staying in the present moment can ensure the child doesn't become overwhelmed by traumatic memory or future anxieties. Tracking what is happening in the client as she is creating helps the therapist observe and maintain mindful awareness and supports the client in staying in present moment experience.

Using mindful observations or questions is naming and knowing what is experienced right now in this moment by the child. When creating mindful questions, the therapist is calling on the energies of the detective and the curious cat. The following are examples of mindful observations and questions:

I am noticing tears in your eyes as you read the part of your poem about your mom.
What do you notice as you reach your arms up to the sky? Does it feel good, yucky, nice, sad?

For young children, it is important to help them find the vocabulary that describes their experiences. We can offer ideas and prompts, but children are always encouraged to return to their bodies and check in to determine if the word is a fit.

Integrating mindfulness in the process of expressive arts therapy supports the work with trauma-related material. In the context of trauma therapy, mindfulness decreases the chances that the child from being triggered into either overwhelming or numbing responses. Inviting the client's awareness to the present moment experience of what is occurring in his body, his art, and these relationships can maintain a grounded approach to trauma treatment.

Mindful observation of here-and-now experience changes information processing. Rather than triggering bottom-up hijacking of cognitions or escalation of trauma-related beliefs and emotions about impending danger, the act of mindful exploration facilitates duel processing. Clients do not get caught up in their trauma-related beliefs or arousal but, rather, study the evocation of titrated components of internal experience, especially the body's responses. Arousal stays within the window of tolerance and associations with traumatic memories begin to shift from automatic and exaggerated reactions to mediated, observable responses.

(Ogden et al., 2006, p. 169)

We want the children we work with to be able to observe what is happening in their bodies and the art, but not to become overwhelmed by it. Children can learn to become curious observers of what is happening in their bodies and in their art.

## A Mindful Attitude of "What Else?"

As noted earlier, we adopt a mindful attitude throughout this work, maintaining awareness of where our attention goes. In any given session, many thoughts and feelings are experienced, sensations are felt, and behaviors are witnessed. As therapists, we are trained to work with and tune into the emotional worlds of our clients. Expressing feelings is important; however, that is only one aspect of the work. Using this resource-oriented approach, the therapist is encouraged to pay attention to signs of resources that the child may not be aware of. The therapist tracks the client's body and her thoughts, feelings, and sensations, looking for signs of power, courage, and strength that could be potential resources. There are many opportunities for the therapist to be curious and to highlight *what else* the client is knowing, other than the fear responses or negative emotions that are most often expressed. Frequently there are shifts and changes that occur in the process of creating. New experiences and information arise that are important to notice, both in the art and in the body of the client. These new experiences, shifts, and changes are the "what else" that the curious, mindful attitude of the therapist can highlight and bring into focus.

This was the case with Conor. As he painted out his fear of doing the trauma story, he sensed himself as small, scared, and powerless. Using a mindful approach, I asked him if he had the impulse to do anything to his image, which allowed for the *what else* he was noticing, which was readiness, inner strength, and courage. These mindful, curious questions were turning points from the familiar fear response to an empowered, taking charge response that not only changed his image but also his present moment body, thinking, sensing, and feeling experience.

### Slowing the Pace

There are multiple dynamics happening within the therapy hour inside the client, inside the therapist, during the creating of the art, and in the relationships between client, art, and therapist. A good principle to follow is to intentionally work at a slower pace, allowing for a more mindful approach and way of being present. Slowing things down allows the therapist to track the body and energy of the client as well as the energy within herself.

When working with children, slowing things down creates space to integrate the learning that is happening and allows time to acknowledge and celebrate the changes. We can slow the process by encouraging the child to take mindful breaths when needed and offering invitations to notice the body's experience through thoughts, feelings, behaviors, and sensations.

While this slowing down can happen at any point in the therapy session, it can be particularly useful after an art expression. A therapist can say, "So we are just going to slow things down a little right now. Let's take a breath together and just notice where your attention wants to go right now." The therapist can also suggest that the child pay attention to what is happening in his body as he looks at his art.

When we invite this kind of noticing, we can also offer a menu of options if the child is uncertain or needs support with identifying potential ideas of what he is noticing. The goal of this noticing is to follow, in a sensory way, the child's experience with creating, to discover potential resources in the body or art, and to follow the lead of the child for the next step in the process. Often, this slowing down will point to where we need to go next and identify what is important to the child's experience.

With younger children, slowing the pace can be more challenging. We want to honor the natural flow and energy within the child, as well as support the child in developing a more regulated body experience. There can be time for both experiences within a session. When the goal is to slow the pace, we can create a safe or special sitting area in the office. We can make a point of teaching the child what this space is about. There may be several purposes for this safe space and for slowing down.

One very active 7-year-old fellow, who would likely never settle throughout the session if not directed, selected a certain chair in my office as his safe place. He was invited to bring whatever he needed into this space. Soon, without prompting, he would gather a pillow, blanket, and stuffed bunny to join him when he prepared his space. For this little fellow, this is where he would go to work on the hard stuff. He would draw, write, and share from this place. As I watched him prepare his space, he seemed to become more focused and ready to engage in this part of the work.

Slowing the pace can allow time for discovery of inner or outer resources. Creating a space in the therapy office, in particular for young children, supports and defines slowing down the pace. Finding this space within the office is done early on in the therapeutic work. It can become many things to the child and to the process.

## THE EAR OF THE HEART LISTENING

> For to listen is to continually give up all expectation and to give our attention, completely and freshly, to what is before us, not really knowing what we will hear or what that will mean. In the practice of our days, to listen is to lean in, softly, with a willingness to be changed by what we hear.
>
> (Nepo, 2005, p. 5)

Nepo's words remind me that "a willingness to be changed by what we hear" is a gift we offer as therapists: to hear the other so deeply that something in both the client and therapist is different. This does not mean we take responsibility for, or lose ourselves, in the other's story. It means we are awake, present, alive, and paying attention to what is said and what is not said. It means we are mindful about what we choose to attend to in the body of the client, the work of art, and in our own bodies as therapists. As therapists, we do not have preconceived ideas about what is needing to happen in the art with the client. However, we might be curious about the shifts and changes that are occurring in the art or in the way a client is working with his art. Together we are witness to something new, freshly unfolding before us. We are in that moment being changed. We can offer something new to this unfolding experience between client, art, and therapist. It is similar to the idea of "beginners mind," where we feel as though we are hearing and seeing things for the first time. In the moment by moment, listening and witnessing, we can be in the experience with our client, each session, and see with fresh eyes what is before and between both of us and the art.

Our ability to listen well is one of the primary processes and resources in the therapeutic relationship. It is a cornerstone. The experience of being listened to offers an experience of being seen and heard. In the true sense of a resource, the gift of listening can create an overall feeling of well-being. Yet, there are two kinds of listening in relationships. First, there is the "ear of the ear" kind of listening, where we listen on the surface, but we are already formulating what we want to say and may jump in and say it before the other is done. Much of our day-to-day communication goes this way.

Then there is the "ear of the heart" listening, the kind of listening that happens in the therapy relationship. This is where we listen to the other to completion. There is breath and pause as part of the listening. We hear beyond words as we watch the body of our client. The way the body speaks the words, how the hands and shoulders tell part of the story. We notice how the eyes open or close, and we notice the tilt of the head. We hear the tone of the client's voice, the energy that goes with the words. When there is so much to take in, we need pause and breathe to know what to attend to in any given moment.

When we work with the arts, we offer this kind of ear of the heart listening as we pay attention to the relationship that the creator has with her art. We watch this relationship develop. How does she take hold of the drum stick and sound the instrument? What kind of intensity is created between drum and client? What happens in the body of the client as she creates? Is there a sense of relief, excitement, playfulness, or tears?

The therapist's body also communicates ear of the heart listening. How are our eyes involved? Do our heads and body posture say, "I am with you, keep going." Sometimes, less is more: fewer words, more of the deep ear in the heart listening that may be offered in the form of a simple gesture allowing the outpouring of the other to bring his words, his art, his knowing forward. Our whole body is a message that can offer a profound sense of being seen by our clients. Words are only one way. Our bodies, and the energy we bring through our bodies, have a language all its own.

Within the energy that comes with ear of the heart listening there lies an eagerness. This eagerness of our listening, this paying attention, says, "I am here and I am present." How we show this, I believe, is an act of love. It is a demonstration of great passion and caring through whole body listening as we "lean in softly." How the therapist shows up in the therapeutic relationship makes all the difference. It is well and good that we have the most updated evidence-based research on trauma treatment, the books, and questionnaires. Yes, that is important. Equally as important is showing up with presence, eagerness, and love. These are some of the most precious resources we can offer.

## WORKING WITH RESOURCES

Now that we have identified resources and cultivated a resource-oriented attitude, there are specific ways of working with the resources in the art. The following sections highlight two ways of working with resources, including framing and amplifying the resource. The final section includes a discussion on how to use resources to manage nervous system activation in the expressive arts process.

### Framing the Resource

In the space of one session, therapists are continually making choices about what to pay attention to, what to let go of, what to highlight, and where to delve further. When using a body-focused, resource orientation to expressive arts, therapists have even more possibilities, including framing what is arriving through the art as a resource in the session. It can be useful to think of the following questions to decide what needs framing:

What are my overall goals with this client?
What are we specifically working on in this session?
What resources or strengths is the client demonstrating?
How does this resource tie into the client's overall goals?

Framing means that the therapist slows down the session, recognizes that something important has just happened, and brings awareness and attention to the experience. Typically, the therapist takes the time to frame the resource in the moment it is noticed, as resources often appear in spontaneous ways. These resources could be something experienced in the child's body, something tangible in the art, or small behaviors that the child may not recognize, such as standing up for herself, asking for what she needs, or demonstrating her bravery. This behavior can be framed by saying, "Something important just happened here and I would just like for us to take some time to be with this." At this point, she may not even be aware of what this is about, which is all the more reason to stop and frame the resource. Once the session has been slowed down and there is increased awareness and focus, identify what resource you have witnessed in your client that is worth framing.

As the resource is identified, the client is invited to notice what it is like to be noticed. We have an opportunity now to invite the client to be aware of her inner world of sensations, feelings, and thoughts about "all of this." Typically, there is a sense of pride and accomplishment as she too becomes aware of the resource.

Keep in mind these can be small behaviors or experiences that are often missed or only acknowledged in a fleeting way. Framing is the opportunity for our client to claim what is hers to claim and to become aware of and build on her repertoire of resources. Framing creates an atmosphere of attunement between client and therapist by helping the client feel seen and heard. Framing also encourages self-attunement through gentle noticing and paying attention to the body while learning about potential new resources.

In one of our first sessions, I asked 13-year-old Gina if she would be able to let me know if she was becoming overwhelmed by something in the session. She stated, "I'm really shy and don't want to make people angry. I'm insecure about what I say and do." This was important information for me to know and to keep in the back of my mind as we moved forward. A few months into our work together, Gina asked me if we could talk about the day her father left the family. Until this point, the work was structured around the sexual abuse by her cousin; what became apparent, however, was that there was another significant hurt that she knew she needed to address. This was a moment to frame and to claim. I slowed things down and acknowledged how important this was that she was asking for something she needed, that she was able to use her voice and express her need. We stayed with the experience by observing what it was like for her to speak her need and have me notice. She acknowledged some jittery sensations, some nervous-like feelings, and relief, all at the same time. We stayed with her body sensations and expanded the good by simply paying attention to the sensations and fully appreciating the whole of her experience. She then stated, "That felt scary but good."

Framing resources is the first step to owning the resource. There are many possible resources to frame, including behaviors, sensations, impulses, or knowings in the body or tangible art products. These choices can be guided by some of the previous questions regarding the overall goals for this particular child. With Gina, I chose to frame her ability to ask for what she needed because this was tied directly to one of her goals of being able to strengthen her confidence in her ability to speak up. Once the resource has been framed, we can now amplify or expand the resource.

## Amplifying the Resource

Amplifying, or expanding, the resources as they emerge is an important process in body-centered expressive arts because it allows the resource to be fully developed for the benefit of the client. The resource is amplified by giving it space through mindful awareness of body–art connections, being curious through gentle questions, and expanded by using other art modalities, as in the following example.

Zahra was 18, with a history of witnessing violence and experiencing physical and sexual trauma growing up in another country. She had been in Canada since she was 10 years old. We had worked together for some time, and in this particular session, as she began to speak about one of the assaults that she remembered, her body began to tremble. At this point, we had already had many conversations about the body and how trauma can stay alive in the nervous system as energy. As she experienced this sensation, she was visibly concerned but not frightened by what she was experiencing. She allowed the tremble to move through her legs and then her hands. When asked what she was noticing now, she identified an impulse to push, moving her hands out in front of her. We stood up, I took a pillow and placed it between our hands and she allowed the impulse of pushing to move from her shoulders, down through her arms, and into her hands. It was a steady, strong push. As she slowed the pushing, she began to notice a relief in her body. Through a slow and mindful process, she was encouraged to notice the sensation of relief.

T: "Did it expand and move or stay in the same place?"
Z: "It kinda stays right here" (pointing to her shoulders and chest).
T: "Does it flow, tingle, or pulse?"
Z: "It flows and kinda swirls around all over here" (again motioning to the upper body).
T: "What happens as you just stay with it?"
Z: "It is like a weight is gone. Like there is sunshine now."

Framing this image of the sunshine was like a turning point in our session. Something fresh and new was emerging. The sunshine was a new resource. I invited her to listen to her own knowing about what art form might capture and/or expand her experience of sunshine in her body. She knew right away she wanted to paint (Figure 4.3). As I watched her dip her

*Figure 4.3* Zahra's painting in response to her newly experienced body sensations. Used with permission.

paintbrush in paint and move it over the paper, her whole body was involved in what looked like a dance. She stepped side to side with wide sweeping arm motions as though she was a partner with the forming image on paper. She began with yellow then added multiple colors. As she used more colors, she noticed a growing excitement in her whole body. She made comments like, "This is inspiring *and* fun!" She delighted in the gold paint as she spread it across the paper. I commented, "I see a big smile on your face as you use more of the gold paint." She said, "Yes, I love using gold and I am excited as I paint. It is like a kaleidoscope on paper. This is like the excitement you feel when you play like a child." She was now connecting with good memories of her childhood that were previously concealed by the intense feelings of fear related to the traumas. I stayed with her in the process by inviting her to notice her body experience as she painted. Once finished with the paint, we gave one-word responses to her image, both of us speaking words that came to us as I wrote them down on paper. I offered these words back to her and she in turn created a poem. She then read her poem out loud:

> The freedom of dance of expression. To be who I am supposed to be. To have fun, to love and to be loved, to care and to be cared for. Happy. To spring forth. To move forward. To help others move forward. Self-awareness. Discovery. To lay the past to rest. To be free of fear. A small piece of the planet but an important piece to those around me. The beauty in me. To show others the love in me. Healing myself. The love I can feel for others. Pride in myself. Calmness, centered. I am the center. I can help people around me if I look after myself. Contentment. Peace. Freedom.

There were a number of elements at work in this example that emphasized a resource-oriented perspective through amplification. These elements include slowing of the pace, creating and allowing space to sense into her body, delighting in the positive sensations and feelings, moving to another art form, and the invitation to return to noticing, over and over again.

## Managing Activation With Resources in the Art

Vera was working on her image that tells the story of how she was impacted by the sexual abuse by her stepfather (Figure 4.4). She remained relatively calm as she drew her image. However, as she began to tell me about her image, she became visibly activated. Her heartbeat quickened and she had difficulty breathing, and then she began to cry and said, "That stuff over there wasn't supposed to happen." I asked her if there was anything she wanted to do to this art piece. She knew right away and asked for more paper. She covered up the part of the image that represented the sexual abuse (Figure 4.5). Immediately, she calmed down, grounded herself, and could continue sharing about her image. She then spoke about the rainbow in the image that represented her sister, who is her resource and is the one who helped her get through it all. Several resources were acknowledged and framed. First was the inner resource of her knowing what she needed to do to calm herself when triggered. She knew she needed to cover up part of her image in that moment. It was her idea and her body that followed suit to actively cover the upsetting part of the image. Second was the symbol of the rainbow that represented her sister, her resource, that she had already incorporated into her image.

It is a delicate interplay between working with the body, the activation in the nervous system, and the art. Each situation is different; however, staying close to and consulting with the

*Figure 4.4* Vera's drawing of how she has been impacted by sexual abuse. Used with permission.

*Figure 4.5* Vera's altered image. Used with permission.

body can guide what needs to happen. In this example, if we went back to the art, and Vera had no idea what to do, my second choice would be to make some suggestions of what she might like to do with the art (e.g., take it down, turn away), and if this still didn't help, then we would work directly with the body and use the strategies and skills she had already developed, such as using her resource cards, belly breathing, standing up and feeling her feet, or moving around in the space. We could work directly with the activation, becoming curious about what she was noticing and what her body wanted to do. Typically, the body knows what it needs to do and often just requires the opportunity to safely respond. Vera knew exactly what she needed to do and responded by using the resources in her art (covering part of her image and bringing her attention to the rainbow) to effectively manage the activation.

## DUMPSTER DIVING: THE THERAPIST'S HEALING AS A RESOURCE

> Like a bird whose broken wing has healed, I sing this constant song: Plunge deep enough into the other and a hidden light will glimmer there between us as we take turns being the wounded and the healer.
>
> (Nepo, 2005, p. 170)

A number of years ago when I had my first house built, the basement needed finishing. My then 75-year-old father and step mom came to visit with the intention of helping to frame and finish the basement. It was a new neighborhood, so many dumpsters stood outside homes in various stages of completion. We needed bits and pieces of lumber, and my father, being the practical and frugal kind of fellow he is, suggested we go dumpster diving. There was a bit of an art to this experience. We would wait until the sun was setting, then we donned our dumpster diving apparel and ventured out in search of thrown away treasures. We framed the majority of the basement with discarded materials found in the dumpsters. It got me thinking about where I looked for treasures, and how some of the most valuable treasures were found in some of the most unexpected places.

Searching for worthy materials in the dumpsters was like taking a leap of faith. One must have the courage (and perhaps a bit of a craze) to jump into a dumpster at dusk, not knowing what you might encounter. This is similar to the faith one must have to face one's own suffering—your own personal dumpster dive to discover the "worthy materials." The dumpster diving reminded me that this was the kind of faith I had when I began my own journey into healing. In fact, the "worthy" material I discovered in my personal dumpster diving was free. It was not from the expensive therapeutic trainings I had taken, but from deep excavating and discovery of what was already there inside waiting to be transformed. I pulled from the shadows of the dumpster the shameful terror along with other ruins and spent time with what I feared most. It was only then that I came to appreciate that there were gifts here in the dumpster and I learned to transform the fears and shame into gifts of compassion, presence, and safety.

Who would believe that childhood sexual abuse and many sexual assaults as an adolescent could become gifts. In fact, in my early adulthood, they were anything but gifts. The untreated trauma of my early life developed into a full blown eating disorder, severe self-harming behaviors, and strong suicidal ideation. In spite of it all, I had completed my bachelor's degree and began working in the field of social work. These symptoms of trauma continued, and I knew that I could not truly fulfill my calling as a therapist until I faced my own suffering and began my personal healing journey. I made a decision to take a year off my work to go to a place that would allow the depth of healing, the kind of dumpster diving I knew I so desperately needed. It truly was a fight for life when the only thing I knew and felt then was absolute darkness and wanting to die.

I found a healing center that I knew was right for me. I left everything behind and entered a battle to save my life. If I knew ahead of time how painful it would be, I am not sure I would have gone, although the living hell I was in was too much to take. I entered an 8-month journey with people I didn't know but trusted implicitly. I believe a miracle happened there. This was truly an experience of transformation. It was based on a tremendous amount of trust in the people I journeyed with and a daily commitment to face what I could not face alone, what I knew I could no longer live in because it was slowly destroying my body and soul. The healing was not only needed with respect to the traumas, but there was an added complexity of growing up in a very Catholic family of seven children in a tiny rural Saskatchewan community. The messages growing up were clear: Children were to be seen and not heard, hell was real, and do not speak unless spoken to.

In the early stages of my healing, I met a nun, "Mary," who was on her own journey in the center. Mary was a seamstress and quilter, and one day in passing she mentioned that if ever I was interested in creating a quilt she would help me. I remember, in that moment, thinking, "Quilt? Are you kidding? I don't even know how to sew up holes in my socks." I thanked her kindly and said I would let her know, yet my inside voice was saying, "I could never even begin to imagine making a quilt."

"Louisa" journeyed with me almost every day during my time there. She was an older woman, also a nun, so very wise and with the kind of eyes that reached into the deepest places in me that needed to be seen. She worked from a place of love, which meant both compassionately hearing and seeing the terrified little girl inside and offering firm, clear boundaries that I also needed at the time. Louisa never gave up on me. No matter how dark it got, I felt her love, and I knew she believed in the life within me that wanted so desperately to live.

Months passed, and at times I was not sure I would make it through alive. Although the healing was not easy, over time I slowly knew something was changing in me. There were pivotal moments in my work with Louisa when the transformation was so powerful, I began feeling that I was living a different life. Something so profound changed during that time and I have truly never looked back. After a long winter, I could sense spring coming. I felt an urging at this point to somehow integrate the changes that I had made as I felt a sense of power from within that I had never, ever before experienced. I needed to do something with this emerging life inside.

It was then that I recalled Mary's offer. I knew I needed to create some kind of quilt. I contacted Mary and asked if the offer was still good. She welcomed me with open arms. I knew *nothing* of the process of quilting. She gave me magazines to look through. Then something caught my eye: a crazy quilt. I laughed as I read the name, feeling the connection to it immediately and knowing somehow that the applique process was what I required to help integrate my experience.

Mary helped me get organized in the upstairs room where the afternoon sun would fill the space with warmth and soft light. The feel of the sun brought a strong sensation of hope in my body, a sign that I was surfacing on the other side of this healing journey in an integrated way. With boxes and boxes of fabric surrounding me, Mary simply said, "Start cutting." I did. I just knew there were images in me that needed to come out to make sense of my 8-month journey and to crystallize what was different in me at that point.

I had recently watched the movie *Jonathan Livingston Seagull*, read the book, and had the cassette tape of the soundtrack by Neil Diamond. This music became the backdrop and the theme songs to my healing experience as seagulls became woven throughout the quilt. Freedom. Striving. Believing. Along with the seagulls, there were butterflies, a sailboat, a child with balloons, a peace dove with a sprig of wheat, a heart surrounded by the community of people holding hands. In the center of the quilt was a rainbow. Hope. Symbols of life, of love, of new beginnings were emerging, but most of all, as these images were embodied through cloth material, I was experiencing a newfound freedom in my body.

There were times when I didn't have a clue what I was doing; however, it seemed at those very moments, Mary would pop her head into the room, listen to my desperation, and then she would simply look me in the eye with all her warmth and compassion and say, "Just trust, Carmen. Trust." And I did. Somehow her supportive, caring words were just what I needed to continue the quilt.

I spent weeks and weeks on that quilt. Spring had arrived. Fresh smells of earth intensified through the thaw and new life was rising and pushing forth through the dirt. Still, over and over, Neil Diamond's words of flight, of sky, of lost and found sounded through the room I inhabited during those months. I remember, toward the end of the quilt making, Mary and I took the bus to the fabric store as we were looking for material to finish the back. As we rode back, I recall the sensation of holding this very big bag of material that seemed to spill over the edges, and at the same time feeling equally as full inside my body with a renewed sense of aliveness spilling out of me. These were all new sensations and new ways of being. I was experiencing my very own body for what felt like the very first time.

The day we put the final touches on the quilt, Mary held it up so I could see it upright. I got the sense, and still do today when I look at it, that it is a child's quilt. Most certainly it was created from the child inside who was once lost, invisible, and alone in the world. There was no mistake, the child in me was guiding the process. However, the images created were very much of being seen and being connected, and they were full of vibrancy and, most importantly, hope. It is certainly not a masterpiece that would grace the walls of a quilter's home, but it is my masterpiece. It is my creation that continues to tell a story of trust, of community, of transformation, and of a passionate belief in God as I knew her then. I knew from my own experience that healing was more than possible. The story of transformation of the caterpillar, to the chrysalis, to the butterfly became embodied in my own story. It was my story. I was no longer the same. I was ready to fly. Fully free.

After completing the quilt, I knew there was still more to do. I knew I needed to write poems. I wrote about the overall theme of hope and about each section of the quilt, including freedom, play, connection, love, and spirit. I knew I needed to take photos. A friend and I drove out to nearby prairie fields where she took photos as I wrapped myself in the quilt to capture the sense of boundary, safety, and protection I experienced with this quilt. Then came the time to share my quilt with and read my poems to the group of people that I had lived and journeyed with over those 8 months. I knew I needed to speak my words. I spoke with shy tentativeness at first, but as I continued speaking, I could feel within me a life force rising up that would never again be pushed down. This remains true to this day.

I was ready to leave the healing center once the quilt was completed, the poems were written, and the process was witnessed by my community. My experience of completing the quilt gave me the most profound sense of integration I could imagine. I knew I was ready. I left my safe place of 8 months and went back into the world. The world looked different as I drove myself across the prairies, back to northern Saskatchewan, with my quilt folded next to me. Fully inhabiting my body now, I walked differently. Truly, nothing was the same.

This full engagement with the arts at that point in my healing was not accidental. Although I did not grow up with an "artist" identity, entering the expressive arts process was simply trusting what I knew I needed. I would not learn about the field of expressive arts therapy for some years to come. Those weeks alone, creating, reinforced and solidified every bit of emotional work I had been engaged in over the previous months. Prior to taking time off work, all I knew was that there was such a hatred for my body and a war that was declared in my internal world. Then, 8 months later, there was a very different landscape. For the very first time, a certain peaceful calm resonated through my whole being as the energy of life was rising up everywhere within me. Engaging with the arts was essential because it allowed me to drop into this very new landscape, claim it, and put into visible form an invisible process. It became tangible through the quilt, and as I gave it voice through poetry, it became real. Like the Velveteen Rabbit. Perhaps that is what happened. That learning to love oneself in this fully compassionate way made me feel "real." I no longer felt invisible to the world or to myself.

Now, 25 years later, I can see how the threads of my past healing experience are keenly woven into the fabric of my current work as three valuable resources. These resources are working from a place of love, believing in transformation, and knowing from the inside the healing medicinal qualities of the expressive arts. First, what I experienced through relationships in the healing center was love. These people were called to lay their lives down for another, and they did this with a sense of compassion and profound love in every interaction I experienced. It was a way of being in a therapeutic relationship that I came to fully embrace in my own work: journeying with others with tremendous love, gratitude, and hope. Second, I experienced such a profound personal transformation that continues to serve as a deep, deep knowing about the possibility for change. I chose to face the suffering and the resulting injuries, and I found the treasure in the dumpster by diving in. Third, the expressive arts showed up spontaneously in my own healing. I know in my own bones what medicine lies in the arts. It is the bringing together of music, fabric, images, poetry, photos, voice, and the power of being witnessed in the process. What I have learned from this journey is that healing from significant emotional injuries is possible, and that there is hope if we have the courage to seek it by diving deep. This is what my story has taught me. And, I do believe we all have a story. It is part of the human condition.

## REFERENCES

Atkins, S., & Duggins Williams, L. (2007). *Sourcebook in expressive arts therapy*. Boone, NC: Parkway Publishers.

Buchanan, J. (2012). *Tune in: A music therapy approach to life*. Austin, TX: Hugo House.

Halprin, D. (2003). *The expressive body in life, art and therapy: Working with movement, metaphor and meaning*. London: Jessica Kingsley.

Heller, D., & Heller, L. (2001). *Crash course: A self-healing guide to auto accident trauma & recovery*. Berkeley, CA: North Atlantic Books.

Heller, L., & LaPierre, A. (2012). *Healing developmental trauma: How early trauma affects self-regulation, self-image, and the capacity for relationship*. Berkeley, CA: North Atlantic Books.

Kabat-Zinn, J. (2013). *Full catastrophe living: Using the wisdom of your body and mind to face stress, pain, and illness* (2nd ed.). New York: Bantam Books.

Levine, P., & Kline, M. (2007). *Trauma through a child's eyes: Awakening the ordinary miracle of healing.* Berkeley, CA: North Atlantic Books.

McNiff, S. (1992). *Art as medicine: Creating a therapy of the imagination.* Boston, MA: Shambhala Publishers.

Nepo, M. (2005). *The exquisite risk: Daring to live an authentic life.* New York: Three Rivers Press.

Ogden, P., Minton, K., & Pain, C. (2006). *Trauma and the body: A sensorimotor approach to psychotherapy.* New York: W.W. Norton.

Rothschild, B. (2000). *The body remembers: The psychophysiology of trauma and trauma treatment.* New York: W. W. Norton.

Steele, W., & Malchiodi, C. (2012). *Trauma-informed practices with children and adolescents.* New York: Routledge.

# Part 3

# An Expressive Arts Four-Phase Model of Treatment

# 5 Introduction to the Expressive Arts Four-Phase Model

There are many excellent resources available with evidence-based practices for the treatment of trauma in children (Blaustein & Kinniburgh, 2010; Cohen, Mannarino, & Deblinger, 2006; Gil, 2006; Gil, 2010; Greenwald, 2005; Levine & Kline, 2007; Malchiodi, 2008; Steele & Kuban, 2013; Steele & Malchiodi, 2012; Steele & Raider, 2009). The treatment approaches vary from play-based, creative therapies to trauma-informed cognitive-behavioral therapy (CBT) and more.

What there appears to be less of are well-defined, step-by-step approaches to treatment that clearly identify the safe, ethical details of how to integrate expressive arts into trauma treatment with children. This does not imply that there is a one-size-fits-all approach to therapy. We need to remain flexible in the work while adapting evidence-based treatment strategies and goals to meet the individual needs of the children with whom we journey.

Within the trauma treatment literature, there are thorough, phase-oriented treatment processes that use structured, evidence-based interventions but make little mention of the body and the importance and potential of working with the body and the arts. The somatically based treatment interventions include detailed processes for working with trauma in adults, but little in the way of working with young people. In the expressive arts literature, there are books that offer creative art or expressive arts ideas and interventions for trauma treatment, but there is less information on providing a safe, structured, coherent approach that can guide the therapist throughout assessment and treatment planning.

This book is an attempt to create a comprehensive framework that is informed by current, evidence-based practices that can guide and support the safe integration of trauma treatment into the therapist's practice with children. This approach brings together a body-centered, expressive arts, resource-oriented approach to trauma treatment in a four-phase model.

The treatment interventions outlined in this book are guided by what is currently known in the interdisciplinary field of neuroscience that studies the nervous system and the brain. The goals of these interventions are threefold. First, we work with sensory interventions to access traumatic material through sensory memories that are typically held in the right brain (Steele & Raider, 2009). Second, we are simultaneously working with the natural pendulation of the nervous system (Levine & Kline, 2007), teaching children to manage body arousal that is triggered by traumatic memory so that they are neither in an overwhelmed nor a numb state while doing the work (Ogden, Minton, & Pain, 2006; Siegel, 2010). The third goal is to help the memories and images that are held in the right brain by using left brain functioning to fully process the memories through verbal and nonverbal means (Stien & Kendall, 2004).

Trauma work with children and teens can feel daunting at times. What is the next step? How do I know if my client is ready to address the trauma? When is enough processing enough? Therapists need a clear, accessible, and evidence-based approach that can meet the complex needs with which children present.

Given that helplessness and powerlessness are often at the heart of traumatic experiences, "interventions must be directed at the restoration of a sense of safety and power" (Steele & Raider, 2009, p. 20). The primary intention of this expressive arts approach to the treatment of trauma and the interventions outlined in these phases were developed with this belief in mind. Restoration of power, safety, and mastery are at the heart of these interventions from assessment to closure.

## OVERVIEW OF THE FOUR PHASES

While the therapeutic process is not a linear one, it is essential to establish certain building blocks that are required to be able to move the therapeutic work forward in a safe and structured manner. The four phases are (1) understanding the child's world, (2) cultivating safety and resources, (3) trauma processing, and (4) reclaiming, reframing, repairing, and reorienting. As we keep in mind that one size never fits all, the present moment needs of our client are the priority. That can mean, at times, that we lay aside the "map" and simply sit with and be present to what our client is needing to say or do in that moment. Further, one phase can cross over to another, so we may end up simultaneously doing assessment from Phase One and skill building from Phase Two.

### Phase One: Understanding the Child's World

Assessment clarifies and highlights the areas where the client is vulnerable and where she is strong, well resourced, and resilient. Assessment also provides the therapist with a baseline from which to gauge progress over time. Keeping in mind the qualifications required to administer certain tests, along with potentially limited time frames, tools were selected based on accessibility and range of information gathered to provide a *good enough* picture of the inside and outside world of the child. Assessment tools range from standardized trauma checklists, to arts-based assessment tools for information gathering, to trauma-specific questionnaires developed to gather details related to *this* child's experience.

### Phase Two: Cultivating Safety and Resources

The primary goal of Phase Two is to ensure the child is stable, safe, and has healthy resources to manage emotions both during therapy and in his world. In therapy, the child learns to use his resources to manage nervous system arousal in response to working on trauma material. Phase Two interventions were created to assist with teaching emotional regulation skills needed to prepare for trauma processing in Phase Three.

### Phase Three: Trauma Processing

Phase Three offers body-focused expressive arts interventions that support safe trauma processing while helping the child heal her relationship with her body. One of the main goals in Phase Three is for the child to tell her trauma story in a safe and regulated way. The second goal of Phase Three is to assist the child with understanding and learning about the body's survival responses in relation to what happened in her body at the time of trauma and what is happening now in her body as she does the therapeutic work. Understanding and knowing what happened then and what is happening now in the body can be empowering as the child learns the language for sensations and can name the body experience of survival.

**Phase Four: Reclaiming, Reframing, Repairing, and Reorienting**

Children live with many problematic thoughts, feelings, and beliefs as a result of experiencing the devastating effects of traumatic events. Often, close relationships need repair and support along the way. The main goals of the Phase Four expressive arts intervention are reclaiming power; reframing thoughts, feelings, and beliefs; repairing relationships; encouraging a future-oriented perspective; and celebrating strengths.

## WORKING WITH SINGLE-INCIDENT AND MULTIPLE TRAUMAS

Some children come to therapy with single-incident trauma, and other children come with knowing only chaos and fear in their young bodies and minds for most of their lives. We need a map to address both kinds of trauma. The process is often less complex for single-incident trauma. The guidelines and principles are similar for both kinds of trauma, in that safety in the therapeutic and caregiving relationships and learning self-regulation skills prior to processing remain the same. However, the individual needs of each child vary.

When children have experienced long-term abuse and/or neglect, it is more difficult to work on specific memories because they have lived in turmoil for much of their young lives. In situations of long-term child abuse, one incident blurs into another. At the end of Phase One, children identify the main incidents of trauma that they remember and write those incidents on puzzle pieces then place them in a wooden box for safe keeping. By the time they reach Phase Three, further incidents may be remembered and more puzzle pieces can be added to the box at that time. Details of this process and how to work with multiple traumas are further explained in Chapter 6 in the section Pieces of My Story Part One: Remembering.

## PHASE GUIDELINES AND PHASE INTERVENTIONS: RATIONALE AND PROCESS

A chapter for each of the four phases follows this introductory chapter. The phases include a range of interventions developed to guide the therapist with meeting the goals of that particular phase. Within each chapter, the rationale and process are described in detail for each intervention. The "rationale" grounds the intervention within the trauma-focused framework, and the "process" includes the details about how to engage clients with this particular intervention. An example of how this intervention was used with a child and/or adolescent often follows. The interventions themselves are found in the Appendices.

## CAREGIVER INVOLVEMENT THROUGHOUT THE FOUR PHASES

Caregiver support is often the bridge that brings the learning from the therapy office into the day-to-day world of the child. This bridge is essential for the child, as is the relationship with his caregiver. The caregiver relationship is key to healing attachment injuries as a result of relational trauma; thus, the caregiver's involvement is of great importance. However, the level of caregiver involvement varies depending on the relationship the child has with his caregiver, the age of the child, and the behaviors that need to be addressed.

During Phase One, we are assessing the relationship the child has with his caregiver. If the adolescent has recently been placed in foster or group home care, he may not have the kind of relationship with his caregiver that would warrant the caregiver attending sessions. In this situation, the child could have the option of identifying someone he would like to have as a bridge between therapy and the rest of his world, and he can begin developing a trusting relationship with a caregiver in his outside world. Some caregivers may simply remain involved in more peripheral ways by providing information regarding general well-being and progress in the group or foster home and identifying any developing strengths or behaviors of concern. However, with younger children, the caregivers are more directly involved in sessions as they are the ones providing external support.

Caregiver involvement in the assessment process includes interviews regarding the child's developmental history, identification of both challenging and positive behaviors, and trauma history/information. Caregivers are also taught how to be witnesses to their child's therapeutic work as they will be asked to be involved in the therapy process. In Phase One, caregivers will be given handouts to complete and will be involved in interviews in which information is exchanged about the child. They will also be involved in a feedback session once the assessment is complete. At times, some children's behaviors are so challenging that consultation regarding how to intervene with these behaviors is required in a more immediate way.

In Phase Two, as the child is in process of learning the many skills required to navigate her world, the caregiver will typically attend the last quarter of every two to four sessions. The child teaches her caregiver what she has learned in the session, and the caregiver has the opportunity to identify any progress the child has made in the home/school environment.

In Phase Three, caregivers may be involved throughout the sessions as the child processes the trauma. Some children, particularly older children, prefer to be on their own, whereas younger children may need or want the support of their caregivers. This preference is child driven. If not involved in the trauma processing, caregivers may be invited in at the end of the session for any updates that will assist them with how to best support their child as a result of the processing. For example, the child may need increased space or nurturing; the caregiver is made aware of any potential triggers; and we review how the caregiver can support the child with using resources as regulation skills. The child is involved in a discussion about what information will be shared with the caregiver, who shares it, and how. The child may want to tell the caregiver, or he may not want to be present and would rather the therapist share the information. The level of detail the caregiver is given is dependent upon the developmental age of the child and the nature of relationship the child has with the caregiver, as described previously in Phase One.

Caregivers are prompted to offer the child authentic encouragement and praise for being brave enough to do this work. These kinds of messages tell the child that the caregivers believe in the child's ability to address the trauma and they recognize the strength it takes to do this work. The caregivers provide reassuring responses that offer the child the understanding that the caregiver is in tune with the child's inner and outer worlds.

Phase Four often includes supportive or reparative family work, when deemed necessary or recommended. Throughout the remaining individual sessions, caregivers attend parts of the session as necessary for updates and/or for integration of what the child is learning, such as cognitive coping strategies, that requires bridging to other parts of her world.

## THE THERAPY PROCESS OVER TIME:
## BEGINNING, MIDDLE, AND END

We may not always know how long we have to work with a client or how many sessions will be available; however, it is beneficial to have a framework that guides the overall work. Regardless of the number of sessions, it can be useful to think of the flow of the therapeutic work as having a beginning, a middle, and an ending with each client. The interventions section is laid out in a sequential way, where each phase of intervention builds a foundation for the next phase. The following is a brief summary of the overall goals for these phases. These will be more thoroughly reviewed under each phase in the chapters ahead.

### Beginning Goals

Assess impact of trauma
Assess nature of caregiver relationship
Identify therapy goals
Establish therapeutic relationship

### Middle Goals

Build skills and resources
Process trauma

### End Goals

Review therapy goals and progress
Reframe thoughts
Repair relationships
Orient to the future, celebrate and provide closure

## NUMBER OF SESSIONS REQUIRED

There are a variety of factors that influence the number of sessions we have with our client. If we work for an agency, the agency guidelines for the expected number of sessions will provide a framework. If in private practice, the amount of coverage from insurance companies and/or our client's financial resources will guide, in part, what we are able to accomplish in the assessment and treatment process. Other factors that determine the number of sessions include the caregiver and/or community support available for the client, the family or client's stability, the client's ability to engage in the process of therapy, and the client's readiness for the work. It is useful to keep these factors in mind as we assess and create a treatment plan for our client.

Our objective is to design the most meaningful and realistic treatment plan guided by the number of sessions we have, or believe we have, at the outset of the therapeutic process. If we enter the process knowing we have only a few sessions, the goals must reflect what can be realistically accomplished within that time.

### Up to Five Sessions

When we begin therapy knowing we have very limited time with a client, our work is to get clear about what the family/child wants and needs. Next, we identify achievable outcomes. Of the four trauma treatment phases outlined, Phase Two, cultivating safety and resources, is the place to start. Understanding and learning how to use resources can be very beneficial for the child and caregiver as they try to successfully navigate the child's world when time is limited.

### Up to 10 Sessions

Having a little more time, and depending on the needs and abilities of the client, we may be able to move into trauma processing if the child is well grounded and has strong attachments to caregivers. If the client struggles with significant attachment concerns, we would likely only work in Phases One and Two, with a focus on strengthening the attachment relationship. Stabilizing concerning behaviors, teaching skills on how to manage emotions, and identifying how the caregivers can provide optimal support to the child would be some of the primary goals.

**More Than 10 Sessions**

If we begin the therapy process knowing or believing sufficient time is available to complete the four-phase process, we can take approximately 3 sessions to complete the assessment and 15 to 20 sessions for the treatment phases. We make decisions about what interventions best suit the needs of each individual client and his family.

## INDIVIDUAL SESSION STRUCTURE: BEGINNING, MIDDLE, AND END

The rhythm and flow of each session is an important part of any therapeutic work. We can think about the session as having the basic form of a beginning, a middle, and an ending. The interventions in the four phases are structured and goal specific. We can take these structured interventions and work with them in the flow of a session.

Creating structured, consistent, and predictable experiences increases the chances of creating a strong therapeutic alliance. Children come to know what to expect of the therapist and what is expected of them. The need to provide a safe and secure therapeutic environment drives the decisions that we make when creating therapeutic structures. There is sufficient support in the literature today for using a structured approach to the treatment of trauma (Cohen et al., 2006; Greenwald, 2005; Steele & Raider, 2009).

Respecting the particular needs of a child on any given day may mean leaving the material or structure and following the need of the client and being present to current, day-to-day issues. However, if this happens on a regular basis, it could be a sign that there is not sufficient stability to move forward with the trauma work at this time. Other needs may take precedence, and this will likely become apparent in the assessment phase.

### Beginning: Connection, Snack, Open Art

The first welcoming minutes are central to relationship building as we greet the child with warmth and attentiveness. We greet her with our eyes and our body in a way that says, "It is good to see you; you are important to me." There are many potential pathways that the beginning of a session can take, but be mindful to keep it to a 10-minute window. Again, these are simply guidelines, and the needs of our client always come first. In the beginning of the session, we can offer a snack and/or drink as we check in about the child's week, allowing us to settle into the space and the comfort of the therapeutic relationship. A general intention for the beginning of a session is to connect with the client's current situation and emotional state and clarify the client's readiness for the work at hand. Depending on the child, this can be a time for open, nondirective art expression as a way of connecting and grounding into the present space and time.

The beginning is also a time when we receive pertinent information from the caregiver regarding what is happening in the child's world from the caregiver's point of view. Because each situation is different, some caregivers will leave information on a voicemail or email before the session. The child is aware that this information will be provided only as necessary and pertinent to the therapeutic work. For many clients, in particular with adolescents, it builds trust when they are involved in this sharing of information whenever possible.

We are continually making decisions about how and when to proceed to the middle phase of the session. Some clients are great storytellers and would like to talk about generalities throughout the whole session. When a client is in a state of crisis, we need to tend to and support him regarding the situation. If this becomes a pattern, we may need to renegotiate the terms of therapy to offer a more supportive counseling approach, rather than a structured trauma approach. However, if it becomes evident that these discussions are more diversions from dealing with the trauma work, we can let the client know that the first 10 minutes will be used to debrief about his week, and then we will move into the middle phase of the session. This message supports a structured and consistent approach to the work. The message can also be a way of letting the client know we will be addressing the difficult material, we believe he is capable of doing that work, and that we, the therapist, know the "map" for the work. Finally, this message is also a way of honoring the therapy goal of trauma treatment.

Some families are in need of extra support, even though they are ready to deal with the trauma. It can be useful to bring in other community resources, such as in-home family support, the school guidance counselor, or a community mental health professional, to support the family with the day-to-day struggles. If the family is able to manage support from both the therapist and another community resource, the boundary of the trauma work is maintained and we are more likely to stay on track.

### Implied Affirmations and Messages

I see you.
You are important to me.
It is safe here.
You are welcome here.
We can play together.

## Middle: The Hard Stuff

The middle of the session is where we do the meat of the work, guided by the interventions as outlined in the four phases. For some children it is important to negotiate the time spent on the hard stuff, in particular at the beginning of therapy as they are becoming familiar with expectations and the process of therapy. Having choices about how much time is spent on the hard stuff gives a sense of power and control over some aspects of the work. We can negotiate what is reasonable for this particular child. It is not a question of *if* we do the difficult work, but *when* and *how much*. Being clear about this expectation from the start gives the message of the therapist's confidence in the child's ability to work through the trauma and the therapist's confidence in the therapeutic map.

More time is required for the middle part of the session as our client's confidence in her ability to tolerate dealing with the hard stuff increases. While we are following a structured framework, we are also engaged with the arts, which can make the tough work more tolerable. We are often working intensely with the creative process, where time is often lost in the flow of creativity. It is our responsibility to ensure there is time for closure.

### Implied Affirmations and Messages

I believe in your ability to work through and face the hard stuff.
Hope exists even in the dark places.
You are not alone.
We are in this together.
Your "team" (e.g., caregivers, friends) are rooting for you!

## End: Grounded and Present

There are two primary goals for the ending phase of the session. The first goal is to ensure there is time for proper closure when doing trauma work, as it can be very activating (Crenshaw, 2006). This means that before the end of a session, we bring our awareness to the child's body to ensure that there is little to no activation left from engaging in interventions that were potentially triggering. We use the intervention handout Managing Activation (see Appendix B) and mark on the client's chart how high her anxiety or upset feelings got in the session and what it was in the session that made it that high. I then ask where she is now on that scale to determine how much work we might need to do to ensure she is feeling grounded, present, and calm in her body and mind before leaving the session. For some clients, too much arousal could mean they disconnect or become numb, meaning we may need to bring their energy up at the end of the session so they become more present and engaged.

Doing a movement activity is highly effective for bringing down any trauma activation that may have been triggered in the therapeutic work as well as bringing the energy up to a more present state. Using a Thumball™ is one of my favorite ways of closing a session. It is a soft, small, soccer-like ball with a variety of movement activities on each ball panel, from jumping jacks to kicking a goal and cheering. Whether working with adults or children, this kind of movement can be an efficient way to move from trauma-activated arousal in the nervous system to a playful, fun, and more relaxed state. We cannot be both upset and playful at the same time. When a child scans her body after playing this game, she often reports noticing playful, positive energy in her body, rather than trauma-related activation.

Creating an art debrief at the end of a session can also be a way of lowering activation and closing a session. The client is asked to scan his body to determine if there is anything that is uncomfortable or leftover from the session that he would like "put out" of himself through creating art. Clients are advised of the time available for this creating. Even though only a short time frame may be available, the process of checking in and expressing through art can be a very effective way of lowering any arousal or bringing the client to the present moment.

These are only two of the possibilities for working with states of arousal or disconnect. It is best to experiment with a variety of interventions and have the child identify which activity works best.

As we come to know our client, we will learn how much time is required to end the session in a safe and regulated manner. If the level of activation is not low enough, we need to take time to find other strategies to decrease or contain the activation until the next session. Generally, when we are working from a body-centered perspective, we are very much in tune with what is happening in the bodies of our clients and we work with modulating sensations and emotions throughout the session. It is a sensitive process that is guided by the specific and unique needs of each client.

The second goal for the ending of a session is to determine what, if anything, the client can take away from the session. Asking this question consolidates what the client has learned and bridges the learning from the therapy world to her everyday life. It is also useful, when appropriate, to share this learning with their caregiver who can support by witnessing the child using this resource, which increases the chances of the client remembering to integrate the resource in her daily life.

### Implied Affirmations and Messages

It is my job to make sure you leave therapy in an emotionally safe place.
We can do hard stuff *and* we can come back to a calm and happy body.
Your body is amazing.
Play and fun are important in our work.

## TEMPORAL ORIENTATIONS: THEN AND NOW/PAST AND PRESENT

Many of the four-phase interventions offer a then–now, past–present orientation. We have conversations and create art that reflect thoughts and emotions from the past, and we pay attention to how those past thoughts and feelings are experienced in the present moment. This orienting from past to present serves to assist clients with placing the trauma experience in the past, while bringing awareness to how their thoughts and emotions shift and change over time. It can bring a sense of hope and positive perspective to the therapeutic work, because many of the experiences were much more difficult or intense at the time they were occurring. The child can "see" in his art and feel the difference in his body between then and now. This past–present orientation also highlights feelings and thoughts that may now be experienced as more upsetting and require further exploration. Typically, these are trauma-influenced thoughts, feelings, and beliefs that need to be addressed when most appropriate in the therapy process.

## WORKING WITH THE BODY'S RHYTHM

Our bodies have a natural ability to regulate between pleasant and unpleasant experiences or feelings at any given moment throughout the day. We can move from feeling calm, to being negatively activated by something or someone around us, and back to feeling grounded again. Levine and Kline (2007) describe this process as pendulation. When a child has experienced trauma, this natural rhythm has been thwarted, resulting in more experiences of high arousal and emotional dysregulation. This back and forth rhythm needs to be restored so that the client can come to know, regardless of how difficult a feeling is, that the feeling will change and she can feel good again.

From this perspective of pendulation, many of the expressive arts interventions offer experience in the back and forth movement between activated and calm body. Experiencing then–now interventions over time can remind children that they are safe now, even though their body experiences can trigger frightening bodily responses in the now. We work with present time, with the body's current experience, to deal with the activation so that the current experience matches knowledge that the client is in the present and safe. Clients are invited to bring the curiosity of the cat to separate the feeling of fear from the sensation, increasing the chances that the child will allow the body to discharge the fight/flight energy that was mobilized at the time of trauma but was not able to be used (Levine, 1997). We separate the feeling from the sensation by staying with and being curious about the sensation, allowing it to move as it needs to through the body. Often there is a sense of relief and good feeling that follows. Having this experience of pendulation builds the child's confidence in his ability to return to a regulated body, thus increasing his readiness to engage in the trauma processing in Phase Three.

## THERAPIST AND CAREGIVER ATTUNEMENT TO THE CHILD

> The process of emotional attunement enables us to achieve a direct connection between our children and ourselves. This alignment is a form of interpersonal integration. At the heart of this attuning is the sharing of nonverbal signals, including tone of voice, eye contact, facial expressions, gestures, and timing and intensity of responses. Being mindful of these signals in our children is paralleled by our own awareness of the sensations of our own bodies. Bodily sensations form an important foundation for knowing how we feel and what has meaning in our lives.
>
> (Siegel & Hartzell, 2003, p. 249)

Wherever we are in the therapy process, attuning to the child and her experiences is the foundation of the therapeutic work. Attunement is our ability to be fully and compassionately present with what the child is experiencing within both her internal and external worlds. We are aware of what she is saying and doing, and we are connected and tuned in to what she is experiencing within, including feelings and sensations. To maintain attunement, we are also aware and tuned in to our own bodies and internal worlds. If we become triggered, we will likely lose the attunement with our client. We must also learn to come back to our own body by grounding ourselves with practices that bring us back to present moment. Feeling the slow, steady inhale and exhale of our breath and noticing the sensation of our feet on the ground can support the regrounding.

We also need to assess the caregivers' abilities to attune to their child. We encourage and coach caregivers to attune to their child's rhythm, their need for expression, and their need for nurturance. Caregivers are supported with learning how to ground themselves as they care for their child and his overwhelmed nervous system. Caregivers may themselves be traumatized or have untreated trauma that has been activated by their child's trauma. Caregivers may need to access their own therapy to best support their child. Therapist and caregiver alike are best positioned to respond effectively to children when they themselves are regulated, calm, and well-resourced with self-care strategies.

## COMPASSIONATE LISTENING

Listening with the ear of the heart is one of the most important gifts therapists can give their clients, as described in more detail in Chapter 4 in The Ear of the Heart Listening section. We offer and model compassionate listening, *and* we teach our clients to listen compassionately to all they are sensing in their inner worlds. Teaching this kind of deep listening can assist clients with becoming more curious about the feelings and sensations that arise in the body in response to the triggers of trauma. In Phase Two, children are taught to befriend the different parts of themselves, including the fearful, angry, and the confused parts in the Learning to Be My Own Best Friend intervention (see Appendix F). We teach clients to be like their own best friends and to learn to listen to and understand the feelings and sensations of the sad, hurt, or angry parts of themselves. We teach them to sit with these feelings and sensations and to be curious, as well as to ask about them and to let the parts know they are hearing the feelings (Cornell, 2013).

## STRUCTURED FLEXIBILITY

As much as these creative interventions are designed to meet specific treatment goals, we also remain open to where the creativity and uniqueness of our clients take us. Children teach us new ideas as they find their own healing pathways specific to their needs. We practice *structured flexibility*; this means we know the therapy "map" and because we know the map, we are able to be in the present moment, allowing the body and the impulse of creativity to also guide the healing process. Eberhart and Atkins (2014) write about the paradoxical relationship between structure and being open to what arises in the art, stating:

> *It is often within a clearly held frame that it is possible to freely trust the process.* Allowing the freedom to trust the process within a clear frame is based on the ability of the change agent to hold the structure in a playful rather than a rigid way.

(p. 135)

The therapist is mindful about which interventions to offer clients, remaining open to altering or omitting as needed, because not all interventions will be meaningful to each child. We can't predict which interventions the child will connect with. At the same time, the therapist remains flexible, following the child's process of creativity and needs in the present moment.

## WHAT TO DO WITH THE TANGIBLE ART

Typically, all art work remains with the therapist to ensure safe keeping during therapy. Having the client's art available at any given time allows for the art to be reviewed, shaped, or shared when necessary. While the child owns the art she has created, it is essential that the therapist, client, and caregiver have a discussion about what to do with the art work when preparing for closure. Sometimes there are specific pieces of art that the client wants to take home to be used as a reminder of something important, or simply because she likes it. When taking any art home, explore and ensure that it will be safe from judgment and protected from unnecessary inquiry. This typically means working with the caregiver to make decisions that are in the best interests of this particular child. Further, it is best to consult with the standards of practice set out by the various regulating bodies that have the clients' best interests in mind, such as the Canadian Art Therapy Association or the International Expressive Arts Therapy Association.

## MODIFYING INTERVENTIONS

Each intervention in the four phases is designed to meet a particular goal for that phase of the therapeutic work. While there may be only one specific art modality suggested for that intervention, a variety of art modalities could be used. The underlying premise is that each intervention should be modified to best meet the needs of the client as you come to know him. If a child has more comfort with or interest in acting things out with puppets instead of drawing, the process of the intervention is modified, staying as true to the theme of the intervention as possible.

## WORKING INTERMODALLY

Although the directive for the intervention may only suggest creating with one art form, moving to another art modality within the same intervention is a natural process in expressive arts. If a child has just painted an image, she may then write a story that goes with the image. Whenever possible, and as time permits, working with another art form, either simultaneously or sequentially, is encouraged. Working intermodally is described in detail in Chapter 2.

## PERMISSION STATEMENTS

In Chapter 2, we discussed the need to offer clients permission statements, inviting them to find safe ways to engage and explore with the various art modalities. Permission statements offered about their trauma experiences are different kinds of statements. Children need to know it is okay to give voice to the horrible things that have happened to them or that they have witnessed. Addressing this issue at the beginning of therapy tells the child early on that he has permission to share what may seem like unshareable experiences. Even when this permission is given, some children still have difficulty and may need to ask permission. One little fellow asked if it was okay if he told me the "yucky stuff" that happened. When I let him know how important it was that he speak the "yucky stuff," he said with relief, "Good, I was worried cause sometimes my feelings just get burped out." An adolescent girl who was sexually abused thought she would be in trouble if she shared or drew her story because she believed she would be drawing pornography. Another young boy asked permission to rip up the picture of the person who abused him. These are very key questions and beliefs that need to be discussed and thoroughly addressed to assist children with more fully expressing without undue stress. Some of these questions can be discussed in the context of boundaries when we address what is acceptable and not acceptable in the expressive arts space.

## MOVING FROM ONE PHASE TO THE NEXT

How do we know when our clients are ready to move to the next phase of therapy? What do we look for? How do we assess their abilities and strengths? At the end of each phase, questions are asked and points are reflected upon to help the therapist discern client readiness to move to the next phase. These questions and points are not rigid; rather they are guides. If there is concern about a point, it deserves further investigation, and time is needed for clarifying what might be in the way or what might be required before moving to the next phase of treatment. If a child is not wanting to close therapy, it may signal that she is experiencing sadness over the loss of connection, and this grief needs to be supported. This doesn't mean we don't close. It does mean we explore more fully to understand and tune into what is present and needs attending to.

Our readiness as therapists can be assessed as well. Are we so afraid to do harm that we avoid addressing the traumatic experiences ourselves? Do we take our clients' avoidance of the trauma as a sign they are not ready? What comes up in us as therapists when we see the pain in our clients as they work through the hard stuff? What are our beliefs about trauma processing, and how do they fit with working through the gradual exposure of trauma work? Understanding what informs and guides our own beliefs about therapy, the change process, and trauma treatment deserves attention.

## THERAPIST HANDOUTS FOR ORGANIZING ASSESSMENT AND TREATMENT INFORMATION

As information is gathered regarding the child's trauma experience, the material needs to be organized in a meaningful way. These handouts, provided in Appendix B, do not replace an outline for a comprehensive assessment and treatment plan; they are tools that can assist the therapist with tracking the process of, progress in, and direction of therapy. Further, they organize information to ensure clear feedback to the caregivers and child. These forms assist and guide information flow throughout the four phases.

### Highlighting Core Issues

*Rationale:* It can be very useful to have one location or form where the therapist highlights the primary issues that need to be addressed. The purpose is to briefly emphasize, in point form, specific issues that come up as you complete the assessment with the child and his caregiver.

*Process:* At the end of each assessment session, take a few minutes to highlight the particular issues that have been flagged that will need to be addressed, and document areas of strength that can be used as potential resources. If any tests have been used (e.g., the TSCC or the BASC), highlight the at-risk or clinically significant scales here.

### Feedback Form

*Rationale:* This form is used to identify the salient themes from the assessment that can be used to offer specific feedback to the caregivers and the child.

*Process:* Once all the assessment forms and sessions are complete, a written report is compiled for the therapist's records. The therapist can add information to the feedback form as she goes along during the assessment, or she can complete the form postassessment. The idea is to succinctly identify the central points that the caregiver will need to hear in order to understand how the child has been impacted by the trauma and how the caregiver can best support the child in the therapy process. The child is also offered information that is meaningful at his developmental level.

Under the Feedback to Child section, we add ideas from the child and her caregivers about the child's strengths and areas that need support. Typically for children 12 and under, the caregiver feedback session is best done without the child, so that the caregivers have the opportunity to clarify any aspect of the assessment in as much detail as they might need, without concerns for overwhelming the child. For adolescents, depending on their relationship with their caregivers, we can jointly decide who needs to be at their feedback sessions. Each situation is unique, calling for careful consideration about who should attend the feedback session.

### Tracking Assessment and Treatment

*Rationale:* It can be difficult to manage everything that is going on in a session, as well as to recall every intervention completed to date and what is left to do. This handout provides an at-a-glance view, highlighting what has been completed in previous sessions and what is next to do.

*Process:* At the end of the session, make a note of the interventions used and the intended direction for the next session.

### Managing Activation—Adolescents/Children

*Rationale:* These two handouts are a reference and tracking guide for both therapist and client regarding the level of arousal that the client experienced in the session related to working on the trauma. There is one handout for children 12 and under and another handout for adolescents. Typically, over time, the client will experience fewer activating feelings and sensations as he gains mastery over trauma triggers. Further, the client will come to trust that at the end of each session, the therapist will try to ensure that he is at a level 1 or 2 on the scale, and the client will not be left with a sense of overwhelm in his body. Tracking and observing activation over time teaches children mindfulness skills and can make difficult trauma work seem more tolerable.

*Process:* The word *activation* is used on these two handouts. However, it is best to find a word that is meaningful to the child and to write that word on the top of the page in place of *activation*. Words such as *upset, yuck feelings, worried, anxious,* or *scary* might be used. We work together with the child to ensure that therapist and client both understand what kinds of feelings we are asking about here. This is the beginning of teaching children a language for activating feelings and sensations. These handouts are used at the end of each session. The child marks on the scale where she was during the most difficult time in the session and where she is by the very end of the session. We make sure that we have sufficient time to address any activation if the child identifies that they are above a 2 on the scale at the end of the session. We can make a note on the form what it was that was most upsetting during the session and what brought the activation down again at the end.

### Artistic Acts of Victory/Mastery

*Rationale:* A child can create art or work with the art in a way that is transforming to the healing of trauma. Through art, a child may face a fear not faced before or give voice to silenced parts of himself that are experienced by the child and witnessed by the therapist as energetic transformations in the body and art of the client. These experiences are called "artistic acts of victory or mastery." Claiming these changes, victories, or masteries supports a resource-oriented approach to treatment, validates the progress the client is making, and emphasizes the good experiences and sensations in the body.

*Process:* When the therapist witnesses an act of victory/mastery, identify and document what the mastery was on the handout. The second step is to check in with the child about how it feels to acknowledge this mastery. Connect the mastery to a body experience, then stay with and delight in it.

**Thoughts, Feelings, and Beliefs Checklist**

*Rationale*: As we come to know the inner and outer worlds of a child, we begin to hear particular thoughts, feelings, and beliefs (TFB) that stand out as likely influenced by the trauma. From the beginning of the first session, we take note of these trauma-influenced TFB that may need to be addressed over time in therapy.

*Process*: Use the handout to track the TFB that stand out as needing to be addressed. During assessment, we are not in a position to address trauma-influenced TFB; rather, we take note of them. While some TFB can be addressed throughout the therapy process, some children will only be ready to address them toward the end of therapy. Typically by Phase Four, children are more regulated, confident, and stable in both body and mind, and they are able to see things more accurately and are ready to hear information that will help them address difficult or challenging TFB.

*Example*

Conor did two sets of victim/survivor images at different points in his treatment process. While this intervention is usually completed in Phase Four, we chose to do this intervention while Conor was working on Phase Two interventions because he talked at length about feeling like a victim to so many things in his life. We began discussing the difference between being a victim and being a survivor, and he created an image in response to this discussion (Figure 5.1). The following is Conor's written response to his image:

> I am a victim who has tripped and fell and I think my life is total hell. I am a survivor who's gone through it all, but despite my suckish life I will not trip and fall. I am a victim with

*Figure 5.1* Conor's painting illustrating his experience of victim/survivor. Used with permission.

a life I've hated, but it's only as bad as I have created. I'm a survivor who forgives and forgets, although some times it's not easy I still do it for my friends and family. It may be hard for this to happen but when it does it makes everyone happy and that is something you can have for free. I am a victim sad and lonely, sit by myself and cry wishing everyone who has caused me harm would die. I am a victim who wants to survive and in order to do this I will thrive.

We can track the various trauma-influenced thoughts and internalizations in his writing. I flagged the statement "it is only as bad as I have created" and added it to the checklist. We can come back to these beliefs at the appropriate time to address them more thoroughly. Sometimes, during the process of therapy, these beliefs shift on their own. This was the case with Conor. Many months later, he did another victim/survivor picture (Figure 5.2) and writing. He now sees that he has tools, he is using them, and he is much more empowered on his journey. He wrote:

He got through and so can you. In that cave is worry and hate and all those who yield to it will die sad and lonely. But if you assess your problems it is easier to live. These are the tools that therapy will give.

Conor had a very different perspective at this point, recognizing what he was responsible for and what others were responsible for. This clarification was vital in the healing and strengthening of family relationships.

*Figure 5.2* Conor's second painting of his experience of victim/survivor. Used with permission.

## INFORMATION HANDOUTS FOR CLIENTS

These handouts, provided in Appendix C, are important to go over with clients prior to the assessment process. First, we let caregivers know about their role in the assessment and treatment process. Second, we need to teach them about sensations and the senses so that children and caregivers have a language for working in this body-oriented way.

### Caregiver Involvement in the Four Phases

*Rationale*: This handout can be reviewed and given to the caregiver in the initial session. It describes the primary ways the caregiver will be involved in his child's therapeutic work. It will provide an opportunity to address any questions or concerns upfront about expectations of caregiver involvement.

*Process*: Review the handout with the caregiver prior to the assessment process. Clarify any questions. Caregiver involvement may look different for adolescents depending on age, needs, and relationship with caregiver. Adolescents tend to be more private and may not want others to see their art, especially when they don't have a strong attachment to their caregiver (e.g., having just moved into a group home). Each situation varies; therefore, adjust the handout as necessary.

### The Inner World of My Body

*Rationale*: There are many new words and concepts that are introduced to our clients. This handout addresses seven main ideas. First is the idea of the inner world of the body, including thoughts, feelings, and sensations. These concepts lay the foundation for the therapeutic work in all four phases.

The second idea is that of tracking thoughts, feelings, and sensations in the body. Tracking teaches children to become more aware of how they experience their inner worlds, and it can increase a sense of mastery in their own bodies. The process of tracking the inner world of the body brings mindfulness to the center of the therapeutic experience.

The third idea relates to increasing awareness of resourcing through the senses. Child and caregiver are encouraged to practice exploring triggering and soothing experiences through the senses. Children are taught to use their senses as resources for grounding and as ways to identify what their triggers are. This experience prepares the child for the handout Reminders of the Trauma.

Fourth is the idea of calm, numb, and activated bodies through the use of the phrases "switched on" and "switched off." It is important that children have a language for these internal world experiences and then are taught how to manage them. When a child is triggered, her awareness is impaired and her feelings and behaviors become trauma-oriented, meaning reacting as if the trauma is happening in the present.

The fifth idea relates to presence and disconnection and the way in which the therapist can help the child increase awareness of his level of presence or disconnect.

Sixth, the parts of the brain and the fight, flight, and freeze responses of survival are introduced. It is beneficial for children to understand that although their bodies did whatever they needed to at the time of trauma (e.g., ran away, hit, or froze), this does not mean they have to continue these survival responses when there is no threat. Children can learn that they have more choices now.

The seventh idea relates to the overall framework and understanding the therapeutic work. Children are told how amazing their bodies are in terms of how they adapt for survival. The body has experienced something very traumatic, and often the child's relationship with her body is in need of significant repair. This resource-oriented emphasis is found throughout the four phases.

These words and ideas are discussed and taught to support the therapeutic work and empower the client. Some children will require very little explanation, while others will need and want to know more. We are mindful about choosing the best vocabulary for each child.

*Process:* Read through the handout to get familiar with the content. Due to the amount and nature of the information on this handout, it can be shared and interspersed over a number of sessions as appropriate. Some concepts may remain as a guide in the back of the therapist's mind. The therapist makes decisions about the what, how, and when of sharing these concepts. What words and experiences could be empowering for this child to know and name? How will these ideas be shared in the most developmentally appropriate way? When is the best time to share and teach these ideas? These are very basic introductions to complex concepts, and further research can provide your client with more information if necessary. Some children benefit from more information on the brain and trauma's impact on the brain.

The information on thoughts, feelings, sensations, and senses is required for all children at this stage in the process because we will be referencing them in the following assessment interventions and throughout the treatment process. Caregivers are involved in these teaching sessions so they, too, can learn the information and follow up with the suggested activities at home. This intervention provides many opportunities for child and caregiver to explore, play, and learn together. These activities can be great ways to increase attunement and a sense of playfulness between a child and his caregiver.

## READINESS TO BEGIN PHASE ONE

As we prepare to understand the world from the child's point of view, we need to ensure that it is the right time to begin the therapeutic process. The following guidelines should be met before proceeding:

1. Ensure the child is safe from further trauma.
2. Verify that basic needs are met (e.g., secure environment, place to live).
3. Resolve any situation that may be contributing to lack of emotional or physical safety.

## REFERENCES

Blaustein, M., & Kinniburgh, K. (2010). *Treating traumatic stress in children and adolescents: How to foster resilience through attachment, self-regulation, and competency.* New York: Guilford Press.

Cohen, J., Mannarino, A., & Deblinger, E. (2006). *Treating trauma and traumatic grief in children and adolescents.* New York: Guilford Press.

Cornell, A.W. (2013). *Focusing in clinical practice: The essence of change.* New York: W.W. Norton.

Crenshaw, D. (2006). Neuroscience and trauma treatment: Implications for creative arts therapists. In L. Carey (Ed.), *Expressive and creative arts methods for trauma survivors* (pp. 21–38). London: Jessica Kingsley.

Eberhart, H., & Atkins, S. (2014). *Presence and process in expressive arts work: At the edge of wonder.* London: Jessica Kingsley.

Gil, E. (2006). *Helping abused and traumatized children: Integrating directive and nondirective approaches.* New York: Guilford Press.

Gil, E. (Ed.). (2010). *Working with children to heal interpersonal trauma: The power of play.* New York: Guilford Press.

Greenwald, R. (2005). *Child trauma handbook: A guide for helping trauma-exposed children and adolescents.* New York: The Haworth Reference Press.

Levine, P. (1997). *Waking the tiger: Healing trauma.* Berkeley, CA: North Atlantic Books.

Levine, P., & Kline, M. (2007). *Trauma through a child's eyes: Awakening the ordinary miracle of healing.* Berkeley, CA: North Atlantic Books.

Malchiodi, C. (Ed.). (2008). *Creative interventions with traumatized children.* New York: Guilford Press.

Ogden, P., Minton, K., & Pain, C. (2006). *Trauma and the body: A sensorimotor approach to psychotherapy.* New York: W.W. Norton.

Siegel, D. (2010). Mindsight: The new science of personal transformation. New York: Bantam Books.

Siegel, D., & Hartzell, M. (2003). *Parenting from the inside out: How a deeper self-understanding can help you raise children who thrive*. New York: Penguin.

Steele, W., & Kuban, C. (2013). *Working with grieving and traumatized children and adolescents: Discovering what matters most through evidence-based, sensory interventions*. Hoboken, NJ: Wiley.

Steele, W., & Malchiodi, C. (2012). *Trauma-informed practices with children and adolescents*. New York: Routledge.

Steele, W., & Raider, M. (2009). *Structured sensory intervention for traumatized children, adolescents and parents* (SITCAP™) (3rd ed.). New York: Edwin Mellen Press.

Stien, P., & Kendall, J. (2004). *Psychological trauma and the developing brain: Neurologically based interventions for troubled children*. New York: Routledge.

# 6  Phase One Guidelines
## Understanding the Child's World

Seventeen-year-old Tammy was sexually abused by her stepfather throughout her teenage years. There was little touching, but there were extensive boundary invasions through watching, inappropriate peeping, comments, and sexual innuendoes.

Nine-year-old David witnessed his father sexually violating his girlfriend in the car where he held them both captive for a 4-hour period.

Seven-year-old Leita was caught in the middle of her parents' high conflict divorce.

How does the impact of trauma vary from one child to another? How does a child experience this level of invasion and disregard for body, mind, and soul? How does a child maintain her own integrity and hope and belief in relationships, in life, and in love? As therapists, how do we come to know the unique perspectives and the private logic of each individual who comes through our office doors? How do we come to know their experiences, their thoughts, and their feelings in a meaningful way as we assist them in healing? We can't assume we know what their experiences might be or what parts of the events experienced were most traumatic until they reveal their perspectives through their words, their art, and their behaviors. Each child brings a world of strengths and vulnerabilities. We must come to know both worlds, harnessing the inherent power that lies uniquely within each child. These strengths can become their resources and allies to cope with and manage the vulnerabilities.

## INITIAL ASSESSMENT

When we meet a child and his current family or caregiving system, we need an avenue to begin to understand the child's world from his point of view. This point of view will include his private logic, including his beliefs and thoughts about himself, his relationship with others and the world around him, and his relationship with his body. Phase One is a multifaceted approach to assessment that includes several standardized tests, an introduction to arts-based assessment, and trauma-specific arts questionnaires designed to elicit information necessary to understand the distinct perspective and experience of this child. We interview the child and the significant people in his world. Through these processes, we see how the pieces of his puzzle fit, and his distinct perspective emerges.

In the assessment process, we are not diagnosing. Instead, we are evaluating behaviors of concern, understanding the impact of trauma, identifying trauma-influenced thinking, tracking body activation, and learning about the child's creativity. We want to know what the world looks like from this child's point of view and identify her therapeutic needs. The information gathered from this assessment phase will guide the rest of the therapeutic process. We will come to know what interventions are a priority, who needs to be included in the various phases, and how to track progress over time. In reality, and as discussed in this chapter, assessment is occurring throughout the therapeutic process; thus, we are noting progress and areas of continued work on a regular basis. If additional issues emerge during the treatment process, any assessment measure can be administered to clarify the concern.

## MULTIPLE TREATMENT PROVIDERS/PROFESSIONALS

When children present in therapy, they may have previously or currently involved treatment providers including physicians, psychiatrists, therapists, and there may be previous assessment reports by psychologists, group home staff, and so on. It is important to gather information from current people in the child's world to garner their insight and perspectives on the current functioning of the child. Working collaboratively with other professionals, including teachers, throughout the treatment process can ensure the best all-around support for the particular needs of each child.

## PROCESS OF ASSESSMENT SESSIONS

Typically, having an initial interview with the caregivers is the place to start. In this session, caregivers are educated about the assessment and therapy process, their concerns are addressed, consent forms are signed, and assessment forms are completed. We have a second session with the caregiver to go over the assessment forms, clarifying and expanding on points if needed. The next session is with the child and caregiver. In this session, we clarify why the child is there and what the "job" of the therapist involves. It is important to be clear about the specific reason the child is there (e.g., by using the words "sexual abuse" or "the accident") so that she will know that the therapist knows about the trauma. The child should be reassured that she won't be talking about the details of the trauma in this session and that the main goal is to get to know each other. We begin by exploring art materials together while learning about the child's likes and dislikes, the activities she is involved with both in and out of school, what she enjoys doing, and things she believes she is good at. As a way of introducing ourselves, both therapist and client engage in art making of our choice that tells something about ourselves, followed by sharing the art.

We are frequently making decisions about what is most critical to accomplish with the time available. As we become familiar with the individual needs of each client, we come to know how much we can ask the child to do within a session. Some children want to get through the handouts quickly, whereas others can hardly manage one handout in a session. Some children need more support with reading and comprehension, whereas others want to complete the handouts on their own. If a session has been particularly difficult for a client, time is needed at the end of a session for "art debriefing." This is an opportunity for the client to express any thoughts, feelings, or sensations that have been triggered in the session, to ensure he leaves feeling calm and regulated.

The order in which the interventions appear is typically the order in which they are completed. The final handout, Pieces of My Story, is one of the last to complete the assessment. We let the child know we are coming to a more challenging topic, but that we believe she is ready to identify the trauma memories. At this point, we have been able to assess the child's ability to manage thoughts of the trauma through a variety of means, including creating images about activated and calm body. If we do not believe the child is ready, we need to do the work that is required to support this child to be ready. The child is assured that she will be learning more skills before addressing these memories so that she will be ready to do the hard work.

## THERAPIST RESPONSE DURING ASSESSMENT VERSUS TREATMENT

In the assessment phase, the primary goal is to understand the world from the child's point of view. We are simultaneously developing a trusting therapeutic relationship as we aim to establish a secure and a supportive holding environment for the trauma work to unfold safely. During assessment, although we may hear many things from the child and her caregivers that may disturb or provoke reactions in us, we are not in the place to challenge or intervene with what we are hearing unless it is a significant safety or behavioral issue or an incident of current, unreported child abuse. In this case, we would need to report to local child welfare authorities. If we hear evidence of trauma-influenced thinking, we make note of them on the Thoughts, Feelings, and Beliefs Checklist and return to them at a more appropriate time, often during Phase Four. Once we can begin to see the world through the eyes of *this* child, we are in a better position to know how to respond and to identify what goals need to be addressed and the order in which they will be addressed.

## OVERVIEW OF ASSESSMENT TOOLS

### Standardized Tests

While there are multiple possibilities when it comes to choosing standardized tests to assess client needs, we are guided by working within the professional boundaries of what we are qualified to administer. Four standardized tests that are efficient and effective for assessing the needs of traumatized children will be reviewed. Consider the following questions to guide what standardized tests might be useful in your own practice:

What behaviors do I need to assess?
For whom am I working, and what assessment forms are already in place?
Are there alternate standardized tests that may supplement my assessment process?
Am I qualified to administer these tests?
Who can I refer to should more specialized testing be required?

### Art Therapy Assessment Tools

While formal art therapy assessments have many known issues related to validity and reliability (Betts, 2005), there are numerous arts-based interventions that are useful for information gathering, understanding the world from the child's perspective, and tracking how the child's perspective changes over time. Two of these assessment tools will be considered here.

### Expressive Arts–Based Information-Gathering Tools

Seven arts-based assessment tools are offered to assist the therapist with understanding how the child has experienced the trauma. Each assessment tool highlights a different aspect of trauma's impact, including how trauma changed the child's world and relationships, how he experienced trauma in his body, and finally, his sense of self in relation to the trauma.

### Questionnaires for Information Gathering

These questionnaires were designed to draw out more trauma-specific information in areas such as perceptions of responsibility and safety, understanding the child's experience of the trauma disclosure, learning about trauma triggers, and exploring a range of emotions experienced at the time of trauma and now. There are four questionnaires designed for the caregivers and eleven for the child.

## STANDARDIZED TESTS

### The Trauma Symptom Checklist for Children (TSCC)

The TSCC is a self-report instrument that rates a number of posttraumatic stress symptoms and related psychological symptoms and includes six clinical scales. The scales are anxiety, depression, anger, posttraumatic stress, dissociation, and sexual concerns. It is a useful measure to evaluate both male and female children between the ages of 8 and 16 who have been exposed to traumatic experiences, including child sexual abuse. There are two versions of the test. The TSCC is a 54-item questionnaire that includes 10 items related to sexual issues. The TSCC-A is a 44-item questionnaire that does not include the sexual concerns items. The test typically takes the child 15 to 20 minutes to complete and can be scored within 5 to 10 minutes (Briere, 1996).

### The Trauma Symptom Checklist for Young Children (TSCYC)

The TSCYC is an assessment instrument completed by caregivers and used to evaluate posttraumatic symptoms in children ages 3 to 12. There are nine clinical scales: anxiety, depression, dissociation, sexual concerns, anger/aggression, posttraumatic stress intrusion, posttraumatic stress avoidance, posttraumatic stress arousal, and posttraumatic stress total. This is a 90-item caregiver report that takes approximately 20 minutes to administer (Briere, 2005).

### The Behavior Assessment System for Children (BASC-2)

The BASC-2 is another valuable tool that provides useful information about children's behaviors and self-perceptions. The BASC-2 is used for children, adolescents, and young adults between the ages of 2.5 and 25 years. There are three different forms: a self-report completed by the child and a parent report and a teacher report to provide a thorough assessment across the various settings the child is part of. There are clinical scales that measure maladaptive behaviors and adaptive scales that measure positive behaviors. The clinical scales include adaptability, anxiety, aggression, attention problems, atypicality, conduct problems, depression, hyperactivity, leadership, learning problems, social skills, somatization, study skills, and withdrawal. The adaptive scales include adaptability, leadership, social skills, and study skills (Reynolds & Kamphaus, 2004).

### Child Sexual Behavior Inventory (CSBI)

When sexual abuse is suspected or disclosed, another assessment tool that is worthy of mention is the CSBI, which is a parent/caregiver report of sexual behaviors of children between the ages of 2 and 12 years. The CSBI is a 38-item report that assesses behavior across nine domains: boundary problems, exhibitionism, gender role behavior, self-stimulation, sexual anxiety, sexual interest, sexual intrusiveness, sexual knowledge, and voyeuristic behavior (Friedrich, 1997).

There are many standardized tests available that could be informative in the evaluation of a child's behaviors as well as evaluating clinical progress over time. The therapist is encouraged to identify the behaviors needing evaluation, then research which tests are within the therapist's professional ability to administer.

## ART THERAPY ASSESSMENT TOOLS

There are a wide range of art therapy assessment tools to consider for evaluation purposes. When making decisions to use art therapy assessment tools for assessing a child's level of functioning or identifying treatment recommendations, it is important to understand that the majority of these tests have issues with poor validity and lack of reliability. Therapists are encouraged to find arts-based assessment tools that can be used to obtain the specific information they are looking for in their clients. These assessment tools can be very useful for information gathering while highlighting areas of further inquiry. They can be valuable tools as you begin being curious about the child's inner and outer worlds, as they elicit powerful stories about the child's perceptions of himself and the people in his life. Two art therapy projective tests that will be discussed are the House-Tree-Person Assessment and the Kinetic Family Drawing Assessment.

### House-Tree-Person Assessment (HTP)

The HTP, developed by Buck (1966), is a projective test for anyone over the age of 3. It invites the client to draw a house, a tree, and a person. Many aspects of these drawings are considered, such as the placement of the images, the size, the color, age, and facial expression. The idea is that the client is projecting aspects of her inner world onto the page through the images created. There are 60 questions that can be asked; however, therapists may choose only some of these questions or design their own questions based on the therapeutic needs of their clients.

### Kinetic Family Drawing Assessment (KFD)

The KFD is a projective test developed by Burns and Kaufman (1972) for children and adolescents. The client is invited to draw a picture of himself and his family doing something, which is followed by asking the child specific questions about his drawing. Characteristics of the drawing, such as placement of figures and inclusion or exclusion of figures or parts of figures, are then examined and rated based on specific criteria. The drawing and questions can be very useful for prompting information about the child and his perceptions of his family.

## EXPRESSIVE ARTS–BASED INFORMATION-GATHERING TOOLS

In this initial phase of assessment, information is required to assist us with understanding, from the child's point of view, how she has experienced the trauma and the resulting impact on her body, her relationships, and her internal worldview of herself and others. With the goal of further understanding the child's private logic, the child is invited to engage with the following expressive arts–based interventions. The interventions are found in Appendix D.

### Map of My World

*Rationale*: Often, genograms or ecomaps are used to illustrate the world from which the child has come. The Map of My Word intervention creates a visual representation of the child's world, the significant relationships in his life, and where he situates the trauma in his world. This intervention acknowledges the presence of the trauma in the child's world without going into detail, allowing the therapist to get to know the world of the client in a nonthreatening way.

*Process*: Usually, we start by sitting on the floor with a large piece of paper, smaller pieces of paper, and markers. The child is invited to write her name in the center of the paper, followed by writing the names of others on separate pieces of small paper, so they can be moved when needed. Symbols to describe the kind of relationship the child has with each person are added next.

If there is time and further information would be beneficial, complete the section Me and My Family and Friends as Objects. Once the child has chosen objects for each person, there are many possible directions. One direction may be writing three words to describe the object (e.g., for pencil—sharp, useful, erasable) that can add another dimension of how this child experiences that person. In addition, the different objects can interact with one another and stories emerge. We become curious observers of these interactions.

Finally, the child is invited to add the trauma. On a separate piece of paper of the size of her choosing, she is encouraged to draw a symbol representing the trauma. Printing the word *trauma* on the paper works as well. Follow the guidelines as outlined on the handout. Working with the image of or the word *trauma,* the boundary, and the people provides important information about the perceptions this child has of her experience of trauma and the impact of trauma on her relationships.

There is no right or wrong way to do this intervention. Think of information that will assist you in your work with this child and modify as necessary. Because this is the assessment phase, information gathering is essential. Make note of anything that would be useful to follow up on with the child or caregivers.

### How Trauma Changed My World

*Rationale*: For some children, being able to express how they have been impacted by the trauma is a relief. It is a nonintrusive invitation that also allows for an exploration of the child's preference and comfort level with the arts. He is not being asked to tell about the trauma, but rather how it has affected his world. This intervention has the potential to obtain pertinent information about how the child views the trauma and how his world currently looks in relation to the trauma.

*Process:* Because this is one of the first art interventions, it is an opportunity to fully explore the various art modalities that the client could work with. At this point, going with whatever feels safest is best. This is the initial stage of developing a trusting therapeutic relationship along with exploring the trauma. This intervention lets the child know that the therapist interested in understanding what he went through, that the details of the trauma won't be discussed at this point, and that the therapist is able to be with him while exploring these difficult experiences through art.

A simple invitation is best: "How did the trauma [use the actual word, e.g., sexual abuse] change or impact your world?" Children tend to understand the invitation and create what is most meaningful to them. For young children, we can ask, "How did the trauma hurt you?"

It can also be beneficial to have the caregiver complete an image of how she believes her child's world has been impacted by the trauma. Sharing this image with the child can bring great comfort, relief, and understanding, as well as an opportunity for the child to clarify his point of view. The caregiver can also feel relief for having an opportunity to share her compassionate understanding with the child in a structured way.

*Example*

Figure 6.1 was completed by Tessa, a 12-year-old girl who experienced physical abuse by her mother and sexual abuse by her father for as long as she could remember. On the right half of the page, she drew a picture of her world when she was sexually abused by her father. She said, "I felt safe and not alone. I could depend on him. I felt the whole world, my dad, is my friend. He said he was teaching me. I knew when he was around I wouldn't get in trouble with mom. The tree represents that I felt stronger. I had hope and happiness I didn't get in other places." She explained that the left side was what it was like when the sexual abuse didn't happen, stating, "I was upset, angry and I would get hurt by mom. I depended on dad for comfort. I would enjoy

*Figure 6.1* Tessa's drawing of how the trauma impacted her world. Used with permission.

his visits with me at night because he would pay attention to me." Seeing the world through a child's image tells a story that is beyond what we might imagine. We can't assume we know how the child experienced the trauma until they show us.

## My Relationships

*Rationale*: Repairing relationships is a vital part of the healing process, particularly when addressing relational trauma. This intervention highlights the salient relationships that have been impacted by the trauma; the temporal differences in the relationships experienced before, during, and after trauma; and the child's hope for the relationship in the future. Through the art, we come to see the child's experience in these relationships and what further work might be required.

*Process*: This intervention could take more than one session, depending how quickly the child works. Some children choose to create all four images, while others choose to create two or three, depending on time and relevance. After the child completes the intervention, we decide together what further therapeutic work is needed in terms of repair, sharing, or doing joint work with the important people in her world. As this is assessment, the repair work is noted and will be returned to in Phase Four. By that time, it may be useful to review and/or have the child redo the Now or Future part of this intervention to see, from her perspective, how the relationships have changed, if at all.

When appropriate, the caregiver can also complete this intervention about his relationship with the child.

*Example*

Thirteen-year-old Eva was sexually abused by her stepfather. Eva and her mother attended some of the sessions together. In one session, both daughter (Figure 6.2) and mother (Figure 6.3)

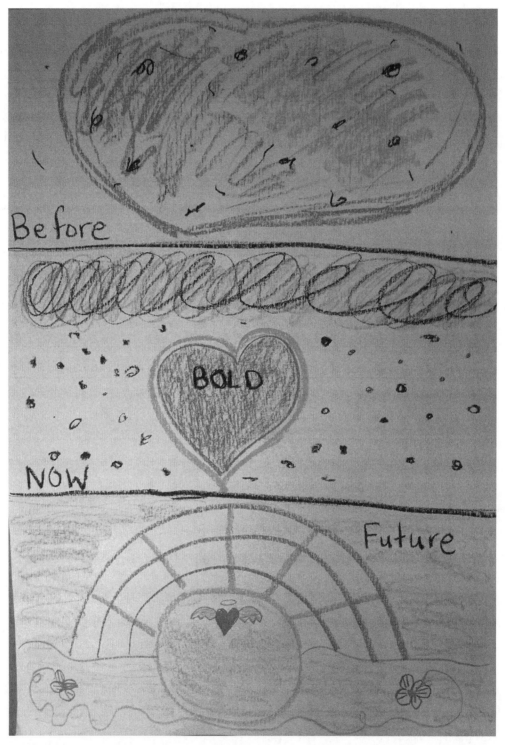

*Figure 6.2* Eva's drawing representing her relationship with her mother before the trauma, now, and in the future. Used with permission.

*Figure 6.3* Drawing by Eva's mother representing her relationship with her daughter before the trauma, now, and in the future. Used with permission.

completed three images each about their relationship before the trauma, now, and in the future. After completing the images, they were each invited to give voice to some aspect of their image or the image as a whole.

### Eva's Written Response

**Before**

I don't know where to turn. I feel lost in feelings. I don't know what to think or say.

**Now**

I feel strange. Not sure of myself. I'm happy I told but I am sad about the results. I am happy my mom will help me through with her love. I feel her protection. I am glad for it.

**Future**

I am glad it is over. Feels better knowing it's behind us. I think my life will be summer and not so glum. I feel that it should be a new beginning. I feel the love around me and the peace it brings.

### Mother's Written Response

**Before**

I am the grey cloud. I feel heavy, tired and confused. I am the purple heart. I am strong. I don't understand. I am the faces and I feel both joy and sadness. I am the traffic light and I feel rushed, hurried. I am always moving.

**Now**

I still feel confused. I feel stronger and have a need to be stronger for Eva. I am the grey cloud and I feel Eva is trying to be brave even though she is angry, hurt, and sad. I feel her sadness and my heart is breaking too. I don't know how this could have happened. We share similar experiences of anger, hurt, sad, and lonely. I don't know how to help her.

**Future**

There is still sadness but less powerful than the sun. The sun has broken through and is strong, bright, and safe. I feel richly blessed, happy that Eva and I figured this out together. We are strong and brave women—the treasure will bless our family. The rainbow promises us happiness and layers of understanding and learning.

### Amazing Body 1

*Rationale*: Trauma lives in the nervous system of the body. Therapy needs to address trauma relationally, somatically, and cognitively to be effective. This intervention serves several purposes. First, it continues to educate and reinforce awareness of sensations in the body, building on the information in the handout The Inner World of My Body. Second, we are teaching mindfulness skills for working with the body in the present moment. Finally, it supports the learning about and maximizing and restoring the natural experience of pendulation (Levine, 1997), that is, moving from a state of activation to a state of calmness.

*Process*: Invite the child to think of something that happened to him that was unpleasant (not trauma related) and map that out on his handout. Together with the child, explore words that describe sensations and discuss how he might capture those sensations by using colors and symbols on the body outline. After he maps it out, track the thoughts, feelings, and sensations as he is sharing them in the present moment, having him pay attention to how he senses them in his body. Then move to the second image, in which he imagines something that helps him to shift to a calmer, happier state. Again, spend time allowing him to explore what expands this sense of goodness.

## Amazing Body 2

*Rationale*: These extra body outlines are available to continue working with the child to support making the connection between content in the sessions and what is happening in the body. Repetition can deepen the child's understanding of the power she has to regulate her body response to trauma triggers.

*Process*: There are times when it is useful to slow things down in the session and invite the child to notice, name, and stay with what is happening in the body. Over time, she can come to notice the way her body responds to certain triggers and start to identify similarities and differences. She can learn to identify and name the activation and bring herself to a calmer place. Drawing her experiences and seeing them on paper can make the inner world more concrete and alive while reinforcing the positive changes that are happening in her body. Drawing these images over time may also be a way of tracking the changes in her body experience as her internal sense of control increases. Be creative with how these images can serve your work with your clients.

## My Body and the Trauma 1 and 2

*Rationale*: The previous interventions prepare the child to complete this one. The child is now invited to think directly about the trauma and map out his body experience. This intervention assists the therapist with assessing the level of activation experienced and identified by the child and his ability to manage the thoughts, feelings, and sensations.

*Process*: The child is given the paper with a human outline and asked to bring up the trauma in his mind right now but not talk about it. If there are multiple traumas, he is asked to think of one of the more upsetting incidents. He is then invited to pay attention to what happens in his body as he brings it up and to map out any thoughts, feelings, and sensations on the outline using symbols, colors, and words. Often the child will automatically make his own key that identifies what the colors and symbols mean. Next, ask how upsetting it is when he brings up the trauma right now, on a scale of 0 to 10, with 10 being most upsetting. We can gauge the level of upset in that moment and monitor how this may change over the course of therapy. The final step is to use another outline of a human body (My Body and the Trauma 2) and have the child think about someone or something that makes him happy and brings a sense of calm in his body, and then have the child map out his thoughts, feelings, and sensations. He may use the body outline previously created in Amazing Body for the calm, happy image, or he can create a new one. Creating a new image assists with expanding and encouraging the use of a number of resources. We now move between calm and activated body in relation to the thoughts of the trauma, inviting the client to notice the changes in his body as he changes his thoughts. We always end with calm body, and highlight for the child how his body is able to go from upset to calm in a few seconds. The child's ability to change the body's experience is identified as a resource.

This intervention could be revisited after the trauma processing in Phase Three to determine how different the experiences are for the child over time.

### Example

Seven-year-old Cori was sexually abused by her teenage male cousin. Figure 6.4 is of her activated body and Figure 6.5 is of her calm body.

The following images are by 13-year-old Gina. Figure 6.6 is of her activated body. After identifying the meaning of each of the colors, she drew a set of wings in the center of the

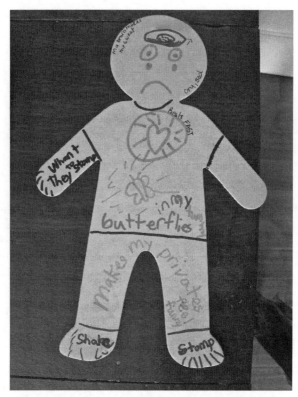

*Figure 6.4* Cori's drawing of her activated body. Used with permission.

*Figure 6.5* Cori's drawing of her calm body. Used with permission.

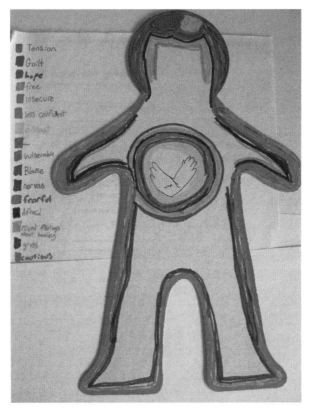

The colors are labeled: Tension, Guilt, hope, free, insecure, less confident, ?, vulnerable, Blame, nervous, fearful, Afraid, mixed feelings about healing, grief, cautious

*Figure 6.6* Gina's drawing of her activated body and the guide to the meaning of the colors. Used with permission.

activated image, saying, "Deep inside me I know I will be free one day of these emotions." This is a powerful example of how spontaneous resources show up in the art and can be used to support the child in their work. Gina returned to this image often because she received a great deal of comfort related to the hope of "being free." This image and these words grounded her through the various phases, in particular the trauma processing in Phase Four.

Figure 6.7 is of Gina's calm body, identifying a range of feelings. After drawing calm body, we stood up and paid attention to what she was noticing in her body. "I am more confident! I notice my posture is better and I am more planted." She continued by identifying that she felt less confused, and the good sensations of calm were spreading through her body.

### Self-Portraits 1

*Rationale*: How a child views herself in relation to the timing of the trauma can give useful information about her resources, her perceptions of self, how these perceptions have changed over time in relation to the trauma, and her hope for the future. She imagines herself before and during the trauma, now, and in the future. The future orientation promotes resilience by reminding the child that there is life beyond the trauma.

*Process*: Self-portraits can be done during the assessment and then again after the trauma processing, in Phase Four, to encourage observation of any changes in how the child represents herself through image and writing. To keep this intervention simple for younger children, we say, "I want you to think about yourself before the trauma happened. If you could draw yourself as anything, what would you draw?" Then continue through the next three self-portraits. If the child is having a hard time deciding, narrow it down and give options, such as, "It could

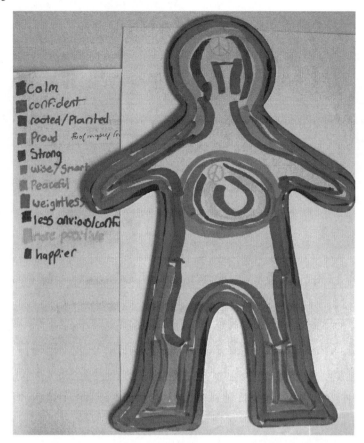

*Figure 6.7* Gina's drawing of her calm body and the guide to the meaning of the colors. Used with permission.

be an animal, a tree, a flower, or a car." Giving alternatives to drawing can also be useful for those who may find other modalities more meaningful. For example, the child may find certain objects in the room that represent her at these various times, or you can invite the child to do a series of body postures or movements for each self-portrait.

*Example*

Eight-year-old Susan, who was sexually abused by her stepfather, drew three self-portraits and a written responses for each.

**Before: Ladybug and Butterfly**

They are easy to trap. All you have to do is step on them to squish them.

**During: Tiger**

You can keep a tiger in captivity and put it in a circus, but at some point they can't handle it and they get mad as it is just too much for them.

**Now: Giraffe**

In the wild when they drink they have to keep looking up to see if there is a predator as this is their most vulnerable position, otherwise the other animals leave them alone. They have some vulnerability, like when drinking, but they have lots of strengths.

We can see, from her chosen images and words, her strengths and vulnerabilities. We can now use these images as potential resources. Susan was encouraged to think about the power of the butterfly and the ladybug (e.g., she noted that they can fly and reach places predators can't reach). As we started to speak about the strengths of the butterfly, ladybug, tiger, and giraffe, Susan sat in her chair a little straighter and she began to speak more confidently. These images became resources for Susan—reminders of her inner strength. She cut out the images and pasted them to canvas. We brought out the canvas during future sessions to support her in the more challenging work.

*Note:* Self-Portraits 2 will be addressed in Phase Four (see Chapter 9).

## QUESTIONNAIRES FOR INFORMATION GATHERING

These questionnaires (provided in Appendix E) are used for gathering information about the child and caregiver's perceptions about the trauma and circumstances surrounding the trauma. The caregiver questionnaires can be given in the initial meeting with the caregiver, or the caregiver can complete them while the child is in session. Information from both the caregiver and the child is important because we see the perceptions the child has about the specific themes related to trauma, including issues of responsibility, safety, disclosure, triggers, and feelings, then and now. The "then and now" aspect to the questions can demonstrate how the feelings have changed from the time of the trauma until now, teaching the child how feelings can change over time.

Deciding to have the child answer the questionnaires on his own depends on the needs of the child. Going through the questionnaires together can increase the likelihood that the child has a clear understanding of what is being asked. Once completed, each question can be reviewed and elaborated on to elicit further pertinent information.

### Exploring Art Modalities and Creativity Beliefs

*Rationale*: Understanding art forms a client is interested in, currently uses, or those that she is opposed to is valuable when using an expressive arts process for the treatment of trauma. This handout is a reminder to explore all art possibilities and it alerts the child that there are many ways we can play and express in this therapeutic process. It also provides an opportunity to explore the child's beliefs about creativity because these will influence the process we engage in. Even if the child does not see herself as creative, we still encourage the use of the arts in therapy. In fact, we create space to hear her notions about her creativity, as well as continue to invite the child to experiment with the arts. In this way, the child may have the opportunity to discover new resources and create updated beliefs about herself as a creative being.

*Process*: Go over the handout together, or have the child complete the handout first and then review together. Reviewing the handout with the caregiver and child together can also offer potentially different points of view about how the caregiver sees the child's creative side.

### Child and Caregiver Trauma History

*Rationale*: Witnessing trauma, another family member's trauma, and current caregiver's personal experience with trauma all play a role in the child's ability to heal. Historical trauma information in the various domains (home and school) helps to identify areas that may need attention in the treatment process. It can be beneficial to have information about the caregiver at the time of trauma and his response to the trauma, as well as the current caregiver's trauma history (particularly if the current caregiver was not the caregiver at the time of the trauma). If the current caregiver has a history of untreated trauma, it may be triggered during the child's process. We also want to know about the caregiver's successes and strengths, as they may be used as resources throughout the therapy process.

*Process:* Gather information from caregivers or guardians. Highlight specific strengths and resources for both the child and the caregiver that could be used in the therapy process.

### Impact of Trauma on Caregiver

*Rationale:* This is a handout for the caregiver only if she was the caregiver at the time the child experienced the trauma. This questionnaire generates some basic information from the caregiver about her own experience of her child's trauma and how she and her child have been affected by the trauma. Further, it can assist with developing recommendations related to how the caregiver can best support herself and her child.

*Process:* This questionnaire, along with other caregiver reports, can be completed in the initial session with the caregiver and reviewed as needed.

### Why It Was Hard for Me to Tell/Why It Was Hard for My Child to Tell (Child/Caregiver)

*Rationale:* It is very difficult for children to disclose what happened to them, particularly if the trauma was relational or sexual. These questionnaires explore the various reasons that the child found it difficult to tell about what happened to him.

*Process:* Depending on the age and needs of the child, these questions may be read to the child. Once finished, go over each item to learn about the thinking behind the answers. We become privy to how the child views his internal power and perceptions of himself and others. The blank spaces can be filled in by the child with the name of the person who hurt the child. Modify the questions to best fit your client's scenario.

### Responsibility Rating Scale (Child/Caregiver)

*Rationale:* Issues related to responsibility come up in a variety of ways for most types of trauma. Often, young people struggle with a sense of being at fault for some aspect of the trauma. Children often share that they believe they could have stopped it. Others feel confused, disappointed, and betrayed by their bodies' responses to the trauma, and they feel that somehow they could have made their bodies do something different at the time of trauma. Understanding a caregiver's or a child's thinking related to issues of responsibility can highlight trauma-influenced thoughts and beliefs that can interfere with healing from the effects of trauma. We can also come to know the resources in their thinking, such as understanding that they feel proud of how they responded and clear about who is responsible.

*Process:* An essential step in this intervention for both the child and caregiver is to review the form and the thinking behind their answers once completed. Reviewing can uncover the intricacies of their thinking and critical details related to responsibility issues. In response to some of the questions on the child's form, children sometimes say they don't know what a parent might think. They are encouraged to make their best guess about what they think others think. Modify questions as needed to suit the scenario of your client.

### Responsibility for the Trauma

*Rationale:* If the previous two questionnaires do not fit the circumstances of your client, use this form to identify the child's thinking related to issues of responsibility. This option allows for a more expansive and open-ended look at the beliefs of the client.

*Process*. The child is encouraged to think about the meaning of responsibility related to the trauma. Use whatever vocabulary is necessary to meet the developmental age of your client to ensure she understands issues related to responsibility. Offer examples to clarify the meaning. Children are reminded that we are interested in *anything* that they might consider to have some responsibility in what happened. Some children need permission to know that it is okay to say whatever they need, even if they think it sounds silly (e.g., like it was the tree's fault when the child fell out of it).

## Safety Questionnaire

*Rationale*: Perceptions and experiences of safety are the cornerstones to progress in therapy, and they are explored in relation to the child's present experiences. This questionnaire can bring to light worries or concerns that the child is experiencing or potential resources (e.g., what the child perceives as safe places/people). It can also identify any practical things that could be put in place to increase the child's current need for safety.

*Process*. Go over the questionnaire together or have the child complete the answers and then review together. This is one exception when we would follow up immediately with the child's caregiver so that he may respond to the child's emotional needs or any logistical changes in order to increase the child's sense of safety.

## Feelings About the Trauma

*Rationale*: Identifying the range of feelings associated with the trauma can tell the child's emotional story of the trauma and more aspects of the child's inner world can be revealed. Working through and expressing emotions connected to the trauma can increase a child's emotional resilience. Identifying feelings then and now can assist the child with seeing how feelings change over time and which feelings need more immediate support, and it places the trauma experience in the past.

*Process*. This questionnaire can be activating for some clients, so it is important to do check-ins as the child is completing the form and take time-outs as needed. Once completed, review the questionnaire with the child to ensure that the meanings of the feelings are understood. The review may happen over several sessions, depending on the child's ability to tolerate the work.

There are many ways to review the information from this questionnaire. We can highlight how some of the feelings are less intense now, and we can be curious about what makes them less. From a resource perspective, we can emphasize the changes and the decreases and how feelings can change over time. Some feelings may be more intense, and we explore together what makes it more intense now. Upon review, it is useful to go over each feeling to hear, from the child's point of view, what it is about that feeling that puts it at a certain number. It may seem obvious why someone might put a 10 for afraid; however, exploring the client's unique story about certain feelings is useful because we may discover something particular to this experience.

## Example

As we went through this handout together, 11-year-old Talia gave the word *paralyzed* a 0 for then and a 4 for now. I asked her to help me understand what that was like for her. She said, "It feels like a push or pull down on me, like I am trying to move forward and I can't." Tears came. We slowed everything down and stayed with the sensation of this difficult push–pull experience. I invited her to create an image that captured that sensation. She drew a heart trying to walk forward but it was being pulled back by ropes. She said, "It hurts and makes me feel sick when I look at it." I asked if the heart had a voice what it might say. She responded, "Help me get free." I then asked what helps the heart, and she stated, "Knowing that one day it will be free." The tears stopped and she took a deep breath. She began to identify the softening and calming in her body, particularly in her shoulders. As we stayed with the softening sensations, she calmed further and felt more relaxed.

### Disclosure Questionnaire

*Rationale*: The process of disclosure can itself be a traumatic experience. Life does not necessarily get better once the trauma is disclosed. In relational trauma in particular, even when the abuse stops, new difficulties can arise and a new crisis can surface if, for example, a family member is removed from the home. While it is essential that the abuse is stopped, it does not necessarily mean everything is fine. Exploring the disclosure experience in cases of child maltreatment is an area that needs careful consideration.

*Process*: Go through the questionnaire with the child to clarify the meaning of the various aspects of disclosure. Explore in further detail areas that are significant to the child. As with all questionnaires, some of the language may need to be changed to ensure the child understands the questions. Modify the questions as needed to fit the scenario of your client.

### Disclosure Picture: When I First Told About the Trauma

*Rationale*: In cases where the child disclosed the trauma, having the child draw or act out in other art forms what happened and what she wished would have happened (if different) can further capture the nuances of her experience. This activity can open many new doors to explore. If the child's experience was such that she wished something different had happened, we can further explore to determine what, if anything, needs to be put in place to increase emotional safety or increase connection between child and caregiver.

*Process*: Whatever art form is used to express the disclosure experience, add thought bubbles or boxes to identify thoughts, feelings, and sensations. Note whether any follow up is needed or further areas of exploration are required.

### Example

Tina disclosed sexual abuse by her stepfather when she was 9 years old. It was investigated and not substantiated, and she was returned home to live with her mother and stepfather. When she was 14 years old, her stepfather went to the authorities and admitted to the sexual abuse of his stepdaughter. Tina said that she didn't have an image for what she wished had happened, only how she felt inside and what is was like when she disclosed 5 years earlier and was not believed. The first image (Figure 6.8) is of her current story, including how she is being "forced" to now go to therapy because the abuser told. She questioned all of her relationships because not one person in her life believed her when she disclosed. She lived in a world where there was no safety and no safe relationship. She said, "My relationships all felt broken."

The second image (Figure 6.9) is of Tina's world at the time she disclosed 5 years earlier. Her experience was one of being blamed by everyone, represented by all the fingers (on the right) pointing at her (on the left). She was blamed for making what other's believed were false allegations and then she had to continue to live with the abuser for 5 more years. We can see, from her point of view, the suffering in both her experience of disclosing and no one believing and her experience of the abuser disclosing and now being believed.

### Trauma Self-Statements

*Rationale*: There are core themes related to the trauma experience that are highlighted in this questionnaire as self-statements. Some self-statements are framed in a more negative tone and

*Figure 6.8* Tina's drawing of disclosure. Used with permission.

*Figure 6.9* Tina's second image of having disclosed and feeling blamed. Used with permission.

others are more positively framed. Having both types of statements acknowledges the experience of suffering (e.g., helplessness) and the belief in one's power and strength.

*Process*: Although this questionnaire is given during assessment, we do not try to challenge or change these beliefs. Rather, we return to the questionnaire in Phase Four as part of the overall review. It can be useful to have the child review the Now scale in Phase Four to highlight what changes, if any, occurred through the process of therapy. In Phase Four we directly address any of the self-statements the child may still struggle with.

### Reminders of the Trauma

*Rationale*: The child will require support with addressing trauma-related triggers. Teaching the child how to manage triggers early on in the therapy process offers a sense of safety for the child and growing confidence in her own ability to effectively manage triggers. Many children are not aware of their triggers, and this handout becomes a work in progress as they come to understand, over time, what events or experiences are reminders of the trauma. The client has already been introduced to the idea of the senses with the handout The Inner World of My Body, and we now further expand her understanding of how the senses can be connected to reminders of the trauma. We explore this idea of "triggers" with the support of her caregiver. Caregivers may be able to provide valuable information about some of the potential triggers that the child may not be aware of.

*Process*: Go over the handout with both the caregiver and the child. We may return to this intervention throughout the therapy process as more information about triggers becomes known to the child.

### Pieces of My Story, Part 1: Remembering

*Rationale*: Completing the trauma narrative is an essential part of trauma therapy (Blaustein & Kinniburgh, 2010; Cohen, Mannarino, & Deblinger, 2006; Greenwald, 2005; Steele & Raider, 2009). This handout is like taking a trauma history, but it is done in a puzzle format that can be more child friendly. The intervention is completed at the end of the assessment phase with the understanding that there has been some establishment of safety in the therapeutic relationship, an understanding of some of the potential triggers, and an awareness of being able to shift from activated to calm body. Completion of this handout is in preparation for the trauma processing in Phase Three.

*Process*: The therapist explains to the child that working on the trauma is like putting pieces of a puzzle together, so that we can come to see the child's unique story. This handout can be cut out by the client so that he has separate pieces to write on. The child is invited to write down the various trauma experiences on the pieces of the puzzle, one incident per puzzle piece. He is encouraged to write only a line about the incident, not the whole incident—just enough so that he will be able to recall what it is about. He can also do a small sketch of the incident. He is asked to rate the incident on a scale of 1 to 10, with 10 being most upsetting when he thinks about it now and 0 being not at all upsetting. He writes that number on the puzzle piece. There may be other upsetting events in his life that he needs or wants to add to the puzzle pieces. Caregivers or guardians may also identify specific traumas the child has experienced. If so, the child is consulted regarding what he wants included on the puzzle pieces.

When there have been multiple traumas over long periods, the incidents blur together. Children can be encouraged to write down themes related to the trauma rather than specific incidents, such as the feelings and sensations in the body when the child was left home alone or would hear the abuser's voice or visit the places the abuse would happen. Sometimes children need support with knowing where to start. In such cases, the therapist can offer some of the following prompts:

> When was the first and last time it happened?
> Were there different places or locations that it happened?
> What was the worst time? Most embarrassing time? Most scary time?
> Was there ever a time when someone saw what was happening?

It is explained to the child that we will not talk about the details of his story at this point, but that these puzzle pieces will be placed for safe keeping in a box that he will prepare. We let the child know that we will return to the puzzle pieces when he is equipped with more skills and is ready to tell his story. The primary purpose, at this point in the process, is to identify the various pieces of the story in preparation for Phase Three. This begins the gradual exposure process by slowly and thoughtfully working with the trauma in a manageable way, thus increasing the child's tolerance of and confidence in dealing with upsetting material.

### Working With Outsider Reports

As we come to know this child, other potentially traumatic incidents may come to our attention through other sources. While the child is the primary source of information, caregivers may know of specific incidents that may be important to include. If there is an open child welfare file, consulting the case manager could identify other potential traumas, such as apprehensions, losses, or reported abuse or neglect incidents.

With information from outside sources such as these, we always come back to the child to have him decide about the appropriateness of adding these identified incidents to the puzzle pieces. We don't assume something is experienced as either good or bad. We might think a particularly "negative" event would be upsetting, yet this may not be so until we understand, from the child's point of view, how he experienced it. We learn about his experiences by asking the child to think of the incident for a few minutes without talking, and having him check in with his body and rate the incident/experience on the same scale from 0 to 10. When checking in with the child, we observe both nonverbal body cues as well as self-report. Some children may say it isn't upsetting and rate it low on the upset scale, but their bodies may give other clues through physiology, emotion, or behavior. In this case, we become curious about what we are witnessing, slow down the process, and invite the child to become curious about what we are seeing in his body and what he is noticing. Often this slowing down and curious approach allows space for acknowledgment about what is really there.

The information from these questionnaires is used to understand the child's experience in relation to the trauma. It is not the time to challenge the child's thinking or negative beliefs that may be identified. It is the time to clarify the information and to ensure that the child's world is understood exactly as it is reported.

*Note:* Pieces of My Story, Part 2, will be addressed in Phase Three (see Chapter 8).

## READINESS TO MOVE TO PHASE TWO

Now that we have a glimpse of the world from the child's perspective, we want to ensure the following guidelines have been met in order to move to Phase Two:

1. Treatment goals are identified.
2. Funding for treatment is in place, if needed.

3. An estimated number of sessions available is identified. This will help determine the depth of the treatment plan and what phases, or parts of phases, will and won't be feasible.
4. Caregivers and child agree with treatment plan.

## REFERENCES

Betts, D. J. (2005). *A systematic analysis of art therapy assessment and rating instrument literature.* Retrieved from http://www.art-therapy.us/assessment.html

Blaustein, M., & Kinniburgh, K. (2010). *Treating traumatic stress in children and adolescents: How to foster resilience through attachment, self-regulation, and competency.* New York: Guilford Press.

Briere, J. (1996). *Trauma symptom checklist for children.* Odessa, FL: Psychological Assessment Resources.

Briere, J. (2005). *Trauma symptom checklist for young children.* Odessa, FL: Psychological Assessment Resources.

Buck, J. N. (1966). *The house-tree-person technique: Revised manual.* Beverly Hills, CA: Western Psychological Services.

Burns, R. C., & Kaufman, S. H. (1972). *Actions, styles and symbols in kinetic family drawings (K-F-D): An interpretive manual.* New York: Brunner/Mazel.

Cohen, J., Mannarino, A., & Deblinger, E. (2006). *Treating trauma and traumatic grief in children and adolescents.* New York: Guilford Press.

Friedrich, W. N. (1997). *Child sexual behavior inventory: Professional manual.* Odessa, FL: Psychological Assessment Resources.

Greenwald, R. (2005). *Child trauma handbook: A guide for helping trauma-exposed children and adolescents.* New York: The Haworth Reference Press.

Levine, P. (1997). *Waking the tiger: Healing trauma.* Berkeley, CA: North Atlantic Books.

Reynolds, C. R., & Kamphaus, R. W. (2004). *BASC-2: Behavior assessment system for children,* (2nd ed). Circle Pines, MN: American Guidance Service.

Steele, W., & Raider, M. (2009). *Structured sensory intervention for traumatized children, adolescents and parents (SITCAP™)* (3rd ed.). New York: Edwin Mellen Press.

# 7 Phase Two Guidelines
## Cultivating Safety and Resources

> Adeptness at returning to a sense of fortitude and competence after feeling vulnerable creates a sense of confidence that is the foundation of healthy self-esteem. It builds inner stability because it is not based on the "ups and downs" of life (external events); rather it is based on a resilient nervous system in action (internal events). This ability of the body to shift out of a state of shutdown, anxiety, aggression, helplessness or feelings of estrangement into a sense of vitality, joy, hope, initiative, and connection is the **best resource** of all!
>
> Levin and Kline (2007, p. 138)

Six-year-old Kali was having difficulty with nightmares and fears. She was now living in a safe home with safe people, but for most of her young life she knew only abuse and neglect. We had been working together for many months, and I had come to know her as being one of the most courageous children I had worked with. Kali had prepared for and attended court on several occasions, and she faced the people who hurt her. She worked earnestly on resourcing for many months, but her fears and nightmares continued. In one session, prior to her final court appearance, Kali shared how fearful she was of the evil devil. I asked if she could draw an image of her fear. When she finished, she was so activated she couldn't look at it, and she physically withdrew from the picture. We took a moment to notice and name what was happening in her body because she had a good grasp of the language for her inner world of emotions and sensations. As she calmed herself, I reminded Kali that there was a part of her that she might have temporarily forgotten about but that I remembered. I shared how I witnessed all the hard work she did to prepare for court and how she had been to court before and, in front of many people, she told the truth about what happened to her, even though she was scared. I reminded her of her bravery. As I said the word *bravery*, her eyes lit up and she sat a little taller. I asked what happened to the fear as she sat up taller, and she said, "It gets smaller and I feel braver!"

We then experimented with slouching and sitting straight, noticing what helped build her bravery. She then went to the gathering drum on the floor and began drumming what she called her "brave song." Kali returned to her original image on the table, and she began changing her drawing, saying, "I want to make *it* scared, not me!" She was no longer scared, but determined, focused, and confident. She was then invited to draw an image of herself at the beginning of the session and how she was now. Kali noticed that in her "now" picture, she was no longer feeling scared; instead she felt happy and brave. She then went on to expand the bravery by having her body traced on large paper then painting the picture (Figure 7.1). Her caregiver attended the last part of the session, and Kali excitedly took her through the whole process. Together they decided that this picture would need to go up alongside her bed, where she would see it as she fell asleep and as she woke up.

This is a powerful example of a young girl learning to regulate her fears by using her body and her art, while at the same time increasing emotional resilience. Kali mobilized her bravery resource to assist her with standing up to her fear. Along with the bravery resource, Kali learned to pay

*Figure 7.1* Kali's painting after expanding her feelings of being brave. Used with permission.

attention to her body, experimented with what body movements strengthened her bravery, used the resource of altering her art, and expanded the good sensations and feelings through the art.

Each intervention builds on previous interventions and serves to create the foundation on which to proceed to the next phase of therapy. Now that the initial assessment is complete, we move into the therapeutic work of creating safe spaces and relationships while teaching regulation skills required to negotiate trauma's imprint. Regulation skills are embedded throughout this four-phase model and are designed to help children and caregivers manage feelings, thoughts, physiological responses, and behaviors. Although we teach specific regulation skills in Phase Two, we build resiliency throughout the treatment process in a variety of ways. Some of these ways include inviting children to increase their awareness of their inner worlds, including thoughts, feelings, and sensations; teaching children to both notice arousal in their bodies and adjust the arousal by lowering or increasing their energy; and teaching children how to effectively communicate their inner world experiences. Expressive arts, by nature, is an action-oriented therapy, meaning we act, move, and take charge of the process in every session. This ability to act and effect change increases a sense of internal locus of control, empowering children to be stewards of their lives.

Learning about, developing, and practicing body and mind resources are the primary goals of this phase. It is empowering for children to be able to have a language to communicate their internal world experiences and to learn how their bodies have the inherent ability to shift sensations and feelings. We teach children and their caregivers about developing internal, external, body, and arts-based resources throughout this phase.

## PHASE TWO EXPRESSIVE ARTS INTERVENTIONS

There are 11 interventions described in this chapter to assist the therapist with using expressive arts to support the child and caregiver. The primary focus of support is developing self-regulation skills while creating a safe therapeutic relationship. The handouts for the interventions addressed in this chapter appear in Appendix F.

### Pouches, Pockets, Bags, and Boxes

*Rationale*: Phase Two is all about creating safety and security. The child is finding ways to manage activation as he moves between activating and nonactivating material. One way of teaching containment is by literally creating containers for the puzzle pieces (discussed in Chapter 6). Containers provide a tangible, safe space to put the "hard stuff," and they act as a temporary boundary until clients are ready to process the puzzle pieces in Phase Three.

    *Process*: There are many ways of creating containers for the puzzle pieces. The child may have his own idea for a container, or you can ask the child to choose from the materials you have available. The containers can be decorated and embellished, and words or symbols can be drawn on or inside of the containers. Allowing choices about the size and shape of the container allows the client to identify what will work best to hold the trauma material. This offers the therapist insight into how the child is sensing the "bigness" of the trauma, and it can be a springboard for further exploration of the child's feelings and thoughts. The following are some ideas of what to have on hand:

1. Pouches: Pouches can be purchased or made with the child. The simplest design is to cut out a circle using material of your choice. Using a plain muslin or canvas cloth allows the material to be painted or drawn on with permanent markers. The size of the circle is up to you. Place objects in the center of the circle. Gather the edges, and tie the pouch closed with embroidery thread, string, or ribbon.
2. Pockets: Using pockets cut from old pairs of jeans can work well.
3. Paper bags and envelopes: These also act as effective containers and are easy to have on hand and embellish.
4. Boxes: Have a collection of boxes for the child to choose from. Small wooden or cardboard boxes are great options.

*Example*

At any given time I will have an assortment of boxes in my office of varying sizes, shapes, and designs made by children (Figure 7.2). Some children find it supportive to notice the presence of the other boxes in the office, knowing that they are not the only ones with trauma stories.

### Setting My Own Pace: Stop, Slow, Go

*Rationale*: Difficulty with impulse control, feeling out of control, and/or feelings of disconnection from their own bodies are common presenting concerns for children who have experienced trauma. Teaching children to use their "brakes" (Rothschild, 2000) when they get too revved up or they feel out of control is an important skill at the beginning of treatment. The main ideas are to help the client become aware of and connect with her inner experience,

*Figure 7.2* Containers for puzzle pieces. Used with permission.

practice returning to a calm enough body, and find a way to effectively communicate what she is experiencing to those around her.

*Process:* Using cardboard, have the client cut out three traffic signs to reflect stop, go, and slow or yield. Have all three visible and on hand to practice using them during the sessions. We teach the child the idea of being too revved up and needing to use brakes, just like we do when riding a bicycle. Practice is done by asking the child to think of something upsetting (not trauma related) and listening to what she is feeling inside to determine which sign best fits with what she "knows" inside. Is braking needed? Just a little? Do we need to stop? Practice often throughout the sessions when needed. Invite the caregiver in and have the child teach what she has learned. The child and caregiver may decide to make another set of signs to use at home to integrate this body awareness skill for emotional regulation.

Adolescents are invited to listen closely to what they are feeling inside and learn to use their voices to slow things down as needed when they start becoming activated. Some teens like the visual of a sign.

*Example*

Josh is a very active young fellow of 7 years. Early on in our work, Josh made his stop and go signs. In one session when he began working on some of the hard things he had lived, I noticed him becoming somewhat distracted when he slowly reached over for the stop sign and said quietly, "I need a break." I was surprised at his ability to so quickly use his new skills. He was letting me know it was becoming too much for him to tolerate. After I acknowledged his success in effectively communicating the need to stop, he took a break, used his resource cards, and then we continued when he showed me the go sign. This process allowed us to work toward increasing his ability to tolerate discussions regarding the more difficult trauma material.

## Learning About Safety

*Rationale*: Safety is not a thought, but an experience known and sensed in the body. There are many kinds of safety, including emotional, physical and psychological. When trauma happens, safety is compromised; thus, reestablishing a sense of safety is the foundation to doing trauma work. Exploring children's experiences of safe and unsafe situations and people brings awareness to what they already know about safety and assists them with learning how they can create a sense of safety in the here and now. Children learn to identify both safe and unsafe experiences by exploring them somatically with these interventions.

*Process*: We do this intervention either with the caregiver or we have the caregiver come in toward the latter part of the session so the child can teach what he has learned by reviewing his work. Sharing with the caregiver is a vital step toward integrating these skills into the everyday life of the child. The first invitation is to explore safe and unsafe feelings and sensations in the body. We then expand this exploration to actual situations in the child's life in which he has experienced both safe and unsafe people and places. Next, we create safe spaces both in the therapy office and at home. The final part of this intervention is to take this learning and use the expressive arts to expand the child's understanding and knowing through story, acting, telling, and drawing. Following the creative impulse of the child is most important. If he has another idea that fits here, we follow his lead.

*Example*

Jenna, who was 12, explored her personal meaning of safety. What stood out for her when working with the theme of safety was how little she said she knew about safe people. She was sexually abused by her grandfather, and it became difficult to know what safe meant because he was supposed to be a safe person. She began by drawing what safe felt and looked like in her body and what unsafe felt and looked like. Jenna shared that it was difficult to draw the images about safe and unsafe feelings (Figure 7.3). She did say that when she feels safe, "My brain no longer feels like I'm going to die. But my mind is always racing, saying, what ifs."

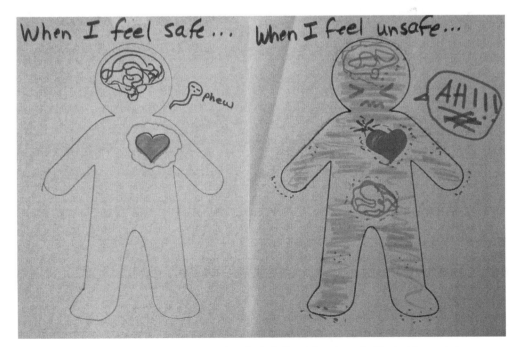

*Figure 7.3* Jenna's drawing of her sensations when she is feeling safe and unsafe. Used with permission.

She identified feeling calm and a sense of relief when she feels safe. When she feels unsafe, she reported feeling shaky, represented by her red dots, and she said that the shaky feelings make her want to run. She said the pink is the adrenaline, "It runs through my body and makes me want to run as well. My brain is hurting and it tells me to fight but my body says no. My stomach hurts and is scared. My heart is beating fast."

This discussion led us to further explore signs of being unsafe in the relationship with her grandfather. She identified the things that made her feel uncomfortable at the time, such as the way he hugged her, took photos of her, and certain things he said. Jenna began putting the pieces together. She began to identify what behaviors and interactions were warning signs. She made a continuum of safe and unsafe people and placed people she knew on the scale from 1, being unsafe, to 10, being safe. As we worked on this intervention, Jenna began to identify other abusive incidents with people who were unsafe.

### Cultivating Hope

*Rationale*: It is essential that we journey alongside of hope. Hope means that we can get through the tough stuff and that life can be good. Grounding the therapeutic work in a framework of hope reminds both therapist and client that there *is* good in the world and that healing *is* possible. We are witness to this each time a child gathers her courage and takes another step toward healing.

*Process*: This intervention can be adapted to whatever age of child you are working with. There are many ideas to choose from on the handout. Go through the handout together with your client and decide together what parts of the intervention the client is interested in completing. Client need, time, and supplies will guide what will fit best for her situation.

Figure 7.4 shows examples of a variety of affirmation cards that can offer teens hope.

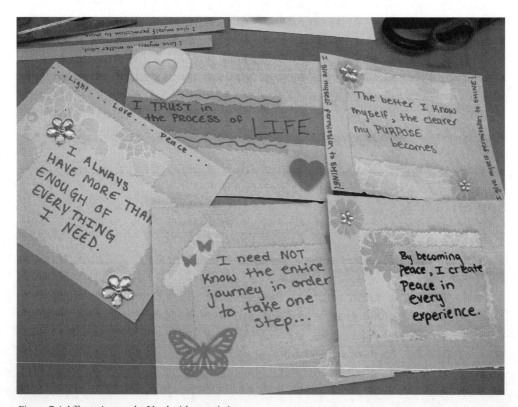

*Figure 7.4* Affirmation cards. Used with permission.

**Building Resources 1**

*Rationale:* Building resources is completed through a series of interventions necessary to prepare the client for the trauma processing in Phase Three. Building Resources 1 is an introduction to inside, outside, and body resources and the process of identifying which resources the client has and which ones are still needed.

*Process:* The child and caregiver are both invited to think about making a list of the various inside, outside, and body resources the child may already have. Next, they identify what resources might be missing and how the caregiver can assist the child with developing them.

*Example*

Lily was 11 years old when we first met. She thoroughly enjoyed creating her own resource list. After developing the resource list, Lily would ask me to read her resource list out loud at the beginning of each session because she loved to hear the words she chose and be reminded of all the people and things that supported her. One of Lily's human resources and inspirations was Martin Luther King, Jr. Lily decided to make her own Martin Luther King, Jr., speech as her testament to stop sexual abuse from happening to other kids. We taped her voice speaking her words and we would play it when she felt the need for this support.

These are her words:

**I Have a Dream**

I have a dream that you should live in a safe environment and walk down the streets without people touching you or harassing you!

You have the right to speak out and to be protected.

Through the hard journey you have been through, know that you are a brave person and you deserve to be you and only YOU.

What do YOU dream?

**Building Resources 2**

*Rationale:* This second resource intervention is working with the resources in an artful way. There are many methods to do this identified in the handout. Creating art with the resources reinforces the power of the resource and acts as a tangible reminder of what the client can use to help deal with upsetting thoughts and feelings. Teaching how to use the resources and encouraging their use outside of the therapy space builds confidence in the child's relationship with his body because the resources assist with regulating and calming distressed emotional states and body activation.

*Process:* There are many ways to strengthen current resources and make reminders of them more present in the daily life of the child. Exploring the options together with the child will determine which art forms he is more drawn to creating with. It can be beneficial to have examples of these resources so the child can see, first hand, what he could create. Practice using the resources is essential to the process. For example, at the beginning of each session, bring out the resource cards, stones, flags, or shrine and have the child connect to these tangible resources in a somatic way. Have them present during the therapeutic work, referring to them as necessary. The child may make extra resource objects so that he can take some with him and use them outside of the therapy sessions to help maintain feeling regulated and grounded. The caregiver is involved in learning how the child may use the resources outside of therapy and encourages their use in daily life as needed.

*Example*

The following images are examples of the various ways clients can create art that represents their resources.

*Figure 7.5* Resource shrines. Used with permission.

*Figure 7.6* Resource flags. Used with permission.

*Figure 7.7* Resource stones. Used with permission.

## Exploring and Healing Boundaries

*Rationale*: When a child experiences trauma, in particular relational trauma, her boundaries have usually been invaded, disregarded, and manipulated. Healing the experience of boundary invasion is part of the treatment plan, and it can be assisted by the therapeutic relationship itself. The therapist can model an overall sense of respect for the child's body, space, and voice in the session to session experiences. This intervention is specifically designed to help the child identify how her boundary has been impacted by the trauma, give her boundary a voice, and sense the integrity of her boundary through experiential activity. The present and future orientation offers hope of healing and moving beyond the trauma with an optimistic future.

*Process*: This intervention needs time and space to be experienced in a way that will be useful to the child and integrated meaningfully in the work. It may be done over a few sessions, woven into other interventions, and referred to throughout the process. Children are encouraged to think of a word that best captures the word *boundary*. Younger children often use the terms "space bubble" or "personal space." They will let you know what word works best for them.

There are four possible drawings for the boundary: before the trauma, how the trauma impacted the boundary, how the boundary looks now, and how the child would like it to be in the future. Choose the ones that are most appropriate for your client, as they all may not fit for everyone, as shown in the following example.

*Example*

Lily created three separate boundaries (Figure 7.8). She couldn't remember a time before being abused, so she created her boundary that represented her life when she was still being abused (top). The middle image represents her boundary now. The bottom image represents her boundary in the future.

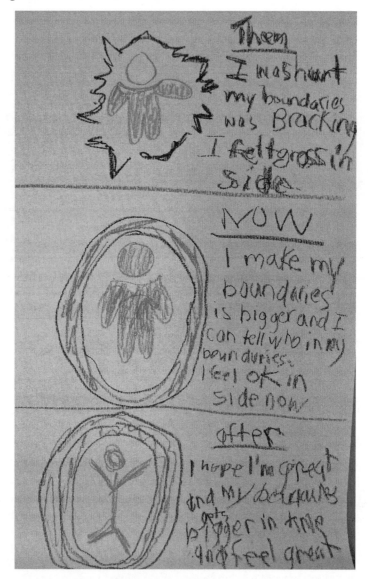

*Figure 7.8* Lily's boundary when she was being abused, now, and in the future. Used with permission.

**Labyrinths, Mazes, and Mandalas**

*Rationale*: Self-soothing interventions are important to introduce as a resource both in therapy and at home. The labyrinth, maze, and mandala all have similar components in that they require little skill and have highly meditative and calming qualities.

*Process*: There are many free Internet sites where you can find and print images of labyrinths, mazes, and mandalas. It's helpful to have a variety to offer. They can be given to clients to take home to be used when a calming activity is called for. Caregivers can attend this session and color one too, so that they are familiar with the benefits of using them as self-soothing tools.

While the process of coloring any one of these patterns is soothing, you might also take this intervention further by inviting your client to give it a name and to write words in or around it that are encouraging to him. If a client needs to be more energized, encourage him to find colors and a shape that brings more aliveness to his experience. He may need to experiment with the various images to determine what works best for his needs in this moment. When finished, he can find a place to put the image at home or leave it in his file to be brought out when needed, if it was agreed to be used as a resource in therapy.

## Learning to Be My Own Best Friend

*Rationale*: Many of us have a difficult time accepting the more demanding parts of ourselves, such as the angry, worried, scared, or hurt parts. When trauma is experienced, children tend to be even more vulnerable to negative thoughts and beliefs that lead them to disown, or at the very least dislike, these aspects of themselves. The various parts of ourselves are expressed through specific thoughts, feelings, beliefs, sensations, and behaviors. It can be beneficial for children to have a way of understanding these parts and to learn to develop the ability to listen to the more difficult aspects of themselves that they often feel shameful about. This intervention is based on inner relationship focusing by Ann Weiser Cornell (2013).

*Process*: This intervention is shared with the caregiver first to ensure that she has an understanding of the process and the ability to support the child by following through at home with the ideas in the handout. The child is then introduced to the process and completes the activities with the therapist. The child teaches the caregiver about the different parts of himself and together they identify ways that the caregiver can assist the child when these parts are present. Check back in from time to time with both the child and the caregiver to determine the progress they are making at home with managing the harder parts. This is not just a technique; rather, it is an ongoing way for clients to learn how to manage the more difficult aspects of themselves.

### Example

Gina created the calm and happy part of herself as a landscape, saying that she loves the open spaces and nature. Gina shared that she could feel a calm peacefulness inside her body just by looking at her image. She used the "I am. . . ." prompt to identify other words for her painting. She wrote, "I am nature, I am the horizon, I am the trees and the earth."

Gina went on to draw some of the other parts of herself that she struggled with. She drew the part of her that often feels lonely, and she explained how this part feels like no one understands her. Gina also drew the part that doubts and questions everything she does, noting how unsettled she began to feel inside as she spoke about these two pictures. I asked Gina how the calm and happy her could help these parts. She immediately took these images and placed them on top of her calm and happy painting. She checked in with her body and noticed how much calmer she felt again. She said she wanted to take her painting of the calm and happy part of her home. Gina said she could use it as a reminder of how to calm these other parts. Gina shared her art with her mom so that when needed mom could remind Gina of her calm and happy part and how it can help her when she becomes lonely, doubtful, or distressed. Gina also talked with her mom about how her mom could assist her when she feels lonely.

## Building Awareness and Resources Through Imagery and Stories

*Rationale*: This intervention acknowledges and validates the body's role in the healing process. The body is a primary resource as children learn to access their strengths and discover what is inside that supports them becoming strong, regulated children. Teaching children about the automatic, instinctual nature of the fight, flight, and freeze responses is helpful and empowering. This handout is designed for both the caregiver and child to work together in playful and adventurous ways in between sessions to strengthen the child's fight, flight, and freeze resources.

*Process*: There are many parts to this intervention. Go over the handout first and decide which parts make the most sense to do with your client based on client need and time available.

Decide on the level of caregiver involvement that is warranted and when the caregiver should be included in the session (throughout or at the end).

The first part normalizes the protective responses of fight, flight, and freeze. The drawing can be done in the session or can be done for homework and reviewed in the next session. The second part is research for the child and caregiver to do as homework. The third part can be done in the session together with the caregiver or alone with the child and then shared with the caregiver at the end as a small performance. Be mindful of going slowly with this part of the intervention. The intention is to bring attention to the child's bodily experience of the protective responses of fight, flight, and freeze and to help her see that what her body did was natural and protective. The goal is to normalize the protective responses and strengthen the child's relationship with self. The fourth part can synthesize the intervention by using a visualization and creating an image in response to the strength and power of the child's protective resources.

Follow up with caregiver and child at the next session about their homework experience.

*Example*

Twelve-year-old Jenna and I reviewed the handout together. As we discussed what protective response she related to most, without hesitation, Jenna identified that it was the freeze response. She asked to paint her experience (Figure 7.9), which was followed with a written response:

*Figure 7.9* Jenna's painting of how she experiences the freeze response in her body. Used with permission.

There once was a place where people use to go and learn about Jenna. One day the people got bored and started vandalizing the statue by throwing things at it, calling it names, drawing on it, and touching it, making it dirty. The statue couldn't do anything to make the people stop. It couldn't speak. After all, it was made of stone.

As Jenna shared her story, she started to realize that the statue and the museum represented herself and her world. She then stated, "I just realized that the girl was me and the whole museum was my body, but my soul wasn't there! It was on vacation!" She was so excited by this revelation that she continued to write a second part to her story:

Then one day a girl saw the place and started yelling at the people and scared them off. She then started cleaning up the place and people started to notice and began helping her. The place was respected again and people got to learn more about the real Jenna.

Jenna appeared very excited as she read the second part of her story. I asked her to notice her inner body experience. She said, "I feel good in my body. I realized my soul wasn't there. All this time I was blaming myself for what grandpa did. I really couldn't move. I was frozen."

## Getting a Handle on Tricky Trauma Behaviors

*Rationale:* Now that the child has learned about different parts of self and the protective survival responses, we have a context in which to deal with tricky trauma behaviors. These are not everyday child behaviors; these are behaviors that are highly distressing to both the caregiver and the child, can be triggered easily and surprisingly quick, and tend to be persistent. Some examples include intense anger, oppositional behaviors, never feeling satisfied, attention seeking, or come close/go away relational behaviors. Children who have been exposed to chronic neglect and abuse over time develop patterns of reactivity due to repeated stressors that trigger the protective survival response reaction in the brain. Whether there is actual threat or not, if the child perceives threat, the reactions ensue. These are behaviors that are ultimately driven by the need to be safe or avoid danger or an attempt to satisfy another unmet need. They will show up in the child's relationships and will be confusing for those around the child. Children need assistance with understanding these experiences, their origin, and how to effectively manage and change the response.

*Process:* Read through the intervention to become familiar with the content. Have both the child and the caregiver present as you go over the framework with the child. We will enlist the wisdom of the inner detective, curious cat, and scientist in both the child and caregiver as this work is grounded in and supported by the attachment relationship. Go through the exercises together, beginning with identifying the behaviors of concern. Once the child and the caregiver have an understanding of the process, decide together which behaviors will be targeted for change. Identify a reasonable goal for behavior change using the process on the handout. For example, the child may decide that he wants to stop having angry outbursts. Ensure that the goal is clear, concrete, able to measured, and the child wants the change. Follow up is essential, and troubleshooting may be necessary.

The level of caregiver involvement, as with all interventions, will vary depending on the age of child and nature of their relationship. The younger the child, the more reliant he is on caregiver support with regulating feelings and behaviors. This intervention requires the direct involvement of the caregiver in bridging the learning from therapy to home. It will be the caregiver who reminds the child of the inner detective, curious cat, and scientist who will assist with the tricky trauma behaviors.

This is not a one-time intervention. Like the previous two interventions, the learning is to be integrated into a framework of understanding oneself and returning to it repeatedly throughout treatment. It may be that the child will not be in a place to manage this level of cognitive exercise until after Phase Three. While these processes are introduced in this phase, the child's readiness is most important and serves as the guide.

*Example*

Nine-year-old Shyla is Kali's older sister. Both girls experienced extreme neglect and physical and sexual abuse by family members. They had settled well into their new home and school, yet some behaviors persisted that were bothersome to both Shyla and her aunt and uncle. Shyla and I read through the handout together. Her inner detective discovered that the behavior that was most difficult was the part of her that would become very argumentative and ask questions she already knew the answers to. When asked what part of her she felt most connected to when this happens, she identified the "abandoned" part, and she drew a picture of this part of herself (Figure 7.10). Shyla identified that the abandoned part felt both angry and sad and her heart felt broken. We then checked in with the curious cat and asked the questions from the Influencers section. Shyla discovered that she was often triggered when she would see other family members getting attention. She could even start feeling those feelings in the moment as she was talking. She remembered that in the past she was so often ignored that she felt as though she didn't exist. We did a then-and-now pie chart and determined that she felt like she was ignored 100% of the time in the past, and now she feels that way a little less than half the time. Her feelings were affirmed by her aunt because her aunt and uncle often tried to ignore this attention-seeking behavior without realizing how it triggered past experiences. We then checked in with Shyla's inner scientist, and together

*Figure 7.10* Shyla's drawing of the part of her that feels abandoned. Used with permission.

*Figure 7.11* Shyla's drawing of her calm and happy part. Used with permission.

we came up with ideas of what her aunt could do rather than ignore the behavior. Shyla was invited to also call on her calm and happy part (Figure 7.11) to determine how it might help the abandoned part. Shyla wrote a love letter, tenderly reminding her abandoned part that she is well loved now by others and by herself and that she will always be there for her. She then painted several wooden hearts that represented calm and love to put over the heart of the abandoned one when needed. Shyla and her aunt went away with a renewed understanding and respect for the abandoned part, along with ideas they would experiment with at home.

## READINESS TO MOVE TO PHASE THREE

Once the safety and resource work of Phase Two has been completed, it is a good time to review the child's readiness for the trauma processing phase. The following guidelines can help you determine if anything more needs to be in place before proceeding to Phase Three.

1. The child has continued physical and emotional safety.
2. The child understands the difference between being safe and feeling unsafe.
3. The child is able to ask for and name safe objects, such as a stuffed animal or blanket, or the teen is using resource cards or other identified resource objects.

4. The child has learned and uses skills for managing arousal with success both in therapy and at home. For example, the child uses strategies such as the stop/go sign or resource cards to help calm and regulate himself.
5. There is security in the therapeutic and caregiver relationships, as reported by both the child and the caregiver.

## REFERENCES

Cornell, A.W. (2013). *Focusing in clinical practice: The essence of change*. New York: W.W. Norton.
Levine, P., & Kline, M. (2007). *Trauma through a child's eyes: Awakening the ordinary miracle of healing*. Berkeley, CA: North Atlantic Books.
Rothschild, B. (2000). *The body remembers: The psychophysiology of trauma and trauma treatment*. New York: W. W. Norton.

# 8 Phase Three Guidelines
## Processing the Trauma

> The weight of treatment outcome research suggests that processing the trauma is essential and necessarily involves the controlled experiencing of the sensations and emotions associated with traumatic memories.
>
> van der Kolk (2003, p. 311)

She sat in the chair next to me, her young body shaking uncontrollably. "I couldn't wait to get here. I have waited for so long to tell someone my story." It was our first meeting, and Renee was 11 years old. A long history of neglect and sexual abuse by multiple family members made up part of her history. I could feel my own body become activated as I witnessed her trembling. I acknowledged she was coming to therapy because of all the hard things that had happened to her, including the sexual abuse. I also acknowledged how long she had been waiting and how her body also had waited a long time, and that I could see it trembling. I let her know that we would have time to get to know each other so that it would be safe to share all the things that she had been holding inside, waiting to tell someone. For now, I asked her if she would like to put all that she was holding into the art, so that the art could help hold it until we were ready to talk more specifically about what had happened. Her body quieted. She nodded and asked to paint. On a large paper, she painted different-sized boxes of various colors to contain the stories she so desperately wanted to share.

This experience with Renee is not typical. Usually, children are less inclined to speak about their experiences, in an effort to avoid uncomfortable feelings or sensations. For Renee, the uncomfortable feelings and sensations could not be tolerated any more. She had tried to let people know what happened to her, but when she did, she was told not to say any more and then was moved from that foster home. By the time she arrived at my office, her young body was needing to tell its own story. We make decisions about what is in the client's best interest at this particular point in the process. I had to decide if I would go ahead and let Renee tell me her story or if I would support her by containing the story until we established some safety in our relationship. This was our first session. There was no relationship between us at that point. I chose to attune to what was happening in her body and acknowledged her feelings and experience of needing to tell someone her stories. I felt the need to be both attentive, acknowledging her need to express, *and* to find a way to create emotional safety that was congruent to where we were developmentally with our therapeutic relationship. This would allow Renee to develop the capacity to manage the intensity of her experiences in a safe and structured process.

The primary goal of Phase Three is to assist children with moving the trauma experience from implicit to explicit memory. "As long as children are unable to talk about their traumatic experiences, they simply have no story, and instead, the trauma is likely to be expressed as an embodiment of what happened" (van der Kolk, 2003, p. 311). van der Kolk emphasizes how the trauma story shows up in the body through "psychosomatic problems." Therapy needs to be organized in a way that children can "learn to observe what is happening in present time and physically respond to current demands instead of recreating the traumatic past behaviorally, emotionally, and biologically" (van der Kolk, 2003, p. 311). If children continue to fear their bodily reactions and feelings related to thoughts of trauma, they will continue to avoid and disconnect from their experiences, preventing mastery over the memory. Memory processing is critical to children's long-term mental and physical well-being.

Now that the work of safety, stabilization, and regulation skills has been established in Phase Two, we move on with processing the trauma more directly in Phase Three. In reality, the processing, by way of gradual exposure, begins with the assessment process. From the beginning, we are assessing the responses of our clients and their abilities to tolerate any mention of the trauma. Processing in Phase Three continues in a more structured and purposeful manner.

Although this is a four-phase approach to trauma treatment, children's lives and experiences do not fit neatly in a four-phase model. This approach provides a framework, in which there are specific guidelines to follow and goals to be met so that the move to the next phase of treatment is done as safely as possible. While linear in approach, there is often a revisiting of experiences and reteaching of skills over time, throughout the process, and with some children, over years. Trauma processing itself is a complex interweaving of exploring trauma incidents while dealing with parts of the child that are triggered and need integration, as well as deepening the use of resources and regulation skills.


## PHASE THREE EXPRESSIVE ARTS INTERVENTIONS

### The Wall

*Rationale*: The closer we get to working on the hard stuff, the more clearly we may sense what I refer to as *the wall* in the client. This is the body's natural way of protecting itself against experiencing negative feelings, overwhelming sensations, and yucky thoughts. The wall can show up in a variety of ways. Some children become angry at having to do this work, try to change the subject, or simply shut down and stop talking. Some children are very aware of the wall, whereas others some seem oblivious to it. Slowing things down and acknowledging the wall allows the therapist and client to work, in a tangible way, with feelings and sensations that might seem difficult to put words to. Once we can "see" the wall (e.g., by building a representation of the wall in the room with pillows or blocks or drawing it in a picture), we can then work with it through the art and the body and honor the very vital role it plays. The work is not to get rid of the wall, but to learn about it and the job it has to do (e.g., protect), to give it voice, and to engage with it in creative ways. As Rothschild (2000) writes, "The solution to a limiting defense mechanism is not in removing it, but in developing its opposite for both balance and choice" (p. 90).

*Process*: The first step is to slow the therapy process down by inviting the child to become aware of something that might be like a wall. As stated previously, it often presents in the client as disinterest in doing or continuing the work, fatigue, anger, and/or frustration. We can acknowledge the wall without judgment and with the determination of the detective or curiosity of the cat. When we bring awareness and acknowledgment to what the child might be experiencing, there is usually recognition that something is feeling scared or worried inside. This is an appropriate time to talk how the body is doing what it is designed to do to protect itself from overwhelm, and it is our job to listen closely to what this part wants us to know. After having learned about befriending the different parts of the self under Learning to Be My Own Best Friend in Phase Two, the child has a context from which to work with the wall.

The second step is an invitation to explore what medium best captures the essence of the wall for the client. With younger clients, it can take the form of a fort, where they can enter into a space that gives them a physical boundary around their bodies. Adolescents tend to draw as a way to illustrate what they are sensing as potential walls.

The third step is to work with the body and the image or structure of the wall. We spend time exploring where in the body the child experiences the wall: what sensations describe it (e.g., heaviness, pushing, tightness), and how it shifts, if at all, when the child stays with it and notices it.

Working with the wall through the art or through the creation of a physical structure, in a body-focused way, provides the client with the opportunity to come to know when the wall is present and really try to understand the job it has to do. When we learn to be aware of its presence in the body, we have the opportunity to give it the deep, compassionate listening that it needs to feel heard. In this way, we come to understand its function and how it has assisted the client in coping with the trauma. Once heard and understood, we can see how the wall has been a resource, and only then can we develop alternate resources to balance the choices.

### Example

Thirteen-year-old Cara had a difficult time preparing to work on the hard stuff of the sexual abuse. Each time we would get close to working on the puzzle pieces, she would say, "No, not today, I am not interested." I acknowledged this lack of interest and how that would come up each time we prepared to do the puzzle pieces. She immediately knew what I meant. I wondered if we could be curious together about this lack of interest. She sensed it like a big block in the center of her belly. She identified closely with the meaning of the wall as I described its potential job to protect. She smiled and was eager to create what the wall was to her and to have me witness what this looked like on paper. She proudly shared her image of the wall, which was heavily guarded by two serious looking men and had barbed wire covering the top of the wall and a lock and chain protecting the door from anyone entering (Figure 8.1). Curiously, I wondered aloud about a key to this lock. Cara said that there was a key, and she proceeded to make a lock and key separate from her image (Figure 8.2). Creating the image

*Figure 8.1* Cara's drawing of how she experienced the wall inside herself. Used with permission.

*Figure 8.2* Cara's drawing of the lock and key used to get into her wall. Used with permission.

of the wall and the lock and key dramatically shifted the way we worked from then on. Each week, as we prepared to work on her puzzle pieces, we would first bring out her image of the wall along with the lock and key. I would wait until she was ready to hand me the key, which became a signal that she was ready to work on a puzzle piece. Something changed in Cara when she completed the image of the wall and the lock and key. It was as though she felt safer and more in charge of her work. As safety increased, so did her openness and willingness to engage in the trauma processing. She said, "The only time it bothers me to talk about this stuff is if someone forces me to talk." Having the choice of whether she would unlock her door or not was critical to her feeling secure and empowered.

### Surfing the Waves

*Rationale*: To provide safe, regulated trauma work, it can be useful to have a visual guide to help a child report what is happening in her body and to stay within a manageable level of activation. Siegel (2010) uses the phrase "window of tolerance" (p. 137), which he describes as a tolerable level of activation that we function within that varies depending on our experiences. Surfing the Waves is designed to support children by staying within a tolerable level of activation in order to effectively complete the trauma processing work. As Siegel (2010) states, "Within our window of tolerance we remain receptive; outside of it we become reactive" (p. 137). The task of the therapist is to ensure that the child is receptive, open, and willing and to be ready to step in to support the child if she moves above or below the window.

It is empowering for our clients to be able to identify when they are numbing or are feeling overwhelmed and to have the power to slow or stop the process as needed and to continue the process when ready. Equally important is the safety created from the presence of a therapist who is paying attention to the child's internal world. "The presence of a caring, trusted other person, one who is attuned to our internal world, is often the initial key to widening our windows of tolerance" (Siegel, 2010, p. 138). We are working to support the child with increasing her ability to tolerate very uncomfortable thoughts, feelings, and sensations and providing the child with the experience that her internal world matters, and we are paying attention and are attuned to this world.

Surfing the Waves is similar to the stop and go signs from Setting My Own Pace in Phase Two. We are now introducing the concept of working within *some* level of activation, not too much and not too little, while using skills to modulate the arousal. Activation is expected because we need some waves to learn to surf; thus, using the concept of waves helps children learn to master activation rather than needing to avoid it.

*Process:* First, read through the intervention. You may use your own words to explain the metaphor of how learning to name, feel, tolerate, and express feelings and sensations can be much like learning to surf waves. We normalize the experience of having some activation and discuss how it is important to be somewhere in the middle, where there is not too much and not too little activation. Have the child draw her own waves. Practice using them on non-trauma-related upsets first, so the child can get a bodily sense of what this feels like to be able to be in charge, be heard, and be more regulated with difficult feelings and sensations. Once the trauma processing with the puzzle pieces begins, the waves are placed on the table in front of the child as a visual cue and resource in the work.

There are many metaphors that could be substituted here, other than a window or waves. The idea of climbing a ladder or working with a thermometer could be used and modified in ways that make sense to your client.

## My Iceberg

*Rationale:* Often in cases of child neglect and abuse, what a child discloses initially, even to the police, tends to be only part of the story that the child experienced. This intervention is only used when there is reason to believe that there may be more to the child's story that was hard to tell. In particular with sexual abuse, because shame and self-blame are so closely intertwined with the experience, there are often aspects of the story that have not been told. My Iceberg can normalize the fact that there may be more to the story that is so very hard to tell. It provides an opportunity to share more of the story in a safe and structured way.

*Process:* Use this intervention prior to engaging in trauma processing as an invitation to discuss themes of shame, embarrassment, and silencing. We can ask children why someone might not want to share the whole story, inviting them to reflect on and be curious about a wide range of possibilities. This intervention gives permission to talk about the "unspeakable," while at the same time connecting with the parts in the child that are potentially very fearful and require a little more support with being seen and witnessed by the therapist. It can be fun to look up images of real icebergs on the Internet or have images available to help children understand the metaphor.

### Example

When Eva completed the Feelings About the Trauma questionnaire, she shared that she often felt responsible and ashamed about what had happened to her. I sensed there was so much more to her story, and I decided to introduce her to the idea of the iceberg. Immediately, Eva acknowledged there was information about what her father did to her that she hadn't shared with the police or written on the puzzle pieces. We discussed how sexual abuse, through shame and embarrassment, silences people. She related to the idea of the iceberg and began drawing her own iceberg, choosing many shades of blue that represented different parts of her story (Figure 8.3). Eva shared that some parts would never be told, other parts would eventually be shared, and there were parts that had already been told. Completing the iceberg allowed her to acknowledge all the parts of her story and to determine what, when, or if she would share them.

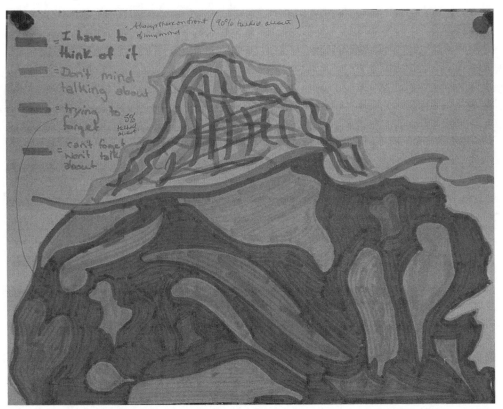

*Figure 8.3* Eva's drawing of an iceberg. Used with permission.

We went on to process the puzzle pieces that she had previously completed at the end of Phase One. Once Eva had processed some of the puzzle pieces, she returned to the image of her iceberg and began sharing the parts she said she would never tell. She identified that she was feeling less afraid and more ready to share these parts. "I was just embarrassed at first. Now I can talk about this," she shared. By working in a titrated way, within her window of tolerance, Eva was empowered to be able to share more than she ever believed she could, steadily building emotional resiliency.

### Tracking Trauma Processing

*Rationale:* As we move through the trauma processing, the child places the puzzle pieces in a box or some other container. These pieces are later burned in the burning pot or disposed of once processed. This form allows the therapist to track, at a glance, the processing of these puzzle pieces and is a reminder of which pieces may need further processing.

*Process:* As the child processes his puzzle pieces, the therapist makes note of the memory/ incident and rates the level of upset prior to processing and the level of upset after processing. Outcome is noted, highlighting observations about the progress made and clarifying what incidents may need further processing at a later date.

### Pieces of My Story, Part 2: Putting It All Together

*Rationale:* This intervention provides the therapist with a structured, step by step guide to processing the trauma pieces prepared by the child in Phase One. This trauma processing tool provides the client choice about what piece she will work on using the arts, and allows the working through of the puzzle pieces within a tolerable level of activation.

It should be noted that some children have their own unique way of conceptualizing how to process the trauma incidents. Creating a storybook with various chapters highlighting both the positive and the difficult memories is another approach taught to me by a 10-year-old girl. We follow their lead when it is an appropriate form of processing. Whichever way the trauma incidents are conceptualized or listed, the key elements of the trauma processing remain. This means that the details of the specific trauma incidents are processed fully, including thoughts, feelings, and sensations.

*Process*. First, check in to determine if there are any new incidents or themes the child has remembered and would like to add to the box. Next, we find a space in the therapy room that feels safest for her to do the processing, inviting her to scan her body to ensure there is a felt sense of safety in the present moment. If not, we do not move on to processing until we have worked with what is needed to increase the sense of safety in the here and now. We bring out the resource cards, stones, or shrine that she has created and put them out in view, reviewing and connecting with each resource and her body experience of that resource. Other resources that may be present are the stop and go signs and the ride the waves image. In the preparation phase, children can also be reminded of their protective figures (e.g., current caregivers, superheroes, angels) that they can name or draw to assist them and refresh a sense of the safety of their boundary or space bubble.

The child is invited to open the container with the puzzle pieces, marking the beginning of the process, and she is asked to choose one puzzle piece to work with. She is then invited to draw an image that shows the hardest part of that incident. As the story is being told through the art, we track what is happening in the child's body. We are moving back and forth between the art and the body, tracking both the content of the story and the energy expressed through the body. We pay attention to and make note of any thoughts or beliefs that may need to be addressed later and any body sensations that need to be acknowledged and tracked now.

The questions outlined in Pieces of My Story Part Two: Putting It All Together can guide the discussion regarding the child's image. Explore all aspects and details with a curious and caring attitude. The child is invited to add thought bubbles for the thoughts, feelings, and sensations regarding the image that represents the trauma.

If the client is having difficulty getting started, she can be offered the handout Resource/Trauma Picture, which has both the image of her strength and the trauma image on the same page. This intervention can get the drawing going by first drawing the part of her that knows she will get through this. Connecting with this part of herself can remind her of her confidence and ability to face the hard stuff that has happened. When there are significant feelings of shame associated to drawing the image, such as in the case of sexual abuse, the child can be asked to draw an image that represents how she *felt* during the incident. We still use the image to tell the details of the trauma story, following the questions on Pieces of My Story Part Two. These two alternatives (resource/trauma image and how the child felt image) are only offered if necessary and when the child is stuck.

Finish the steps outlined in the handout. The final steps involve returning the puzzle piece to the box, closing the lid signifying the end of this processing, followed by active engagement with the arts to increase a sense of empowerment and lower potential activation.

### Working With Activation and Disconnection

Sometimes we work further with the art to deal with disconnection or activation that is troubling. In previous sessions, Talia had already successfully worked on many puzzle pieces. During one session, Talia struggled with doing the puzzle piece, saying, "Do I have to?" We both became curious about what this part might need. We created space to compassionately hear the part that was feeling particularly afraid that day. When asked what that part might need, Talia knew immediately what she needed to do. She painted a safe place for her scared part, painting a treehouse high up in a tree in the middle of a forest. She was completely calm once finished. She went from a 9 out of 10 on the upset scale to a 1 of out 10. She smiled, felt in charge, and sensed her courage of having faced this difficult feeling, and she was able to continue with the puzzle pieces.

Joey (7 years old) discovered his own resource to deal with the activation associated with working on the puzzle pieces. He decided to create a separate box for his fears. Each time he prepared to talk about his story, he drew a picture of his fear, then put it in the box. At the time he made his box, Joey told me that this box "transforms the fear into love." This ritual regulated the fear and connected him to the courage it took to work on his puzzle pieces.

Alternately, we may need to support a child who disconnects and numbs when he is activated. Here, we will want to work slowly with the body and pay attention to when the child starts to drift away. We then experiment with anchoring back in the present, engaging with skills that increase tolerance to staying present. Creating a human outline and mapping out the process of disconnection can itself be anchoring. We then use this image as a guide and a reminder to alert the child when this begins to happen again. The goal is for the child to eventually learn to catch the disconnection as it begins to happen and to use her skills to stay anchored in the present.

### Number of Sessions

This process, in particular when there are multiple traumas, can take many sessions. Some clients want to do more than one piece in a session and some can tolerate only one. What seems to happen over time is that the client becomes increasingly desensitized to the content, is more familiar with and less afraid of her body sensations, and has a greater sense of confidence as she continues to face the challenging memories through the structured puzzle piece process. Often, the intensity on the upset scale drops for the other puzzle pieces as she begins this process. Have the child check in on the upset scale when a new puzzle piece is started to determine if the number has changed from the time she first wrote it back in Phase One.

### Example 1

When Eva came to one of the last pieces of the puzzle, she noted that she had given this particular puzzle piece a rating of 8 when she first wrote it down at the end of Phase One. "Now when I read it out loud I understand it differently. My dad told me that when this [the sexual touching] happens again that I need to tell him to stop. But why should I be the one stopping it? And if I don't, then is it my fault? Now I am no longer embarrassed. I am seeing more and more how he turned this around and made me feel like it is my fault." It was a 0 out of 10 when we got to this puzzle piece. She spoke about the incident without activation.

### Example 2

Kelly, who was 16 at the time she was working on her puzzle pieces, primarily experienced sensations instead of feelings in her body as she remembered and drew the trauma images. For each of her 10 puzzle pieces, we worked with the images and sensations, stayed with them until they had an opportunity to be acknowledged, and then the intensity of the sensation subsided.

As Kelly processed one of the incidents, she began to notice a sensation of what she described as panic, and she said, "I could have done more to try to get away. I feel guilty that my brother can't live with us now. It felt good and wrong and confusing." In this short period of time, a number of thoughts were noted and added to the Thoughts, Feelings, and Beliefs Checklist. We would address those later on; in that moment, we continued to follow her body. As she spoke about how she felt trapped, I noticed her hands forming a fist. We both became curious about her hands as I wondered out loud what her hands were wanting to do. She immediately said, "Push!" She played with the various ways that pushing felt right and good in her body, checking in with the sensations as she experimented by slowly pushing against the wall, shaking out her hands, and, at her request, putting on music to dance out any related energy.

*Example 3*

There are times when the child is not in the frame of mind to do the puzzle processing. We then work with what has come up in the body around the "no." Twelve-year-old Jenna had been working with the puzzle pieces over a few sessions; this day, however, she said she just couldn't do it. I invited her to check into her body about what this was like. She described it as a push–pull sensation in her stomach. She drew out the experience she was having in her body (Figure 8.4). She identified that there was a part of her that wanted to give up but that there was a weight, like an anchor in her belly that holds her up and tells her to keep her going. In the upper right image, as seen in Figure 8.4, was a message, "Keep holding on, it will get better." She identified that she was drawn to the heart and how the heart reminded her to keep going on, "Like there is someone there to help me." She then checked in with her body and noticed a sense of relief. It was important that we listened to the parts inside that needed us to slow the process and reconnect with her inner resources. She was ready to continue with the pieces the following session.

On another occasion, Jenna chose a puzzle piece to work on, but had a difficult time drawing the sexual abuse that happened. Together we decided that she would draw how it felt when it happened (Figure 8.5). She explained that she felt like a puppet, like she was being

*Figure 8.4* Jenna's drawing of her inner sensations. Used with permission.

*Figure 8.5* Jenna's drawing of how it felt when she was sexually abused. Used with permission.

used, "I felt gross in my stomach. Not a little bit but big." After drawing her image, she was grounded and able to continue writing and expanding on this part of her trauma story using the questions in the handout.

### Art Debrief

After a child works on a puzzle piece, he will be given the opportunity to debrief, through art, in response to anything left over in his mind or body from working on this trauma incident/theme. The child is invited to check in his body and create a response to whatever he is noticing, be it a yucky or positive feeling that needs expression. Both experiences are valuable to acknowledge and work with.

### Example

Figure 8.6 is an art debrief by fourteen-year-old Conor after completing a puzzle piece.

### Sharing With the Caregiver

For very young children, the caregiver is present during the trauma processing. Older children can decide what they would prefer. However, once the puzzle pieces are finished and the story is written, the caregiver is invited to hear the child's story through words and images. Before the joint session, the caregiver is prepared and supported in her own session to ensure she is

*Figure 8.6* Conor's painting of an art debrief after completing a puzzle piece. Used with permission.

able to be present to the child's work. We close the joint session with both child and caregiver drawing an art response. The caregiver creates an art response related to how she is moved by her child's work. The child is invited to create art in response to how it was to have her caregiver witness his story.

*Example*

Gina expressed being nervous and scared to share her story with her mother. She felt guilty about the sexual abuse happening with her older cousin, she felt responsible for putting her mother in this situation, and she was worried that her mother would be mad at her and that she wouldn't understand. These were all significant feelings that were addressed with her mother prior to sharing the puzzle pieces. It also allowed the opportunity for her mother to share how difficult it had been for her to offer support to her daughter because there seemed to be a wall between them since the disclosure. Sharing the trauma story is a vulnerable enough experience for a child; therefore, we address any perceived worries or barriers in the attachment relationship to clear the way for as much support between caregiver and child as possible.

Gina prepared her trauma story by taking all the images created in response to the puzzle pieces and creating a visual time line. The images visually told her experience, with the documentation of her thoughts, feelings, and sensations written next to the image. It was a difficult process for both mother and daughter. Her mother, although ready and present, found it distressing to witness the hurt, confusion, and suffering that Gina experienced. Gina was ready, yet nervous, as she shared the details of her story. One of the most powerful parts of the session was witnessing how her mother discovered a way around the wall and was able to offer Gina comfort and compassion that had been difficult for her to express outside of therapy. In this session, Gina's mother shared with Gina her own history of sexual assault when she was a teen.

For the first time, Gina began to believe that her mother might be able to understand some of what she went through. This was a pivotal session for their relationship. At the end, both completed an art response to the session. Gina's mother shared that she has felt numb since Gina disclosed and that she hasn't been able to express any feelings. She drew an image of the sun weeping, creating an ocean of tears, sharing how awful she felt that she wasn't able to stop the abuse. Further mother–daughter work continued in subsequent sessions.

Gina's art response was a bird leaving the cage, singing, "I believe I can fly!" She smiled and identified feeling both relieved and hopeful. As difficult as the process was, she felt she could now move on because her mother could now know and understand what she went through.

### Resource/Trauma Art

*Rationale*: There are times, even when all the resources and other supports are in place and there has been sufficient skill building, when it is difficult for a child to begin creating the trauma image. This intervention can be used to actively refresh the child's relationship with his inner resources or strengths.

This intervention can also be used for a variety of struggles that a child may encounter as a result of the trauma. For example, a child who was not believed about the sexual abuse could create an image of that struggle and an image of his strength, and then bring the two images together. Often, there is an empowering response when, in the art, the child is able to have power over the struggle, have a sensory connection to his strength, and have the ability to alter the images however he wants. Through this process, the child can recognize and experience in a bodily way his own inner strength when dealing with adversity.

*Process*: Invite the child to create art that represents an inner resource or strength that has assisted him so far in the therapeutic work and will continue to assist him with getting through the trauma processing. Offer examples if needed. Once he has created the art and connected with the resource in a somatic way, invite the child to now draw or create the trauma art (or other struggle), following the directives on the handout. Finally, invite the child to bring the two images together. Discuss how his strength has influenced the trauma/struggle.

### Example

Bella was a strong and vocal young 15-year-old. Yet, when it came time to process the puzzle pieces, she found herself stuck. I invited her to think of her strengths that had brought her this far in the process. She made her own list of strengths then drew an image to represent them (Figure 8.7). Bella shared that at the center of her body, she felt truly alive. She wrote positive messages on the bottom, including, "This too shall pass" and "Keep creating from the rhythm of your heart. Surely, you'll shine like a star." Bella identified strongly with her optimistic nature, and as she shared her image, she felt this strength grow stronger as she talked about it. She said she was now ready to draw the trauma image. Bella took the main theme from several of the puzzle pieces and drew one image (Figure 8.8). She identified that she was the purple in the center and the squares represented all the people who have hurt her in her life. She took the time to go through the details of the primary incidents of sexual abuse, clarifying her thoughts, feelings, and sensations related to each square. Bella spent several sessions with this image and process, and when she was finished, she was asked if she would like to bring these two images together. Bella was excited as she cut the purple center, representing herself, out of the trauma image and placed in the center of her strength image (Figure 8.9). She explained that she added teal arms around the purple part to protect and comfort it. Bella appeared noticeably relieved and energized as she reported, "I knew I had the strength in me to talk about this stuff, I just needed some help."

*Figure 8.7* Bella's drawing of her strength. Used with permission.

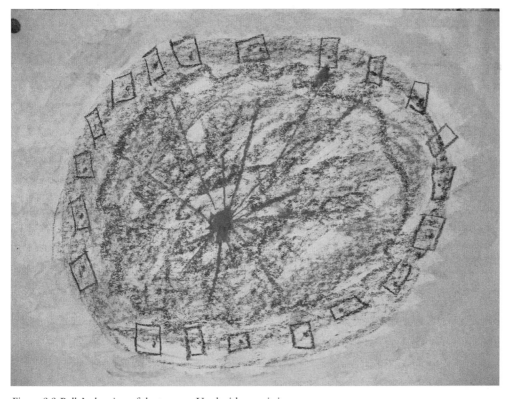

*Figure 8.8* Bella's drawing of the trauma. Used with permission.

*Figure 8.9* Bella altered her two images by combining them. Used with permission.

## Time Lines and Road Maps

*Rationale:* As noted earlier, the primary tasks in Phase Three are to help children develop the skills to stand up to and master trauma memories and organize the trauma story in a meaningful, coherent way. At this point, the child has completed the puzzle pieces, created the story, and shared with her caregiver. We now want the child to situate the trauma in the context of her life that clearly places the trauma in the past. There are many creative possibilities for this to be done. Creating a time line or road map are two ideas that will be explored here.

*Process:* The time line is a visual image in which the child outlines both positive and negative life events on a line beginning from birth to the present day. It is a useful way to really see the child's story. A long line is drawn on paper, with positive life events documented above the line and the difficult events below the line. The child places the puzzle pieces below the line then adds positive memories and events above the line. The final part of the process is to make the line long enough to add dreams and hopes for the future. This intervention is best done with the caregiver (though the child can decide), who can assist by reminding the child of positive memories as well as witness the child's documented story, reinforcing how the trauma was a part of her life and it is now in the past. This experience can also support the caregiver with placing the trauma in the past and can offer a future-oriented perspective.

A second option is to create a road map. This intervention includes drawing out a long road and placing the trauma incidents along the way, adding positive life events pre- and post-trauma. The child then considers the various resources (internal, external, and body) that she has used to cope with the trauma, adding these next to the trauma incidents through symbols, words, and colors. The child can imagine the trauma incidents as obstacles encountered on the road and the resources as the various ways she has managed to overcome the obstacles. The final steps are to invite the child to identify what she has learned from the trials and imagine the possibilities of where this road might lead her, again ending with an optimistic future-oriented perspective.

The questions at the end can be asked or modified for both the time line and road map. The child is invited to tell the brief story (without all the details, but in a coherent way) that describes her journey. We want the child to end the intervention by considering the things she has learned on this journey and where it is leading her. Both questions can assist with building emotional resilience by standing back and developing a more optimistic perspective that, although the trauma happened, it is only a part of the whole story, there are lessons learned from it, and good things are coming.

## Honor and Transformation

*Rationale:* Now that the child has completed the difficult task of processing the trauma, it is useful to put closure on this part of the work. Closure is vital for several reasons. First, it is encouraging because it marks a transition, a moving forward in the process and achievement of therapeutic goals. Second, the child has completed a very difficult part of his work, and we must honor the courage it took to do this work. A small ritual can provide a rite of passage to the next phase of the work that can be marked in simple ways, as described next.

*Process:* There are two parts to this intervention. First, there is doing something with the puzzle pieces. It can be ripping up the pieces of the puzzle, watering them down, or squishing them. Some children like the idea of shredding the pieces, then working them into clay and making something beautiful or making something ugly that, when dry, can be smashed, broken, or thrown away.

I often do a small burning ritual that is like a rite of passage for many children. We go outside to the backyard and rip the puzzle pieces then put them in what I call "the burning pot." It is a small, ceramic, outdoor pot that is used to burn citronella candles, which is perfect for burning puzzle pieces. I am in charge of lighting them on fire, and we watch the smoke take away the hard stuff of the memories. Once done, I take the ashes, and we add them to the garden. We speak of how something so bad could be of use for something good: nourishing the garden.

The second part of this intervention is transforming the box that contained the puzzle pieces, by painting, writing on it, or redecorating it in some way. Discuss how the container held the hard stuff for a long time, and now it is free to be made into something else. For some, it may need to remain the same; for others, it will be important to transform it and then use it for other things.

There are choices about when this intervention is completed. It may make sense to complete this intervention immediately after the puzzle pieces are done because some children voice their eagerness to want to get rid of the puzzle pieces. For many children, it is done at the end of Phase Three to truly mark the transition from Phase Three to Phase Four. Do what makes the most sense for this child.

*Example*

When Susan first created her box for the puzzle pieces, she drew an image of the person who abused her and put it in the photo frame that was on the box (Figure 8.10). After the trauma processing, she repainted her box and drew an image of a butterfly to replace the other image (Figure 8.11). "I feel more free now," she said as she shared the changes she made to her box.

## My Body: Four-Part Process

Now that the trauma story has been processed, the focus moves to healing the child's relationship with his body. We identify and address distressing and empowering thoughts, feelings, and sensations. Each intervention can be completed on the small body images on the handouts. However, it should be noted that these interventions could also be done progressively on one

*Figure 8.10* Susan's box that contained the puzzle pieces. Used with permission.

*Figure 8.11* Susan repainted and altered her box after the trauma processing was over. Used with permission.

large body outline. The child is invited to lay down on a large piece of paper and have her body traced. From there, each of the interventions is completed on that outline, taking the time to process any body movements, feelings, or resources that are revealed.

## My Body, Part 1: What My Body Did at the Time of the Trauma

*Rationale:* Victims of trauma often experience feelings of betrayal by their own bodies. There can be a sense of disappointment, concern, or shame that their bodies didn't do what they wanted them to do. This intervention supports children by identifying what happened in their bodies at the time of the trauma, thus providing them with the opportunity to integrate the previous learning regarding the survival responses of fight, flight, and freeze.

*Process:* Children can be told that these next interventions are to help with/heal their relationship with their body. The client is invited to think back to the trauma and remember what his body did while the trauma was happening. He is encouraged to think of thoughts, feelings, sensations, and actions and then to map these experiences on an outline of a body with colors, symbols, and words. Pay attention to what comes up in the body of the child while he is mapping this out. When there are multiple incidents, have the client focus on one of the more difficult incidents.

### A Note on Sexual Abuse

When a child has been sexually abused, he can have conflicted feelings if his body felt good when being touched. Children often feel embarrassed about having these feelings, so it is imperative that this is normalized and that the child understands that our bodies are made to feel good when touched in a sexual way. If a child who was sexually abused does not identify these feelings, it can be useful to let the child know that some children feel good when touched and how this can be confusing. Doing so can open a door that a child may find too difficult to open on his own. Often, children feel tremendous relief to be able to acknowledge and understand their bodies in this way.

Some children may act out sexually towards other children. Further assessment and treatment is required for children who develop sexual behavior problems. Sexual abuse–specific treatment is required for both the child and the caregivers about how to address and respond to these behaviors appropriately (Johnson, 1999; Silovsky, 2009).

### Example

Thinking back to what her body did at the time of the trauma, Gina recalled feeling like running away, shaky, guilty, dirty, sick, and insecure (left side of Figure 8.12). She identified the following as some of her thoughts at the time of the abuse:

> I acted like I was just having a bad dream.
> I acted like nothing was happening and that it would be over soon.

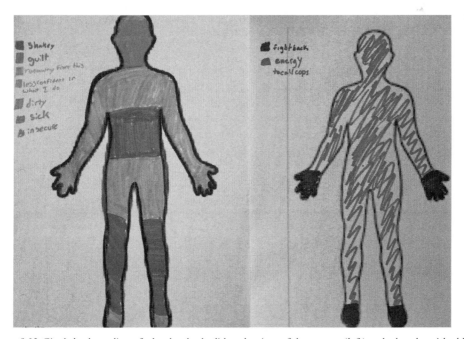

*Figure 8.12* Gina's body outline of what her body did at the time of the trauma (left) and what she wished her body did at the time of the trauma (right). Used with permission.

**My Body, Part 2: What I Wished My Body Did**

*Rationale:* Children sometimes wish they could have done something different during the trauma. Some clients even talk as though they were superheroes that overthrew the villain. This may be due to feelings of guilt or helplessness that they somehow let something happen to them and they have a need to reframe and reclaim power. Allowing clients the opportunity to explore what they wished their bodies did or could have done can be a powerful experience.

While similar to "wished," asking the child what her body "wanted" to do can also evoke strong expressions of acknowledging the wanting but not being able to carry it out. Again, addressing these thoughts, feelings, and sensations allows integration of the meaning of survival responses and allows children to act on the energy in their bodies *now*, as they speak about the wanting.

*Process:* The client is encouraged to imagine what her body might have wanted to do and to draw and write this on the body outline. Once she has completed it, we work with the body and identify sensations and feelings that come up in the present moment as the child speaks about her image. We work with the sensations or actions that the body has the impulse to do now. There can also be spontaneous movement and actions that happen as the child discusses the wanting. It is important to go slow and stay with the experience in the body.

*Example*

On the right side of Figure 8.12 is Gina's image of what she wished her body did. Gina stated, "I wished I would have called the cops right away and fought him back and told him to leave me alone." As she spoke these words, her hands went up in front of her as though to push something away. We experimented with this movement, finding ways that felt good in her body to move her hands out. As Gina played with various ways of moving her hands and arms away from her body, she felt relief rush through her neck, shoulders, arms, and hands. "Now that felt good," she said.

**My Body, Part 3: My Body's Voice**

*Rationale:* Silence and fear of speaking are often part of how one is effected by relational trauma. This intervention offers the client the opportunity to give voice to the parts of the body that have been hurt and highlights the then and now time orientation, increasing the client's awareness of how things may have changed over time since the trauma.

*Process:* Using the body outline, the child identifies through words, shapes, and images the hurts that happened to his mind, body, and heart. Next, he is invited to *imagine* what those parts that have been hurt might say if they had voices. He is encouraged to write on the outline both what they might have said at the time of the trauma and what those body parts might say now. Remember to track the child's body response in the present moment as he is working on these interventions. Often, we witness important body movements that can be worked with as they are happening, feelings that need further expression, and resources that can be amplified.

*Example 1*

Six-year-old Kali was sexually abused by her father. She completed several of the interventions on one paper (Figures 8.13).

*Figure 8.13* Kali's body outline of what her body did at the time of the sexual abuse and what she wished her body did. Used with permission.

**What my body did at the time of the sexual abuse:**

> I felt gross.
> My neck, arms and legs would freeze, like I couldn't move.
> My tummy had bubbles.

**What I wished by body did then:**

> I wished my heart would get so small and me too.
> I wished I wiggled away.
> I wished my hands would slap and hit him and my feet would kick and stomp him.

**If my body parts had a voice they would say:**

> My heart: Gross!
> My privates: Stop.
> My bubbles in my tummy: Don't do that to her.
> I would say: Stop!

*Figure 8.14* Gina's drawing of giving her body parts a voice. Used with permission.

*Example 2*

Gina gave her body parts a voice in Figure 8.14 and wrote her message in a card that she could open and read. She wrote:

> My Heart—I feel pain, like half of me is not there.
> My Mind—Just thinking of the abuse hurts.
> My Eyes—When my mind thinks of it, it brings me to tears and seeing it I wish I was blind.
> My Legs—I wish I could kick him and run somewhere else in the house.
> My Hands—I wish I just hit him or pushed him off my body.
> My Mouth—I wish I yelled and screamed for help, hoping someone would hear me.

*Example 3*

Fourteen-year-old Kara was sexually abused by multiple perpetrators within her family. Figure 8.15 is in response to what her body did during the abuse. She identified feeling confused and paralyzed, like she couldn't move or stop what was happening, "I felt there was no feeling in my heart. Like it was in a cage."

Kara's next image (Figure 8.16) is what she wanted to do.

*Figure 8.15* Kara's image of what her body did during the abuse. Used with permission.

*Figure 8.16* Kara's image of what she wanted her body to do. Used with permission.

She wrote the following response to this image:

> These people keep coming closer . . . they move in and in until they're on top of her. They get into her mind. They exploit her body. They taint her soul. They take over the territory she thought was only hers. They weigh her down. She has to stop walking. They get so heavy that she falls to her knees. Suddenly she's lying flat on the floor while the people just keep weighing more. Her breathing gets shorter, still they come. Oh how they suffocate her, she's now gasping for air. They weigh more and more and more, she takes the last gasp of air and holds it in for a second . . . when she lets her breath out in defeat she barely says, "Get off of me. . . ." He does. "Get off me," she says again. They do. Suddenly she can breathe again, "Get off me!" She says louder. She breaths in deep. "Get off me!" She yells. They all move away. "GET OFF OF ME!!!" She screams, throwing her hands in the air. Suddenly she realizes they've listened to her. She learns what she weighs alone, without the extra baggage. She looks down and sees her heart for the first time. (It's bleeding all over, but she knows she can fix that.) She throws her arms in the air again, and she screams, "I'M ALIVE!" Finally, she bursts open with feeling.

Kara then gave voice to all the parts of her body that were hurt by the abuse. She created an image that was taller than she was. She wrote at length, giving every body part, including her chest, thighs, back, vagina, eyes, mouth, and arms, a chance to be heard by speaking out. The day she completed her picture and writing I invited her to notice what it was like to be finished. She said, "When you find your voice you need to get it heard!" A few months later, Kara asked to work further with this piece. She called this her "breakthrough piece," saying, "I acknowledged the burdens I had to get over and captured all the issues and dealt with them. I haven't tuned out or numbed since doing this piece. I just feel okay." She then ripped off parts of her image to keep in her journal and burned the rest.

## My Body, Part 4: Caregiver and Child Session

*Rationale:* Some caregivers have their own trauma that is triggered due to their child's trauma. Caregivers are encouraged to address these issues in their own therapy. For the purposes of supporting her child in this therapeutic process, an individual session is recommended to assess the caregiver's readiness to witness her child's work and to prepare herself emotionally for this experience so that she is able to be as present as possible for the child. Further, if relevant, it is an opportunity for the caregiver to process her own experience of not having been able to prevent the trauma.

*Process:* Details of the process are outlined on the handout. Caregivers who were part of the child's life at the time of the trauma are encouraged to acknowledge the lack of protection, even if they couldn't have changed the trauma, stopped it, or known about it. From an attachment point of view, this acknowledgment can repair the rupture of the child not having been protected. In some situations, this may be a larger issue (e.g., when the caregiver did know about the abuse and didn't protect). Further therapeutic work will be warranted in these situations.

The joint session between caregiver and child is primarily for the child to be witnessed by the caregiver and to allow for repair that is needed between child and caregiver. If appropriate, the caregiver can share her image with her child to illustrate how they have both been hurt by what has happened. For some children, it can be a way of knowing they are not alone in their hurt. If there are concerns that the child could not handle this sharing, it may not be fit to do this part of the process. However, it is also an opportunity to witness the child's response to the caregiver's pain and, if needed, to address any aspect of that dynamic that would be healing to their relationship (e.g., parentification concerns). I have had many caregivers respectfully and appropriately share the effect the child's trauma had on them. The sharing can be very healing for the caregiver–child relationship because the child is typically not aware of how much the caregiver wanted to protect the child.

*Example*

Seven-year-old Joey was severely sexually abused by his uncle. He did all three parts of the interventions on one outline of his body on a large piece of paper. He began by filling it in with words and images about what his body did at the time of the abuse. He drew tear drops streaming down his face and wrote "sad, cry."

Next, Joey wrote what he wished his body did or said at the time of the trauma:

Mouth: Mom, help me!
   I should tell mom about this.
   I should tell mom that someone is hurting me!
Arms and legs: I wished they moved.
Private parts would say, Stop hurting me! Cry, cry, cry, cry.
Feet: I wished they would run, run, run.

The following is what the body parts would have said now:

Brain: Wow, I am so happy I told.
Heart: When I told the truth everything was better and better.
Private parts: I am glad he is in jail and can't hurt me anymore.
Muscles: I feel proud that I am strong.
Eyes: I feel glad to see the light now that he is gone.

Mom attended the joint session. As he shared his image and told her about what his body parts wanted to do, he made that motion with his own body. When he came to the part about what his feet wanted to do, he began running on the spot very quickly, then looked at his mom, and spontaneously ran over to her and fell into her open arms. This was one of the most moving moments to witness. This little fellow wanted and needed the security of his mother and now he allowed his body to do what it needed to do in this moment to not only discharge energy but also to be witnessed by his mother and for her to be able to receive and hold him. Later in the session, his mother took a marker and responded to his writing and drawing by attaching band aids to the hurt parts and by adding the following nurturing comments:

I am so sorry I didn't know what was happening and didn't protect you.
I wish I could take away your hurt.
I see how sad and hurt you were.
I am so glad you told.
You are such a brave little boy.
I am proud of you.

Mom also shared her image of how she was hurt by Joey being hurt. She identified what her body wanted to do and say:

Arms: I want to hug Joey!
Heart: I am crying. I'm sad for Joey and want to hug him.
Eyes: We are so mad and sad.
Mouth: How could uncle do that!
Hands: We want to push uncle away from you.

Mom held Joey in her lap as she read her words. When she read the nurturing comments, she slowed down, looked him in the eyes and spoke the words directly toward him.

**My Expressive Arts Bravery Story**

*Rationale:* This intervention is an opportunity for the child to acknowledge, claim, and celebrate his strengths by expressing his brave story with whatever modalities interest him. The story is about his bravery, determination, tenacity, spirit, and courage to have lived through the trauma and faced it head on in therapy. This story becomes the "final act" of processing the child's story through self-directed expression, revealing his grit and strength of character.

*Process:* The child is invited to embody this theme of courage through story and other art forms. All the potential expressive arts options that are available to express this story are reviewed. Sharing of this story often elicits feelings of competency, mastery, and inner power. As the child shares or enacts his story, we remember to work with what is rising in the child's body as he completes the story. Noticing his thoughts, feelings and sensations and expanding and staying with the good are part of the process.

Once the story is ready to be shared, we decide who the child would like to have his story witnessed by. Typically it is the therapist and caregiver as witnesses. After the story is shared, the therapist and caregiver create an art response about how they are moved by the child's expressive arts bravery story.

Children have expressed their bravery stories in so many ways. One teen wrote a song, brought her guitar, and played it during the session. Another chose a specific song to dance her story to. Joey acted out his story using his mom and myself as part of the "cast," using various hats to depict the different "characters" in his story. He then wrote a song called "Good-bye Stranger. I Don't Need You in My House Anymore." Gina wrote her expressive arts bravery story in the form of a booklet. She said the story identified all the parts of her journey, including living with an alcoholic father, him leaving the family, the sexual abuse, and the help and healing.

## READINESS TO MOVE TO PHASE FOUR

Now that the trauma processing of Phase Three has been completed, the following guidelines can be considered to ensure the child is ready to move beyond the trauma and into the final phase of trauma treatment.

1. There is regular and consistent use of regulation skills/resources as reported by the child and caregivers.
2. The child was able to process main trauma incidents and create a comprehensive narrative.
3. The child is able to recall the traumatic incidents without moving into overwhelm or disconnect.
4. The child reports low levels on the upset scale for the trauma incidents.
5. The child is able to see that both positive and negative life events are part of her story.

## REFERENCES

Johnson, T. C. (1999). *Understanding child's sexual behavior: What's natural and healthy.* Oakland, CA: New Harbinger Publications.

Rothschild, B. (2000). *The body remembers: The psychophysiology of trauma and trauma treatment.* New York: W. W. Norton.

Siegel, D. (2010). *Mindsight: The new science of personal transformation.* New York: Bantam Books.

Silovsky, J. (2009). *Taking action: Support for families of children with sexual behavior problems.* Brandon, VT: The Safer Society Press.

van der Kolk, B. A. (2003). The neurobiology of childhood trauma and abuse. *Child and Adolescent Psychiatric Clinics of North America, 12,* 193–317.

# 9 Phase Four Guidelines
## Reclaiming, Reframing, Repairing, and Reorienting

Seven-year-old Josh created many pictures of the experiences of the physical, emotional, and sexual abuse by both of his parents. In Phase Three, after processing the trauma, he took the pictures, carefully cut himself out of each one, ripped the rest of the image, worked the ripped pieces into clay, and then threw out the clay. Josh carefully took the small pictures of his scared and sad parts, glued them inside of an envelope, drew three happy faces, then wrote on the front, "Safe Place. I am not sad anymore. I am safe and loved" (Figure 9.1). He could open and close the envelope, giving an increased sense of safety. He then drew what he called his "power image." It was a picture of himself with "a superhero boundary" around his body. We continued to work with these images throughout Phase Four, clarifying questions about why hard things happened to him, beliefs that there was something wrong with his body, and residual feelings of fear. This was a critical step in the process of reclaiming safety and power. He affirmed what he knew now, writing on his power image, "I know more now than before. I have a nice family. I get fed well. I watch appropriate shows. I have love and care." These were strong acts of mastery that encompassed many aspects of the themes of Phase Four of reclaiming, reframing, repairing, and reorienting.

At the heart of all interventions in this expressive arts, four-phase trauma treatment model are the goals of mastery, empowerment, and safety. By Phase Four, children will have repeated experiences of being able to manage and regulate their bodies' physiological and emotional survival responses. This, along with regular, somatic experiences of safety over time, mean the child will be focused less on survival and will be more present for the tasks at hand. There should be fewer mid-brain dominant trauma triggers and increased access to neocortical functioning. Children are now better positioned to engage in the more cognitive aspects of Phase Four interventions.

Consolidating gains is at the core of Phase Four interventions, providing opportunities for children to strengthen and integrate the learning thus far. More specifically, there are four goals that support the consolidating of gains. First is the goal of reclamation. To reclaim is to take back, save, and rediscover what was lost. While much can be lost in the experience of trauma, much can be reclaimed in the process of healing. Children in treatment are engaged in the reclaiming of their right to be free, happy, and alive in their child bodies. The interventions throughout all four phases are an invitation for children to reclaim their power and resources, moving from a state of helplessness to one of empowerment. In Phase Four, there are many review-based activities that call for mindful reflections on the progress achieved to date, assisting with sorting through the gains and identifying work yet to be completed.

Second is the goal of reframing. Children are now ready to challenge and reframe trauma influenced thoughts, feelings, and beliefs that have developed over time that are no longer of service. Having completed the work of trauma processing through sensory, experiential interventions, children will have better access to executive functioning skills to manage the more cognitive aspects of reframing. We review the handout Thoughts, Feelings, and Beliefs Checklist, then we work with the art to explore, challenge, and reframe. This process involves not only reframing trauma-influenced thoughts, feelings, and beliefs, but also includes the

*Figure 9.1* Josh's image of his scared and sad parts tucked away in a safe place. Used with permission.

reframing of the larger picture, which is placing the trauma in the past and learning to be fully immersed in the present.

Third is the goal of repairing. Repairing is a critical function of strong and healthy attachments. Together with the child and caregiver, a review is completed by identifying what relationships in the child's world remain in need of repair. While much repair will have been completed by this point, relational repair goals are set and followed through on as needed. The level of relational repair work will vary for each child and family.

The fourth goal is reorienting to the future. Much of the work has been focused on the past experience of trauma, though it is grounded in present moment experience. In Phase Four, there is an emphasis on reorienting, which means looking ahead, and building on a future-oriented perspective as the client moves beyond the trauma work. Children are involved in a process of reorienting through a variety of arts-based interventions that appeal to the children's curiosity of what lies ahead. The future orientation restores a child's belief that he is more than the trauma and his life can be reclaimed.

These four goals of reclamation, reframing, repairing, and reorienting are carefully woven through each intervention in Phase Four. The hope is that children leave the therapeutic process with a renewed sense of mastery, empowerment, and safety both within their bodies, their relationships, and in the world around them.

## PHASE FOUR EXPRESSIVE ARTS INTERVENTIONS

### Therapy Review: What's Left to Do

*Rationale*: The first step in Phase Four is to complete an overall review with the child. This review will guide the final phase of therapy by identifying the client's progress and the areas left to address.

*Process.* With the child and caregiver, review some of the handouts that were given in Phase One. In particular, review Feelings About the Trauma; Trauma Self-Statements; and the Thoughts, Feelings, and Beliefs Checklist. Clients can rate themselves again on some of the statements and feelings now that they have addressed the trauma in more detail. The child, caregiver, and therapist jointly form the final therapeutic goals.

Deciding on the priorities in Phase Four will, in part, depend on the number of sessions available. Identify problematic thoughts, feelings, and beliefs and family relationships or other areas of therapy that still need to be addressed. At this point in the therapeutic process, some of the trauma-influenced beliefs and thoughts may have shifted and changed. Some remain to be addressed, discussed, and worked through both individually and with caregivers.

We can find creative, arts-based ways to deal with the thoughts, feelings, and beliefs. The approach taken will depend on the child and what we have come to know about what works best for her to process experiences. The following is an example of one way of working with the remaining thoughts, feelings, and beliefs that the client experienced as troubling.

### Example 1

Gina and I reviewed the progress she had made and what areas of work remained. She highlighted a number of thoughts and feelings that still were troublesome to her, including the following:

- I could have stopped the abuse.
- My body felt good but in my mind I know it was wrong.
- I feel embarrassed by what he did.
- I feel insecure in what I say and do.

When Gina first started therapy, she shared how she felt insecure in what she says and does. We revisited this belief at the beginning of this phase by drawing her experience of this belief before therapy and now (Figure 9.2). She realized as she drew this image just how far she had come from feeling insecure, self-conscious, scared, and shaky to feeling flamboyant, open,

*Figure 9.2* Gina's drawing of a negative belief before therapy and now. Used with permission.

happy, brave, and bubbly. She noticed the sensations fill her body as she spoke about how she feels now. We continued to work with each belief in this way.

*Example 2*

Joey loved to act out scenarios and experiences with puppets, hats, and other available props. When we reviewed some of the trauma-influenced thoughts, beliefs, and feelings that we added to the handout throughout our time together, Joey shared that he felt different about them now. He decided he would take each one and act out how he felt before and how he felt now. Joey spent time thinking about how he felt different now and asked me to write down his ideas as identified below. He called this process using his "talk back voice," varying the timbre as he spoke. He would use a different hat for both then and now. Joey invited his mother into the session to have her witness him acting out the many different thoughts and feelings. Some of the thoughts and feelings included:

### Then

I could have stopped uncle.

### Now

I was too scared and too little.

### Then

He would make deals with me. Are deals okay?

### Now

No, deals are not okay, he tricked me!

### Then

I am worried that uncle is mad at me.

### Now

I am mad at uncle! He had no right to hurt me!

## My Healing Journey

*Rationale*: This is a good time to review where the child sees himself in the healing process. My Healing Journey helps the child see that there is a beginning, a middle, and an end to the formal therapeutic work and that it is a process. The child's art can capture the review about the progress he has made and what is yet to be done from his point of view.

*Process*: The child is encouraged to express this healing path or journey in whatever art form he would like. We can offer an array of art materials to symbolically illustrate this path, or the child can act it out using the space in the office as part of the journey. Having some percussion instruments available can bring the journey alive through sound.

*Example*

Gina created an image of her healing journey (Figure 9.3) with many obstacles that needed to be overcome. She also created the tool that was needed to conquer the obstacle and placed the tool next to the obstacle. She stated, "All I had to do was to find a way to use them" (e.g., the rocks needed a pick axe, the snakes a whip, the fire needed water). When she got to the part where there was a break in the ground, Gina said, "I need a pogo stick to get across the break in the ground. This is where I am. I am moving home with boundaries and I am going through

*Figure 9.3* Gina's drawing of her healing journey. Used with permission.

the door as I have the key!" She was excited about the progress she made and identified feeling more confident in herself and her ability to speak and stand up for herself.

### Self-Portraits 2

*Rationale*: Self-portraits are a great way to get a snapshot of how the child is viewing himself at this point in the therapy process. While there are many ways to do a self-portrait, this one is different from the self-portraits from the assessment phase. Here, the child is invited to complete a four-part process. This allows for a thoughtful, integrative process, often revealing areas of growth and areas needing further support.

*Process*: The child is invited to draw herself in three ways. First as an animal, second as a tree, and third as a landscape. The final step is to bring all three images together and create one image. When the final image is finished, the child is invited to do a written response to the image, such as giving something in the image a voice or a dialogue between the child and some aspect of the image. It could be a story or a poem. Once these various modalities have been used, the session may be closed by being curious about what the child has learned from this process. Often, in the writing, we can identify particular thoughts, feelings, or beliefs that may need to be addressed or simply acknowledged.

### Example

Riley, a 15-year-old girl who was physically and sexually abused by her mother's various boyfriends, drew herself first as a landscape (Figure 9.4), then as a tree (Figure 9.5), then as an animal (Figure 9.6). Riley then took all three self-portraits and created one (Figure 9.7). She created a written response to each image.

*Figure 9.4* Riley's image of herself as a landscape. Used with permission.

This landscape is open, like the horizon. There is beauty in the setting sun. So much space to move.

*Figure 9.5* Riley's image of herself as a tree. Used with permission.

I am an apple tree. These trees provide apples to everyone. They are protective.

*Figure 9.6* Riley's image of herself as an animal. Used with permission.

Cats are beautiful and they are wise.

*Figure 9.7* Riley combined all three self-portraits and made one. Used with permission.

The sunset shows that I am a calm person and love nature. The tree has had a very hard life, but it still has fruit. This means I am healing. The kitty is so very wise, she stays close to the healing tree that offers her protection. Sometimes, when feeling hurt, she hides up high in the branches. Her green eyes speak of wisdom and hope.

## Sexual Abuse–Specific Interventions

The following two interventions are sexual abuse specific and have been included to address two issues directly related to sexual abuse. One issue relates to living with the secret of sexual abuse, and the second issue is related to living with the abuser in the same home or when the abuser is a close relative or family friend.

### Secrets

*Rationale*: When children live with secrets, they can come to question themselves and their integrity, and the trust between themselves and others is compromised. This intervention is designed to explore this specific issue and acknowledge the stress that children live with regarding the secret of sexual abuse.

*Process*: Take the time to explore the client's full experience of what it meant for him to keep the secret and then tell the secret. The first image acknowledges the various aspects of the child's experience on all levels of thoughts, feelings, and sensations while keeping the secret. The second image captures the child's experience of telling for the first time. The third image helps the child see what, if anything, is different in his body and mind now, after he told. Next, work with the images by asking the child to identify the differences between the three experiences with regard to thoughts, feelings, and sensations. Bring this awareness into the present moment by asking what he is noticing now as he speaks about each image.

### My Inside/Outside Stories

*Rationale*: When sexual abuse happens in families or with close family friends, it can be as though the child lives in two worlds. The inside world is where acknowledgment of the sexual abuse lives, including the sensing of when the abuse will happen; the watching and waiting; the orienting to the nuances of meaning in behavior of the abuser; and the wave of emotions, thoughts, and sensations. Then there is the outside world, where everything appears normal and fine. It is as though the sexual abuse does not exist in the outside world. This intervention is an opportunity for the client to address the body's lived experience of both these worlds. Exploring the stories through art can assist the client with understanding these two worlds.

*Process*: The primary therapeutic work is creating space to explore the two stories through some art form. The child can decide which story she would like to begin with. Under the Written Response, she can decide if she would like to write the answers or discuss directly. Remember to go slowly because awareness of the body is included in the processing of the stories and the questions. Psychoeducational information can be beneficial at this point. For example, it can be important information for children to learn about the body's natural response to being touched (e.g., our body is made to feel good when touched) and the offender's strategy to manipulate and trick children.

### Example

Jenna was sexually abused by her grandfather. She spent a great deal of time with her grandparents both in her home and at their home. Jenna knew exactly what her inside and outside stories were like: "I lived two lives for many years" (Figure 9.8). Jenna drew her outside world (right) and inside world (left). She wrote the following:

> When everything was happening on the outside I made everything seem fine like I was a normal little girl like nothing ever happened. I wore my hair in pigtails. I smiled. No one questioned me.

*Figure 9.8* Jenna's drawing of her outside and inside worlds. Used with permission.

On the inside I felt furious, depressed and disgusted in myself. So on the inside around my heart I felt like everything was gone. Like I was hanging by a couple threads, like everything was pitch black.

Another variation of the inside/outside worlds is the discrepancy between what the client will show on the outside and what she is living on the inside. As Gina shared more about her story of the sexual abuse by her cousin, it became apparent that what she showed on the outside to her cousin when it was happening was very different from what she felt on the inside. She drew the image in Figure 9.9 as a representation of what she experienced on the inside throughout the time the sexual abuse was happening. She then added her outside world, what she showed her cousin while the abuse was happening, in the small images inside the larger images. She used her image in the joint work she eventually did with her cousin so that he could understand the truth about her inner experience and how her outside world response was about survival.

**Before Therapy and Now**

*Rationale*: This invitation can illustrate the client's perspective of the changes he has made in the therapeutic process. Before and now art helps consolidate the changes that have been made and supports the child with claiming the changes. It is empowering for the child to "see" the changes and to acknowledge, through his own art making, what is different in his world. The therapist is invited to concurrently create a before and now art response. By offering her own view, through the art, the therapist creates an opportunity for attunement and the "I see you" mirroring that is important in the therapeutic relationship. Caregivers, when appropriate, can also be invited to create the before and now image of their child.

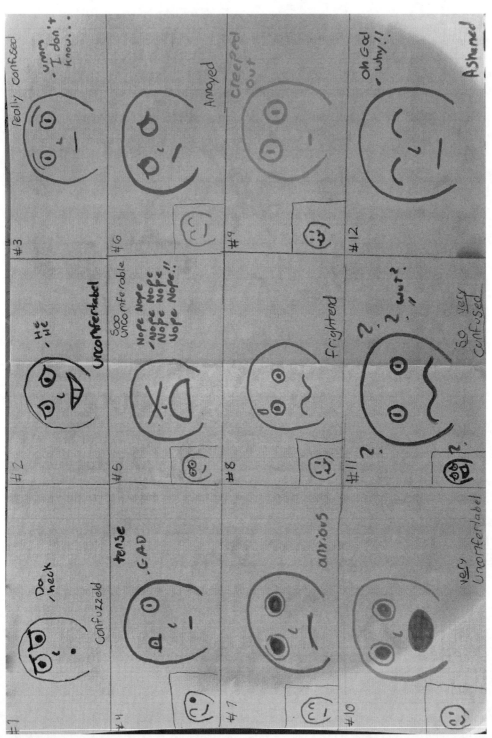

*Figure 9.9* Gina's drawing of her inside and outside worlds. Used with permission.

*Process:* If possible, the client is given little prompting, and he is invited to create two pieces of art from the invitation: "Draw an image that represents how your life was before therapy and then a second image that represents how your life is now." We may begin this invitation by remembering how his life was before coming to therapy. The therapist encourages the child to think about certain areas that were troublesome before and where he has seen change and growth. There are many art forms that could be used for this intervention. The child is encouraged to choose the most meaningful one.

The therapist and caregiver, when fitting, are invited to create a before/now art response regarding the growth and changes they have witnessed in the child. The therapist and caregiver do art alongside the child, both sharing their art when ready. This can be a very heartfelt experience for child, caregiver, and therapist.

As seen in the following examples, there are typically good sensations that arise in their bodies as children review their experiences before therapy and now. We can work with what has arrived in the art and anchor in their bodies the new, fresh, positive experiences through mindful awareness of the sensations, thoughts, and feelings they are now experiencing.

*Example 1*

Eleven-year-old Renee painted her body's experience before and after therapy (Figure 9.10). Renee shared that before therapy she was scared, had no one to talk to, and felt hurt, hopeless, and shaky in her body. Now, after 8 months of therapy, she said she is smiling, she has someone to talk to, there is a weight off her shoulders, her body is no longer shaky, and she has hope in her

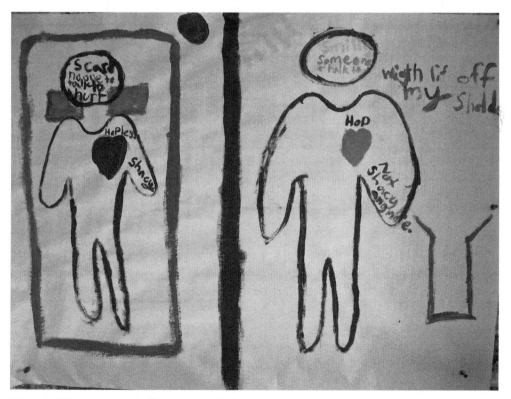

*Figure 9.10* Renee's painting of her experience before therapy and now. Used with permission.

heart. She reported feeling a shift in her body as we were looking at her image. She said, "I no longer feel shaky or have butterflies or feel anxious when I think about what happened to me."

### Example 2

Seven-year-old Joey created a before therapy image (Figure 9.11) and an after therapy image (Figure 9.12). He identified that before therapy, "Bad stuff was spreading everywhere in my body. My heart shrunk because it was hurt. My thoughts were full of the bad stuff that happened." About his after therapy image, Joey stated, "I'm so happy. These different colors are everywhere, shining like a rainbow. I am filled with joy."

The following is an example of my art response to Joey before and after therapy. There are times when, as therapists, we develop strong connections with the little ones we work with.

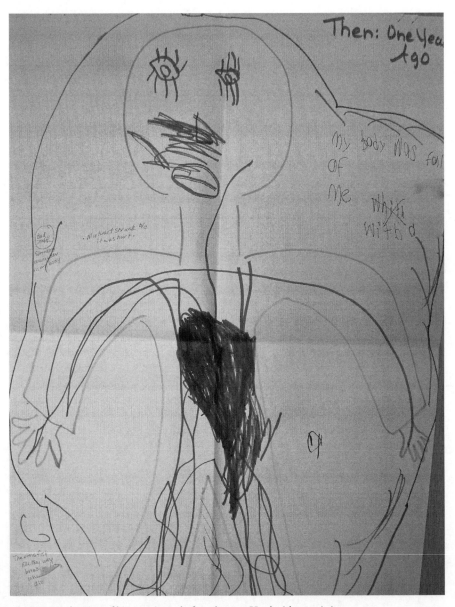

*Figure 9.11* Joey's drawing of his experience before therapy. Used with permission.

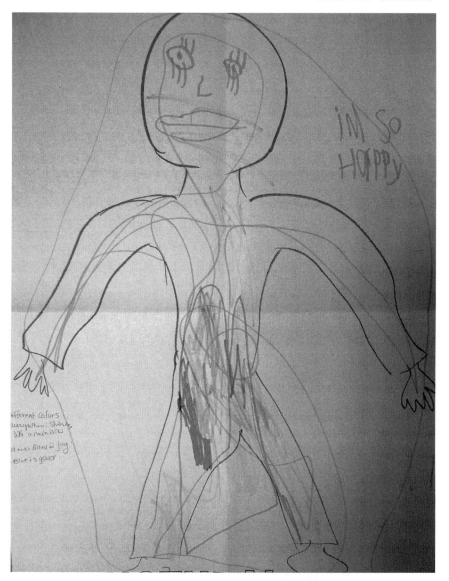

*Figure 9.12* Joey's drawing of his experience now. Used with permission.

This was so with Joey. I often marveled at his beyond-his-years wisdom. He possessed a sense of awe at the world around him, and he had the ability to make heartfelt connections with the people in his life. I witnessed Joey grow over a full year of working together. I was moved by his ability to learn to trust and to do the very difficult trauma work while maintaining a hopeful and joyful presence. I looked forward to offering an art response. I recalled how Joey often talked about feeling the "bad stuff" in his heart and how his heart hurt. I decided to respond by creating two hearts. The first image was of a very sad heart, which represented him before therapy and showed how I thought his heart might have felt from all the hard stuff happening. The second image was of a happy heart that represented all the joy and happiness that I saw in him now. I asked Joey if he would like to do something with the hearts. He wondered if we could rip up the sad heart. We did. Joey led the experience in a playful way, ripping it into tiny pieces, laughing as he threw the pieces in the air like confetti. After collecting the ripped pieces and throwing them in the garbage, Joey took the other heart and gently hugged it close to his chest, saying, "This is a special heart," and he asked if he could keep it.

**Evidence of Growth**

*Rationale*: At this point in the process, there have been many opportunities to acknowledge the child's growth and changes. This intervention focuses specifically on the growth that has come from adverse events in the child's life, reinforcing resilience and a resource-oriented perspective. Now we "mine" the rich learning that has come from the hard stuff the child has experienced. Some children are readily able to identify the wisdom that they have come to know, whereas others will require more support to glean from what they have learned.

*Process*: There are many ideas to explore on this handout. Read through the handout ahead of time and explore with your client the ideas that interest her. Throughout therapy, we pay attention to the changes and growth noticed in our client, such as the small acts of achievement, joy, delight, pride, or satisfaction. We can offer our thoughts as our client explores what she sees as evidence of growth. Remember to ground the learning in the body and delight in the positive sensations and feelings that the child identifies.

*Example 1*

Seven-year-old Shari was being raised by her aunt because her mother was not able to parent her due to mental health issues. Shari and I talked about how much she had grown through our work together. As we read through the handout, the words that had meaning for Shari were *brave* and *strong*. She asked if she could create a doll. Once finished, she put two glass hearts inside a pouch and attached it to her doll (Figure 9.13). This doll was the keeper of the

*Figure 9.13* Shari created a doll that represents how strong and brave she is. Used with permission.

two hearts, one heart for herself and the other heart for her mother. Shari said that this doll shows how strong and brave she is to remember the love her mom has for her.

*Example 2*

As Gina started feeling stronger and more confident in herself, she was able to identify how she had grown from the hard things that happened to her. After reading the handout, Gina played one of her favorite songs that captured the changes and growth she was experiencing. She chose a line from the lyrics and created her own poem with this line. She wrote her new poem inside her box that previously held the puzzle pieces during the trauma processing (Figure 9.14). She now calls this her "hope box." This was her way of both naming and claiming her growth and transforming the box.

> All these feelings stuck inside
> Cage them in and don't let them fly
> That's the rule I wanted to abide
> letting all the good die.

*Figure 9.14* Gina recreated her box after the trauma processing. Used with permission.

This will happen no more
my feet are planted firmly on the floor
These inner feelings will be caged no more
now you're gonna hear me roar.

## Victim–Survivor–Thriver

*Rationale*: In Phase Four we are consolidating changes. In particular, clients are reclaiming a sense of powerfulness through every creative action they engage with, which in turn supports the task of reframing trauma-influenced beliefs. Introducing the concepts and experiences of victim, survivor, and thriver can identify the ways in which the client is changing. For example, she may acknowledge being pushed around less by the effects of trauma and becoming more empowered in her life to act from her own volition. She may start to experience herself speaking out more, challenging her belief that she has no voice.

*Process*: Choose the interventions on this handout that are best suited for your client. Begin by having discussions about what it is like to be a victim of trauma and the kinds of thoughts and behavior that go with that identity. The meaning, thinking, and behaving that go with being a survivor of trauma are also explored. Being a thriver is often a new concept to children, so time is taken to find ways to explain the essence of being a thriver after trauma or to find a word that is meaningful to the child.

The following can be used as a guide when discussing the meaning of the various experiences of victim, survivor, and thriver:

> *Victim* is a noun that describes the impact that an event has had on a person, for example, how the person has been harmed or hurt by an outside event, such as an accident or a harmful action by another. It is of great importance that the nature of the harm is named and acknowledged. This naming is essential to being able to move forward from a victim identity.
> A *survivor* is one who has come through the event or action. Strengths and resources need to be claimed and acknowledged as residing within the child, reflecting the inherent power the child possesses to have coped with and moved on from the trauma.
> To *thrive* is to flourish, to become fully alive, and to move beyond an associated identity to a bad event that happened. Children who are thrivers know that there are ups and downs in life, but there is an overall sense of optimism for the future and joy in the present.

The next step can be inviting the child to create an image that goes with each word. This way we come to see, from her point of view, what these words mean to her and how she identifies where she is in the process. Often what is revealed in the art work is the progress that has been made and possible aspects of therapy that are yet to be addressed. Embodying the meaning of each word by walking in the space like a victim, then survivor, and then thriver can be fun and playful and can teach, in a somatic way, the differences in these identities.

The final invitation on the handout is to understand, from the child's perspective, where she would visually place the trauma in her world. For younger children, it could be more productive to use visual props for this exercise. The child can choose a toy or object to represent herself and another to represent the trauma. Use a hula hoop to symbolize the child's world, or draw a large circle on paper. Play with moving the objects and having the child get a felt sense of where the trauma currently lives in her life.

### Example

Gina created three images to represent victim (Figure 9.15), survivor (Figure 9.16), and thriver (Figure 9.17). Gina wrote a written response that follows each image.

*Figure 9.15* Gina's drawing that represents the experience of being a victim. Used with permission.

### Victim

The world seems like it has ended. Can these wounds be mended?
Dark thoughts, life tied up in knots.
Can this be fixed? Emotions all mixed!

*Figure 9.16* Gina's drawing that represents the experience of being a survivor. Used with permission.

### Survivor

Halfway there, people are starting to care.
Wounds almost gone, here comes the sun!
I'm starting to feel the love, the magic pouring down from above.

*Figure 9.17* Gina's drawing that represents the experience of being a thriver. Used with permission.

### Thriver

I'm soaring high, the bad is saying good-bye.
Smiles appear everyday and in every way.
I love the confident new me. This is who I want to be.

### Beyond the Trauma: Action Figure and Doll Making

*Rationale:* Creating a doll or action figure (such as a superhero) can be a powerful experience and resource, reorienting the client to a future without the trauma.

For females, the invitation is to create a doll that represents the part of the child that was never touched by the trauma. The idea alone can be challenging, yet refreshing and exciting. The possibility can help combat feelings of contamination that can go hand in hand with many kinds of traumas. The child is invited to imagine that perhaps, somewhere inside, there is a part of her that was not contaminated by the trauma. This intervention has the potential to bring alive lost places and parts of the child to the surface. It is an opportunity to connect with who she is outside of view from the trauma lens. Our attention is now shifting to future-oriented time, imagining life without the dark veil of trauma and all the possibilities that exist from this new place. Even younger clients can imagine and tap into the excitement and happiness that lie within them, outside the trauma experience, waiting to be acknowledged and brought to life through the arts.

If the trauma processing was not completed in Phase Three, it is not recommended to do this intervention, as it may be even more difficult to imagine this possibility when so much of the trauma is still alive and easily activated in the body.

Boys or girls are invited to create superheroes with stories about their special powers and how they have triumphed over adversity. Creating a superhero can invite the child to think about his own inner power and abilities. Further, it can build and claim resiliency, that is, the ability to stand up and take action. Like the superhero, he can identify problems and find solutions.

The different themes for males/females are only guides. In consultation with your client, you will know what theme makes the most sense and how best to modify the intervention.

*Process:* Cloth bendable dolls (see Further Resources in Appendix J) are great forms to start with. They can be painted or embellished in whatever way suits the child. It is easiest to use a glue gun to embellish the figure with material, beads, yarn, and ribbon. Hair can be made with funky colored yarns. Some young people like to write words on the body of the doll before embellishing it.

Superheroes can be constructed from a variety of materials, including cloth bendable dolls, paper towel rolls, pipe cleaners, or Plasticine. Inviting the child to use his imagination to create the superhero can be very exciting and encourages a playful and involved process. For children who are interested in computer-generated art, and if a computer is available, there are many websites designed for children to create their own personal superheroes.

Once the doll or superhero is created, encourage the child to name the doll and write a story about it. Female adolescents are encouraged to consider writing the doll's "birthing story," that is, how the doll came to be in the world, exploring her purpose and hopes for the future. For the superheroes, the child can tell the story of how it came to be, what special powers it possesses, and the hero's main purpose. For younger children, "Write the story that goes with the figure" is a good enough prompt.

### Example 1

Bella created a doll that represented the part of her that was never touched by the abuse (Figure 9.18). She shared that she loved creating the doll and that it reminds her that she is more than just the abuse. Bella named the doll Annika and wrote the following birthing story:

> She comes from the earth, the trees, the leaves, the rivers, the wind. She is freedom. She lives her life to the fullest, living off the land. Traveling, day by day, she lives in the present, taking only wisdom and great memories from her past. She is forgiveness, she is gratefulness, she is the logic, but as well, free mind. She shares her gift with women, she does not judge. She came from the earth, to watch over and lead us to eternal happiness. She bears her soul for all to see. How they react is their choice, for she knows who she is, and is content with that. She expresses her feelings loudly and no matter what, loves herself above all.
>
> She dances in the wind, and dances in the rain, for all season, all weather is for her to experience. She is a child of the earth and that is where she remains.

*Figure 9.18* Bella's doll that represents the part of her that has never been touched by the sexual abuse. Used with permission.

## Example 2

Nine-year-old David created his own superhero action figure (Figure 9.19). He named him "Three Puffy Eyes," and his story reads like this:

> Hi, my name is Three Puffy Eyes. My super power is sight. It allows me to spot people who are hurting other people badly and that is what I do. So make a difference by not being mean.

## Expressive Arts Review

*Rationale*: Taking the time to bring out all the art work the child has done over the course of therapy provides the opportunity to see the progress and growth in tangible and expressive forms. Further, it provides the client with the opportunity to make decisions about what she wants to do with the art she has created. Clients decide what they want to keep, leave behind, or throw away.

*Process*: The caregiver is typically invited to this art review, although the child can decide what is best for her. The client's art is displayed throughout the therapy room. Each art piece is observed, and all written responses are read, being mindfully present to all the creations. After

*Figure 9.19* David's action figure that he called Three Puffy Eyes. Used with permission.

the art is witnessed, the therapist, caregiver, and client complete art responses to their experience of witnessing the journey.

*Example*

After 8 months in therapy due to sexual abuse by her father, and about 13 large paintings and creative writings later, 14-year-old Eva and I displayed all her paintings around the room. In preparation for closing our therapeutic work together we were reviewing all her art work. She read the poems and stories that accompanied each piece of art. After reading and witnessing all her images, we both stood in silence, honoring the intense healing journey she had been engaged in over the 8 months. After the silence, I asked Eva if she had any impulse to do something with all her paintings, such as rip, cut, tear, or shred some or parts of her images. Eva did not need further prompting. She asked for scissors and pipe cleaners. She cut out and kept small parts from some of her paintings and created a hanging mobile (Figure 9.20). Once done, Eva wrote the following final poem:

### The Pieces

> The pieces, they hang there, swinging, and rocking. Dangling amongst the air.
> Cut from the pictures of the beautiful hope and the ugly truth.

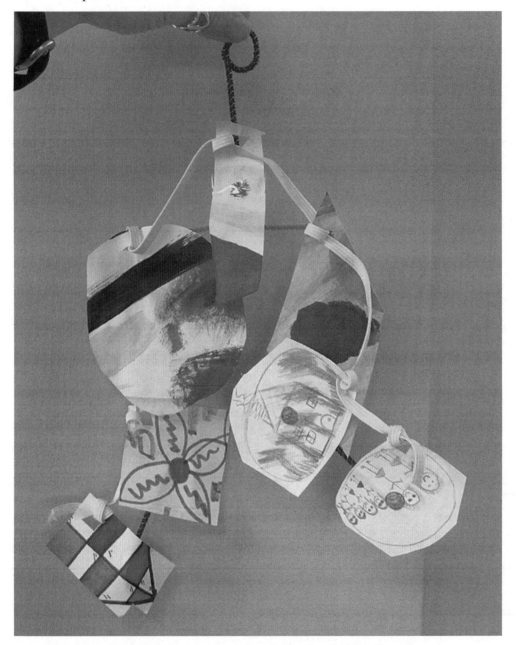

*Figure 9.20* Eva's mobile created as an art response to her therapy journey. Used with permission.

The pieces, the reminders, the memories of old things happened and new
things beginning.
Just pieces you say. To you they are paper pieces cut by scissors.
To me I see the meaning and memories.
The bitterness & hope brought to paper by marker, paint, and pencil.
I see the emotion that made this art, art. I can feel the presence of all of "it."
So listen, feel, hear, and let it wash over you till you too share the "it."
Till all of us UNDERSTAND the "it."

Eva then invited her mom into the session to hear her final poem and see her mobile, her
final art piece. Her mom and I both completed art responses to her final art creations. Her

mom responded by creating a pipe cleaner mobile with a person entwined in a large heart. Her mom shared, "The person represents you, my girl. You are strong and courageous. The heart is mine and I want you to know that my love will be with you always."

My art response to Eva was the poem below.

**I Believe in You**

> I see you. I see the "it."
> You helped us all see the "it."
> And you are so much more.
> I saw you paint, draw, express, and cry.
> I cried too, at times. We celebrated. We played, laughed and danced.
> Thank you.
> Thank you for bringing to the world a better understanding of what "it" is and how to heal.
> I see you. Your beauty and strength.
> I believe in you.

**Celebration or Ceremony**

*Rationale*: Working through trauma takes courage and trust. It also takes commitment and tenacity on part of the child, caregiver, and therapist to build relationships that can endure the stressful and trying journey of healing from trauma. Taking the time to co-create a celebration honors the client's process, hard work, and helps reorient to the future. The celebration can be simple, encompassing activities that are most relevant to the child.

*Process*: The intention of the celebration is to honor the child's healing journey. The child can decide if he would like to have his caregivers involved. In the session prior to the celebration, go over the handout with the child and discuss the points that you feel are most appropriate for this client. Both therapist and child may have things to prepare for the celebration. Taking time for preparations makes the meaning of the celebration more powerful because it gives the message that this celebration is important enough to put forethought and energy into. The closing can be as simple as making "celebration" play dough with fun colors and sparkles, or it can be a more ritual type of celebration.

*Example*

At 17 years of age, Danielle knew what was most meaningful to her. She put a great deal of thought into what her celebration would look like. She wrote a letter to herself from her wise self and read it as part of her celebration. She brought music and some of her art to display, along with a special candle and other meaningful objects. I brought a small pouch with stones. Together, we wrote words on the stones that would serve as reminders of her special qualities and strengths.

## READINESS TO CLOSE THERAPY

Preparing the child for closure is an important part of the therapeutic work. Although there can be factors beyond our control that determine the timing of closure, the follow guidelines can be considered when intentionally preparing to close therapy.

1. The child feels ready to close.
2. The child feels some confidence to continue using what she has learned in therapy.
3. The child is managing behaviors, impulses, and triggers at home and at school.
4. Both child and caregiver report a readiness to move on.

# Appendix A
## An Expressive Arts Four-Phase Model

### CHECKLIST OF THE MAIN MAP

**Therapist Handouts for Organizing Assessment and Treatment Information (see Appendix B)**

\_\_\_\_\_ Highlighting Core Issues
\_\_\_\_\_ Feedback Form
\_\_\_\_\_ Tracking Assessment and Treatment
\_\_\_\_\_ Managing Activation—Adolescents
\_\_\_\_\_ Managing Activation—Children
\_\_\_\_\_ Acts of Victory and Mastery
\_\_\_\_\_ Thoughts, Feelings, and Beliefs Checklist

**Information Handouts for Clients (see Appendix C)**

\_\_\_\_\_ Caregiver Involvement in the Four Phases
\_\_\_\_\_ The Inner World of My Body

**Phase One: Understanding the Child's World**

Arts-Based Information-Gathering Tools (see Appendix D)

\_\_\_\_\_ Map of My World
\_\_\_\_\_ How Trauma Changed My World
\_\_\_\_\_ My Relationships
\_\_\_\_\_ Amazing Body 1
\_\_\_\_\_ Amazing Body 2
\_\_\_\_\_ My Body and the Trauma 1
\_\_\_\_\_ My Body and the Trauma 2
\_\_\_\_\_ Self-Portraits 1

Questionnaires (see Appendix E)

\_\_\_\_\_ Exploring Art Modalities and Creativity Beliefs
\_\_\_\_\_ Child and Caregiver Trauma History
\_\_\_\_\_ Impact of Trauma on Caregiver
\_\_\_\_\_ Why It Was Hard for Me to Tell
\_\_\_\_\_ Why It Was Hard for My Child to Tell
\_\_\_\_\_ Responsibility Rating Scale (Child)
\_\_\_\_\_ Responsibility Rating Scale (Caregiver)
\_\_\_\_\_ Responsibility for the Trauma
\_\_\_\_\_ Safety Questionnaire

_____ Feelings About the Trauma
_____ Disclosure Questionnaire
_____ Disclosure Picture: When I First Told About the Trauma
_____ Trauma Self-Statements
_____ Reminders of the Trauma
_____ Pieces of My Story, Part 1: Remembering

**Phase Two: Cultivating Safety and Resources (see Appendix F)**

_____ Pouches, Pockets, Bags, and Boxes
_____ Setting My Own Pace: Stop, Slow, Go
_____ Learning About Safety
_____ Cultivating Hope
_____ Building Resources 1
_____ Building Resources 2
_____ Exploring and Healing Boundaries
_____ Labyrinths, Mazes, and Mandalas
_____ Learning to Be My Own Best Friend
_____ Building Awareness and Resources Through Imagery and Stories
_____ Getting a Handle on Tricky Trauma Behaviors

**Phase Three: Processing the Trauma (see Appendix G)**

_____ The Wall
_____ Surfing the Waves
_____ My Iceberg
_____ Tracking Trauma Processing
_____ Pieces of My Story, Part 2: Putting It All Together
_____ Resource/Trauma Art
_____ Time Lines and Road Maps
_____ Honor and Transformation
_____ My Body, Part 1: What My Body Did at the Time of the Trauma
_____ My Body, Part 2: What I Wished My Body Did
_____ My Body, Part 3: My Body's Voice
_____ My Body, Part 4: Caregiver and Child Session
_____ My Expressive Arts Bravery Story

**Phase Four: Reclaiming, Reframing, Repairing, and Reorienting (see Appendix H)**

_____ Therapy Review: What's Left to Do
_____ My Healing Journey
_____ Self-Portraits 2
_____ Secrets
_____ My Inside/Outside Stories
_____ Before Therapy and Now
_____ Evidence of Growth
_____ Victim–Survivor–Thriver
_____ Beyond the Trauma: Action Figure and Doll Making
_____ Expressive Arts Review
_____ Celebration or Ceremony

# Appendix B
## Therapist Handouts for Organizing Assessment and Treatment Information

**HIGHLIGHTING CORE ISSUES**

TSCC (or TSCYC)
  At-risk scales
  Clinically significant scales

BASC
  At-risk scales
  Clinically significant scales

Other tests


Behaviors to address (in order of urgency)


Relationships (areas of strengths and areas in need of repair)
  Family
  Other caregivers
  Child

Impact of trauma


Strengths/resources
  Inside
  Outside

Other points to consider from the questionnaire forms

## FEEDBACK FORM

### Feedback to Caregivers

Summary of findings/treatment issues:

Treatment recommendations:

Who will be involved to ensure successful treatment:

Strengths/resources (in child, family):

### Feedback to Child

Strengths:

   As you see them:

   As caregivers see them:

   As I see them:

Areas that need support:

   As you see them:

   As caregivers see them:

   As I see them:

Treatment recommendations:

Who will be involved:

# TRACKING ASSESSMENT AND TREATMENT

Date: _____ Session theme: _____
Interventions: _____
Next: _____

Date: _____ Session theme: _____
Interventions: _____
Next: _____

Date: _____ Session theme: _____
Interventions: _____
Next: _____

Date: _____ Session theme: _____
Interventions: _____
Next: _____

Date: _____ Session theme: _____
Interventions: _____
Next: _____

Date: _____ Session theme: _____
Interventions: _____
Next: _____

Date: _____ Session theme: _____
Interventions: _____
Next: _____

Date: _____ Session theme: _____
Interventions: _____
Next: _____

Date: _____ Session theme: _____
Interventions: _____
Next: _____

Date: _____ Session theme: _____
Interventions: _____
Next: _____

## MANAGING ACTIVATION—ADOLESCENTS

Put a square around the number that shows how difficult it was to talk about the trauma today.
Put a circle around the number that shows for how you felt at the end of the session.

Session date:_____ Session theme: _____

| No Anxiety | | Somewhat Anxious | | | So-So | Very Anxious | | Extremely Anxious!!! | | |
|---|---|---|---|---|---|---|---|---|---|---|
| 0 | 1 | 2 | 3 | 4 | 5 | 6 | 7 | 8 | 9 | 10 |

Session date: _____ Session theme: _____

| No Anxiety | | Somewhat Anxious | | | So-So | Very Anxious | | Extremely Anxious!!! | | |
|---|---|---|---|---|---|---|---|---|---|---|
| 0 | 1 | 2 | 3 | 4 | 5 | 6 | 7 | 8 | 9 | 10 |

Session date: _____ Session theme: _____

| No Anxiety | | Somewhat Anxious | | | So-So | Very Anxious | | Extremely Anxious!!! | | |
|---|---|---|---|---|---|---|---|---|---|---|
| 0 | 1 | 2 | 3 | 4 | 5 | 6 | 7 | 8 | 9 | 10 |

Session date: _____ Session theme: _____

| No Anxiety | | Somewhat Anxious | | | So-So | Very Anxious | | Extremely Anxious!!! | | |
|---|---|---|---|---|---|---|---|---|---|---|
| 0 | 1 | 2 | 3 | 4 | 5 | 6 | 7 | 8 | 9 | 10 |

Session date: _____ Session theme: _____

| No Anxiety | | Somewhat Anxious | | | So-So | Very Anxious | | Extremely Anxious!!! | | |
|---|---|---|---|---|---|---|---|---|---|---|
| 0 | 1 | 2 | 3 | 4 | 5 | 6 | 7 | 8 | 9 | 10 |

Session date: _____ Session theme: _____

| No Anxiety | | Somewhat Anxious | | | So-So | Very Anxious | | Extremely Anxious!!! | | |
|---|---|---|---|---|---|---|---|---|---|---|
| 0 | 1 | 2 | 3 | 4 | 5 | 6 | 7 | 8 | 9 | 10 |

Session date: _____ Session theme: _____

| No Anxiety | | Somewhat Anxious | | | So-So | Very Anxious | | Extremely Anxious!!! | | |
|---|---|---|---|---|---|---|---|---|---|---|
| 0 | 1 | 2 | 3 | 4 | 5 | 6 | 7 | 8 | 9 | 10 |

Session date: _____ Session theme: _____

| No Anxiety | | Somewhat Anxious | | | So-So | Very Anxious | | Extremely Anxious!!! | | |
|---|---|---|---|---|---|---|---|---|---|---|
| 0 | 1 | 2 | 3 | 4 | 5 | 6 | 7 | 8 | 9 | 10 |

Session date: _____ Session theme: _____

| No Anxiety | | Somewhat Anxious | | | So-So | Very Anxious | | Extremely Anxious!!! | | |
|---|---|---|---|---|---|---|---|---|---|---|
| 0 | 1 | 2 | 3 | 4 | 5 | 6 | 7 | 8 | 9 | 10 |

Session date:_____ Session theme: _____

| No Anxiety | | Somewhat Anxious | | | So-So | Very Anxious | | Extremely Anxious!!! | | |
|---|---|---|---|---|---|---|---|---|---|---|
| 0 | 1 | 2 | 3 | 4 | 5 | 6 | 7 | 8 | 9 | 10 |

Session date: _____ Session theme: _____

| No Anxiety | | Somewhat Anxious | | | So-So | Very Anxious | | Extremely Anxious!!! | | |
|---|---|---|---|---|---|---|---|---|---|---|
| 0 | 1 | 2 | 3 | 4 | 5 | 6 | 7 | 8 | 9 | 10 |

## MANAGING ACTIVATION—CHILDREN

Circle the number that shows how hard it was in our session when working on the trauma. Underline the number that shows how you felt at the end of our time.

Session date: _____ Session theme: _____

| Easy | | Okay | | | So-So | | Hard | | | Very hard!! |
|---|---|---|---|---|---|---|---|---|---|---|
| 0 | 1 | 2 | 3 | 4 | 5 | 6 | 7 | 8 | 9 | 10 |

Session date: _____ Session theme: _____

| Easy | | Okay | | | So-So | | Hard | | | Very hard!! |
|---|---|---|---|---|---|---|---|---|---|---|
| 0 | 1 | 2 | 3 | 4 | 5 | 6 | 7 | 8 | 9 | 10 |

Session date: _____ Session theme: _____

| Easy | | Okay | | | So-So | | Hard | | | Very hard!! |
|---|---|---|---|---|---|---|---|---|---|---|
| 0 | 1 | 2 | 3 | 4 | 5 | 6 | 7 | 8 | 9 | 10 |

Session date: _____ Session theme: _____

| Easy | | Okay | | | So-So | | Hard | | | Very hard!! |
|---|---|---|---|---|---|---|---|---|---|---|
| 0 | 1 | 2 | 3 | 4 | 5 | 6 | 7 | 8 | 9 | 10 |

Session date: _____ Session theme: _____

| Easy | | Okay | | | So-So | | Hard | | | Very hard!! |
|---|---|---|---|---|---|---|---|---|---|---|
| 0 | 1 | 2 | 3 | 4 | 5 | 6 | 7 | 8 | 9 | 10 |

Session date: _____ Session theme: _____

| Easy | | Okay | | | So-So | | Hard | | | Very hard!! |
|---|---|---|---|---|---|---|---|---|---|---|
| 0 | 1 | 2 | 3 | 4 | 5 | 6 | 7 | 8 | 9 | 10 |

## ACTS OF VICTORY AND MASTERY

Date:

    Act of victory/mastery:

    Sensations:

    Thoughts:

    Feelings:

Date:

    Act of victory/mastery:

    Sensations:

    Thoughts:

    Feelings:

Date:

    Act of victory/mastery:

    Sensations:

    Thoughts:

    Feelings:

Date:

    Act of victory/mastery:

    Sensations:

    Thoughts:

    Feelings:

# THOUGHTS, FEELINGS, AND BELIEFS CHECKLIST

Date:

Thought, feeling, belief:

Date addressed:

Outcome:

Date:

Thought, feeling, belief:

Date addressed:

Outcome:

Date:

Thought, feeling, belief:

Date addressed:

Outcome:

Date:

Thought, feeling, belief:

Date addressed:

Outcome:

Date:

Thought, feeling, belief:

Date addressed:

Outcome:

Date:

Thought, feeling, belief:

Date addressed:

Outcome:

# Appendix C
## Information Handouts for Clients

### CAREGIVER INVOLVEMENT IN THE FOUR PHASES

Your participation in your child's therapy is essential. Depending on your child's needs, you will be invited to participate in various ways. The following highlights some of these ways:

1. The assessment process

You and your child will be invited to complete some questionnaires and to create simple art interventions as part of the assessment.

2. Helping with homework

Your child will have homework that you will be invited to support her with. She will be learning new skills in therapy, and you will be invited in for part of the session so that she may teach you what she is learning. You are asked to help her practice the new skills at home.

3. Addressing your own trauma

You are here because your child has experienced trauma. You, your child, and I are part of her healing team. Some caregivers want to fix the problem. If this is true for you, just notice your impulse to want to fix the issue or make it go away and allow that impulse to be. Do not act on it. Rather, stay present to whatever is coming up in you that may also need support. If you have had your own trauma, it may be triggered in this process. That is completely normal, especially if you have untreated trauma. It is important to ask for help and get therapeutic assistance for your own issues. The more grounded you are, the more of a resource you can be to your child by offering a calm and regulated presence.

4. Witnessing your child's art

Your child will engage in various forms of art making, including visual art, creative writing, music, drama, or movement. You will be invited, at various times in the process, to witness your child's art. Witnessing is a particular way of offering presence to your child by:

- Listening to her stories without interruption
- Being aware of "Why did you . . . ?" kinds of questions, because they tend to be more judging and have potential to shut down your child
- Being curious without intrusiveness
  - Tell me more about this.
  - I am so moved by your story, it really inspires me.

5. Witnessing your child's suffering

You have been or will be witness to some of the very hard things that your child has experienced. It is important that you address your worries or concerns with me prior to joint sessions with your child, so that you can be ready to witness her experience of the trauma.

It is not easy to witness the suffering your child has experienced, in particular if you are seeing some of the images your child has created. The following are some ways of being with your child in this process:

### Acknowledge Emotions, Thoughts, and Sensations

I see how hard this was and is for you.
You were so very scared.
I notice how your shoulders really tighten when you tell me about. . . .

### Compassionate Support in the Now

I am with you right now.
I wonder what might happen if you and I both take a deep breath.

### Open-Ended Questions

Tell me more.
Tell me what is happening right now as you pay attention to. . . .
How can I help you now with . . . ?

6. Response art

You may be invited at different points in the process to create response art. This does not mean you need to be an artist. It means you will explore and respond in the language your child is using, which is the language of the arts. Responding through art slows down our own thinking and allows for a more mindful response to what we are witnessing. Creating simple art is enough and can be powerful. This process can help your child feel truly seen and heard.

## THE INNER WORLD OF MY BODY

In our work together, you will learn certain words to explain what happened to you and what happens in your body when we talk about the hard stuff. The following are some of those words and ideas that will be helpful to know.

### My Inside World

Your inside world is made up of thoughts, emotions, sensations, and our five senses.

> *Thoughts* are what we are saying to ourselves in our heads or out loud.
> "When can I go and play outside?"

> *Emotions* are the feelings we have inside related to what happens to us. They help to tell the mood we are in.
> "I feel so happy now that we have a puppy."

> *Sensations* help us describe the physical things that we feel in our bodies.
> "I feel a lump in my throat and butterflies in my tummy when I have to speak in class."

What are some emotions and sensations that you are already aware of?

Between now and the next time we meet, for homework, you and your caregiver will come up with a list of feelings and sensations and bring the list to the next session.

Here are some feeling words:

happy, sad, excited, disappointed, frustrated, hopeful, worried, angry, playful, grateful, peaceful

Here are some words for body sensations:

shiver, goose bumps, cold, warm, nauseous, heavy, light, floating, tightening, drained, knots, expanding, numb, prickly, shaky, pounding, throbbing, bubbly, butterflies, hungry, flowing, calm

### Tracking My Inside World

There many different things you can track. If you were a hunter, you might track the paw prints of an animal to find its location. In our work together, tracking means you pay attention to and become curious about the things you notice in your body and mind. Some of the things you track are:

- Thoughts (what your mind tells you, "I wonder if. . . .")
- Feelings (a state of being, such as mad, sad, glad)
- Sensations (how the body feels, such as heavy, cold, tingly, tight, hungry, prickly)

For example, when I think about my cat, I feel happy, warm, and tingly in my heart area.
You are encouraged to learn how thoughts, feelings, and sensations are each experienced differently in your body. Here are some tips:

- Go slowly.
- Bring awareness to your breathing.

- Exaggerate any sensations that are noticed. (Have fun with this!)
- Connect words to sensations.

You and your caregiver are asked to take some quiet time together to pay attention to your bodies and minds. After you sit for a time to listen, make a list of the thoughts, feelings, and sensations as you track them in your body and mind. Share your lists with each other.

### Senses as Triggers and Resources

You have five senses, and you can explore sensations through your senses. Reminders, or triggers, of the hard stuff that happened can be experienced through our senses. For example, one young person became very scared when she would hear people raise their voices, because it reminded her of her mom being hurt by her dad. Other things that can be triggering are sounds, certain types of people, loss, times of day, or teasing. When you are triggered, you can have a hard time managing your feelings, speaking clearly, or understanding what others are saying.

It is also important to remember that good memories can also be triggered by your senses, such as remembering your best friend when you hear a song you both liked, or thinking about being at your grandma's house when you smell cookies baking. These positive triggers are resources, meaning they can help you feel better by remembering them.

Here are some ideas to do at home with your caregiver. You might choose one or two to practice. Remember, notice the sensations in your body as you learn about the different senses, paying particular attention to what experiences sooth or calm you and which ones make you uncomfortable.

1. Sight: Together with your caregiver, go through magazines and cut out four pictures that you like and four that you don't like. Explore what sensations come up in your body as you talk about each of them. Looking around you, can you find things that excite you (e.g., tickets to a concert) or make you bored (e.g., homework)?
2. Taste: Have your caregiver arrange six very different things for you to taste without looking. You will guess what they are and see how many you get right! They might be sweet, salty, spicy, cold, warm, chewy, soft, or crispy. What sensations do you notice with the different tastes?
3. Touch: Have your caregiver arrange a box with six different things for you to touch without looking, so that you can guess what they are. There can be a range of textures such as soft, hard, cold, warm, prickly, delicate, heavy, light, rough, silky, and so on. Again, notice your body.
4. Smell: Have your caregiver arrange six different things for you to smell without looking. You guess again! There are all kinds of things to smell, such as essential oils, spices, flowers, and scented markers.
5. Hearing: What are some things that you hear that annoy you (e.g., fingernails on a chalk board, a revving motor cycle engine, a crying baby, screamo music)? What soothes you (e.g., soft music, a trickling brook, birds singing, cats purring)? What body sensations go with each?

Together with your therapist and/or caregiver, start to make a list of resources that you discovered are soothing. Use these resources when you need to feel more calm and peaceful. It might be a touch of a stuffed animal or soft music. It is from a calmer place that you can best understand yourself and others and make good choices. Once calm, you can then remember the trauma is no longer happening, you are safe in this moment, and you can sort out what triggers the more difficult behavior.

When you have been hurt and/or scared by another person, you can become very sensitive to other people's reactions, such as body language, tone of voice, or facial expressions. You may become very frightened by a certain tone of voice, even if you are not threatened in this moment. Together with your caregiver, begin to create a list of experiences that trigger you, noting what feelings, thoughts, or sensations you have. You can add these ideas to the handout Reminders of the Trauma.

## From Switched On to Calm Body

**Switched on:** Getting "switched on" is what happens in the body when you are triggered by the hard stuff. It is like a lot of feelings, thoughts, and sensations get turned on in your body all at once. These are the things that happened in your body at the time of the trauma when your body was preparing to protect you. Sometimes, you may react very quickly to something that reminds you of the trauma before you even know if you are threatened. Add to the lists below to indicate your own experience, or check off things that you have experienced when you think of the hard stuff.

Examples:

| Body | Thoughts | Emotions |
|------|----------|----------|
| heart beat increases | I can't think about this | fear |
| sweaty hands | I still care about that person | sad |
| feel tightness | I feel numb/nothing/bored | mad |
| butterflies | I hate talking about this | guilty |
| shaking | I just want to forget | confused |
| muscles tense | I wish this would all go away | worried |

**Switched Off:** Getting switched off is the opposite of getting switched on. It is like not having any feelings about what happened to you. *Numb* or *bored* are words that some young people say describe it best. Often times there are not many thoughts about it, or the thoughts that come are pushed away, or children simply say, "I don't know." Sometimes when you feel switched off, you may need help getting energized and connecting with the things and people around you.

**Calm Body:** Having a calm body usually means you are feeling good, comfortable, and content. Below are examples of what the body might experience and some of the thoughts and emotions that can go with it. Which ones have you experienced? Anything different?

Examples:

| Body | Thoughts | Emotions |
|------|----------|----------|
| slow breaths | I am okay | happy |
| relaxed | I am safe | relief |
| warm hands | I am in charge | confident |
| like a wet noodle | I like . . . | grateful |
| calm tummy | I am looking forward to . . . | love |
| shoulders down | I can . . . | hopeful |

**How to Get to Calm Body:** If your body starts to feel "switched on" and you need to be more grounded, it is my job to make sure that you return to calm body. You will use strategies to remind you that you are in the present day, not back in the trauma. You will use all your resources, including good sensory memories, to help your body slow down and remind you that you are safe from harm right now. Over time, your self-confidence will grow as you learn how to calm yourself using your resources.

## Presence and Disconnection

### Being Here or Not Being Here (for children 12 and under)

Of course you are here in this room with me! What I mean is something different. Being here means you are listening, sharing, and aware of your feelings and your body. Not being here can be like going off in a daydream. It might be thinking about what you will be doing after this appointment or what happened in school earlier today. Sometimes young people have a hard time staying with the work we are doing in therapy because it can be tough.

We will track your thoughts, feelings, and sensations. That means I will be checking in with you about all these things that you are noticing in your body. This will help us learn how your body and brain works and how you can learn to feel better and in charge while we are working on the hard stuff.

### *Ideas to Help Feel More Here*

If I notice you are not all here, I may invite you to do some of the following:

- Stand up and walk in the space
- Find five puppets (or whatever objects are available), and bring them to where you are sitting; then, give the objects names, and tell me what you like about each one
- Draw an outline of a person adding color, symbols, or words that show this disconnection
- Tell me a story about your favorite pet, animal, person

You may also have ideas about what can help you feel more here. We will practice these ideas and discover which ones work best for you.

### Presence/Disconnection (for adolescents)

During our sessions, it is important that we are both present to what we are doing. Being present or having presence means, "I am here and I am paying attention to what is happening right now in this room and in my body." However, some young people report feeling far away, distant, and have difficulty paying attention to what is happening in the moment. I call this feeling "disconnected." Sometimes I will notice when my client becomes less present or "disconnected" in the session. For example, he might look off in a different direction or have a faraway look in his eyes. I will check in with you if I notice this. Usually it means that what we are working on might be too overwhelming so we need to slow things down and pay attention to what you are noticing is happening in your thoughts, feelings, or your body. You will learn to track your inner experience throughout the various phases of treatment so that you are able to identify when you are present or disconnected and what triggers the disconnect.

### *Ideas to Help Get Present*

If I notice you are not very present, I may invite you to do some of the following:

- Stand up and walk in the space
- Name five things you like in this space

- Draw an outline of a person adding color, symbols, or words that show this disconnection
- Choose a song to listen to that makes you happy

You may also have ideas about what can help you become more present. We will practice these ideas and discover which ones work best for you.

**Our Brains Have Three Parts**

**Reptilian brain:** This is the oldest part of the brain and is the first part to develop. It helps our bodies stay well by controlling the temperature, breathing, hunger, and many more things! This part of the brain is very concerned about survival. It is the part of the brain that is in charge when we are super scared. In those moments we don't think, we act! For example, if you looked down and saw that there was a snake at your feet, you probably wouldn't think, "Hmm, should I move?" Most likely your body would just move. Very quickly, I might add!

   **Mammalian brain:** This is the part of the brain that is involved with our emotions and memory. If we are very upset about something, we are likely thinking less and feeling more. It is this part of the brain that is in charge when we are very anxious, sad, or angry.

   **Primate/thinking brain:** This part is our logical brain that helps us make decisions, think, and act.

   **Homework:** You and your caregiver can look up information on your brain to learn more about it and how it can help you understand what is happening inside when you get scared from the hard stuff that happened.

**What Our Bodies Do When Scary Things Happen: Fight, Flight, Freeze**

So now that you know the three parts of your brain, here is what happens when something very scary happens. Usually, your body will do one of three things: either fight, flight, or freeze. If you can fight, you will fight; if not, you will likely try to run away (flight). If you can do neither, you will freeze, meaning your body feels like it can't move. You don't get to choose this, just like you don't choose to breathe—your body just does it. Your reaction of fight, flight, or freeze is the same. It just happens because the old reptilian brain just acts automatically to help you stay safe. Your body is doing exactly what it is made to do: survive! We will work with these ideas more in Phase Two with the handout Building Awareness and Resources.

**Your Body Is Amazing!**

Your body is so important in our work together. It is where all your good things and resources are stored *and* where the hard stuff lives, too. I will be asking you lots of questions about "noticing" your body and what is happening in your body. We will come to see how your body is truly a resource because it is able to adapt and survive through really difficult things. We will also learn how to take care of the hurt that still lives inside your body.

**Our Sessions**

In our sessions together we will start with something easy (like a snack or fun activity), then do some of the harder stuff, and then end the session with something positive and fun. We will go back and forth between the easy stuff and the hard stuff, but it is my job to make sure you are in CALM body before you leave at the end of the session.

# Appendix D
## Phase One: Expressive Arts–Based Information-Gathering Tools

## MAP OF MY WORLD

You have your very own special world that you have grown up in. It is like your own unique map. Each person's map will look different because we all have various stories to tell about our experiences. Find a way to create your own map that can help show the following:

### Me

Write your name in the center and decorate it any way you like. With words or symbols, add all the things you love to do, are good at, or are interested in.

### Me and My Family and Friends

Draw concentric circles around your name.

Think of the important people in your life, including family and friends, then write each name on a small piece of paper. Place them somewhere in the circles. The closer they are to your name, the more connected they are to you emotionally.

Create a key that shows what kind of relationship there is between you and each person on your map (e.g., a star might mean close, lightening could mean difficult, or a broken line could mean distant). Draw the symbols on small pieces of paper, and place them between you and each person.

### Me and My Family and Friends as Objects

Find objects in the room (e.g., miniatures, puppets) to represent you and your family and friends. Place the objects on their names, including one for yourself. Name three qualities of that object. Share your thoughts about each object and how they have come to represent this particular person.

### My World and the Trauma

On another piece of paper (you decide how big it needs to be), draw a symbol of the trauma or just print the word *trauma* on the paper. Where would you place it on the map? Draw a boundary around the trauma. What does the boundary look like? What do you notice in your body as you draw the boundary? What difference, if any, does it make for the trauma to have a boundary?

Come back to the people in your life. Where would they be placed before the trauma? Where would they be placed after the trauma? Where would you place them now, if different? Where would you like them to be placed if you had a choice?

## HOW TRAUMA CHANGED MY WORLD

There are many ways to express how the trauma has changed or impacted your life. First, explore the art materials and then come back to your body. What materials are you drawn to? Is there an impulse inside that guides your decisions about what to use and how to express your inner experience? You may paint, draw, use clay, create symbols, do a collage, create mandalas, dance, listen to or write a song that has meaning, or write a play and act it out. What medium makes sense to you in how you can express this part of your story? What materials do you need (e.g., size of paper, puppets, or musical instruments)?

### Option

Invite your caregiver to create art that shows how she believes you have been impacted by the trauma. Decide if you would like to share your art first, or if you would like your caregiver to share first.

## MY RELATIONSHIPS

Some relationships have been hurt by the trauma, and some relationships may become closer because of the trauma. Make a list of the relationships that you feel have been affected in any way by the trauma.

Chose any art medium to show the relationships before the trauma, during the trauma, now, and in the future. Art choices include paint, clay, collage, drama/stories/poetry, creating or sing songs, playing an instrument, using puppets, or creating a dance/movement. Your caregiver can also do this activity.

## AMAZING BODY 1

Think of something upsetting that happened to you in the last day or so. Draw on this outline with symbols, colors, and words what you notice in your body when you think of this.

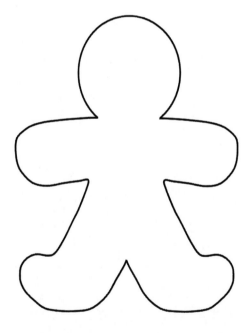

Think of something that makes you happy. It could be an activity, a person, an animal, or a good memory. Draw on this outline with symbols, colors, and words what you notice in your body as you think of this.

Look at the changes! Wow, you are able to change the sensations in your body with your thoughts! Your body and mind are amazing!

## AMAZING BODY 2

Make many copies of this body image and use this outline often to practice learning about the connections between your thoughts, feelings, and body sensations. For example, if something is upsetting you, use this outline to write out your upsetting thoughts; then show your feelings and sensations with symbols, colors, and words and where they are located in your body.

## MY BODY AND THE TRAUMA 1

Using the body image here, or on a cardboard body outline, and map out the following:

1. Bring up the trauma in your mind. Don't tell me about it, just notice what happens in your body when you think about it (sensations, feelings, thoughts).
2. On this image, draw and/or write the things you notice in your body. For example, you might use symbols, colors, or words to represent sensations (e.g., shaking, nervousness, sweaty hands, heart pounding), thoughts, and feelings.
3. On a scale of 0 to 10, with 10 being the most upsetting, how upsetting is it right now when you think about the trauma? Write this on the paper.
4. Now think about something or someone that makes you feel happy, calm, or peaceful. On the handout My Body and the Trauma 2, map out what you notice in your body, including thoughts, feelings, and sensations.

**MY BODY AND THE TRAUMA 2**

**SELF-PORTRAITS 1**

You can draw these self-portraits, or you can find things in the room that represent you at these times. You might even do a series of body postures/movements for each self-portrait. Make one self-portrait for each of the following times:

Me before the trauma (as animal, creature, tree, landscape, symbol, bush, flower, kitchen utensil, vehicle, etc.)

Me during the trauma

Me now

Me in the future

# Appendix E
## Phase One: Questionnaires for Information Gathering

**EXPLORING ART MODALITIES AND CREATIVITY BELIEFS**

There are so many ways to do art! Put a check mark beside the ones you like, put an X next to the ones you don't like, and put a question mark beside the ones you don't know much about.

Visual art

| | | | |
|---|---|---|---|
| drawing | pencils | pastels | markers |
| clay | collage | painting | crafts |

Dancing (what kind?)


Drama/acting/improv


Creative writing or other forms of writing

writing poems
writing stories

Reading/speaking

reading poems
speaking poems
telling stories
reading stories

Music

playing instrument(s)
singing (even if it is in the shower)
listening to music
your three favorite musicians

your three favorite songs

**Creativity and Me**

I am a creative person (why or why not):

My creativity is supported by (people, places, etc.):

Two things that influenced my creativity (positive and/or negative):

Secretly, I LOVE to (some art form, such as dance alone in my room):

I wish I was better at:

If I were better at this, I would:

# CHILD AND CAREGIVER TRAUMA HISTORY

Details of current trauma (identify how you know of these details):

Child's response to the trauma (identify any ongoing behaviors of concern):

Caregiver's response to trauma (If you are not the original caregiver, is there anything known about the original caregiver's response?):

Child's other past traumas (medical, losses, separations, deaths, neglect, etc.):

    Identify whether treated or untreated

    If treated: when, approach, outcome

Current caregiver's past traumas:

    Identify whether treated or untreated

    If treated: when, approach, outcome

Geographical moves:

    Dates/reasons for the move:

School

    School(s) attended (dates and reasons for move):

    Academic concerns/strengths:

    Social concerns/strengths:

    School-related traumas (e.g., bullying) or successes (e.g., awards):

Significant family life events (e.g. crises, deaths, illness):

Sibling or biological parent trauma:

Witness to trauma:

## IMPACT OF TRAUMA ON CAREGIVER

1.  How have you been impacted by your child's trauma?

2.  What feelings have stayed with you or are hard to shake since the trauma?

3.  What feelings do you have toward your child since the trauma?

4.  How do you cope with these feelings?

5.  Who is your main support to help you deal with these challenges?

6.  What has been the biggest struggle for you since the trauma?

7.  What helps take care of your own hurt?

8.  If you have a trauma history, has it been triggered since learning about your child's trauma?

# WHY IT WAS HARD FOR ME TO TELL

| | 0 = Not true | 1 = A little true | 2 = Somewhat true | 3 = Very true |
|---|---|---|---|---|
| 1. I thought my parents would be angry at me. | 0 | 1 | 2 | 3 |
| 2. I didn't want to bother my mom or dad. | 0 | 1 | 2 | 3 |
| 3. I thought my mother would be upset. | 0 | 1 | 2 | 3 |
| 4. I thought my father would be upset. | 0 | 1 | 2 | 3 |
| 5. I thought our family would break up. | 0 | 1 | 2 | 3 |
| 6. I thought my parents wouldn't believe me. | 0 | 1 | 2 | 3 |
| 7. I didn't want to be upset. | 0 | 1 | 2 | 3 |
| 8. _____ told me not to tell. | 0 | 1 | 2 | 3 |
| 9. I thought _____ would be mad. | 0 | 1 | 2 | 3 |
| 10. I was scared that _____ would have to leave the home. | 0 | 1 | 2 | 3 |
| 11. I was afraid _____ would be in trouble. | 0 | 1 | 2 | 3 |
| 12. I was worried _____ might hurt me. | 0 | 1 | 2 | 3 |
| 13. I was afraid I would get into trouble. | 0 | 1 | 2 | 3 |
| 14. I thought I had done something wrong. | 0 | 1 | 2 | 3 |
| 15. I had mixed-up feelings. | 0 | 1 | 2 | 3 |

## WHY IT WAS HARD FOR MY CHILD TO TELL

|  | 0 =<br>Not true | 1 =<br>A little<br>true | 2 =<br>Somewhat<br>true | 3 =<br>Very<br>true |
|---|---|---|---|---|
| 1. She/he was afraid that you and your spouse would be angry. | 0 | 1 | 2 | 3 |
| 2. She/he didn't want to bother parent(s). | 0 | 1 | 2 | 3 |
| 3. She/he worried the family might break up. | 0 | 1 | 2 | 3 |
| 4. She/he was scared _____ would have to leave the home. | 0 | 1 | 2 | 3 |
| 5. She/he worried she/he wouldn't be believed. | 0 | 1 | 2 | 3 |
| 6. She/he was afraid _____ would be in trouble. | 0 | 1 | 2 | 3 |
| 7. She/he worried _____ might hurt her. | 0 | 1 | 2 | 3 |
| 8. _____ told her/him not to tell. | 0 | 1 | 2 | 3 |
| 9. She/he thought _____ would be mad. | 0 | 1 | 2 | 3 |
| 10. She/he was ashamed. | 0 | 1 | 2 | 3 |
| 11. She/he thought he/she would be seen as damaged. | 0 | 1 | 2 | 3 |
| 12. She/he was afraid to get into trouble. | 0 | 1 | 2 | 3 |
| 13. She/he is too shy to tell. | 0 | 1 | 2 | 3 |
| 14. She/he didn't know it was wrong. | 0 | 1 | 2 | 3 |
| 15. She/he didn't think it would do any good. | 0 | 1 | 2 | 3 |

## RESPONSIBILITY RATING SCALE (CHILD)

| No Responsibility | | Somewhat Responsible | | Half Responsible | | Mostly Responsible | | Totally Responsible |
|---|---|---|---|---|---|---|---|---|
| 0 | 1 | 2 | 3 | 4 | 5 | 6 | 7 | 8 | 9 | 10 |

1. Using the 0–10 rating scale below the question, **circle** the number that shows how much you believe you are responsible (at fault for) for what happened between you and _____.

   Put an X over the number that shows how responsible you think_____ is.

   0      1      2      3      4      5      6      7      8      9      10

2. **Circle** the number that you think your mother would give you, and put an X over the number that you think your mother would give_____.

   0      1      2      3      4      5      6      7      8      9      10

3. **Circle** the number that you think that your father would give you, and put an X over the number that you think your father would give_____.

   0      1      2      3      4      5      6      7      8      9      10

4. **Circle** the number that you think_____would give you and put an X over the number that you think she/he would give herself/himself.

   0      1      2      3      4      5      6      7      8      9      10

5. Circle the number that you think your best friend (or someone you really look up to) would give you, and put an X over the number that you think she/he would give_____.

   0      1      2      3      4      5      6      7      8      9      10

6. Is there someone else that has some responsibility for what happened? **Yes   No**

   If yes, who?_____Circle the number would you give this person.

   0      1      2      3      4      5      6      7      8      9      10

# RESPONSIBILITY RATING SCALE (CAREGIVER)

*Note:* **v = victim; o= offender**

| No Responsibility | | | Somewhat Responsible | | Half Responsible | | Mostly Responsible | | Totally Responsible |
|---|---|---|---|---|---|---|---|---|---|
| 0 | 1 | 2 | 3 | 4 | 5 | 6 | 7 | 8 | 9 | 10 |

1. Using the 0–10 rating scale below, **circle** the number that shows how much you believe _____(o) is responsible for what happened with _____ (v). Put an X over the number that shows how responsible that you think _____(v) is.

   0    1    2    3    4    5    6    7    8    9    10

2. **Circle** the number that you think _____ (o) would give him/herself, and put an X over the number that you think _____ (v) would give him/herself.

   0    1    2    3    4    5    6    7    8    9    10

3. **Circle** the number that you think _____ (o) would give _____ (v), and put an X over the number that you think _____ (v) would give _____ (o).

   0    1    2    3    4    5    6    7    8    9    10

4. **Circle** the number that you think the other parent would give _____ (o), and put an X over the number that would be given to _____(v).

   0    1    2    3    4    5    6    7    8    9    10

5. Is there someone else that has some responsibility for what happened? **Yes No**

   If yes, who?_____Circle the number would you give this person.

   0    1    2    3    4    5    6    7    8    9    10

## RESPONSIBILITY FOR THE TRAUMA

Who/what is responsible for what happened? Draw as many people or things needed in order to answer this question. Show how much each person/thing is responsible by giving each a number on the following scale:

| No Responsibility | | Somewhat Responsible | | Half Responsible | | Mostly Responsible | | Totally Responsible | |
|---|---|---|---|---|---|---|---|---|---|
| 0 | 1 | 2 | 3 | 4 | 5 | 6 | 7 | 8 | 9 | 10 |

## SAFETY QUESTIONNAIRE

1.  How safe do you feel from this happening again?

    Not Safe at All      A Little Bit Safe      Somewhat Safe      Safer      Totally Safe
    0       1       2       3       4       5       6       7       8       9       10

2.  What do you need to increase your feelings of being safe from this happening?

    From your mom?
    From your dad?
    From yourself?
    From _____?

3.  Where (physical location) do you feel safest? Why?

4.  Who is in charge of keeping you safe? Why?

5.  Who helps you feel safe from this happening again?

6.  What helps you feel safe from this happening again (e.g., stuffed animal, being in your bedroom, talking)?

7.  Do you think you can stop this from happening again? Yes No Maybe
    Explain further.

8.  How confident are you that you could stop this from happening again?

    Not Confident      A Little Bit Confident      Somewhat Confident      Totally Confident
    0       1       2       3       4       5       6       7       8       9       10

9.  How confident are you that your parents could stop this from happening to you again?

    Not Confident      A Little Bit Confident      Somewhat Confident      Totally Confident
    0       1       2       3       4       5       6       7       8       9       10

10. What would you do to stop this from happening again?

## FEELINGS ABOUT THE TRAUMA

Please rate, out of 10, how intense the feeling was for you then (when the trauma was happening) and now.

| | I Don't Feel This At All | | So-So | | The Most I Could Ever Feel | |
|---|---|---|---|---|---|---|
| 0 | 1 | 2 | 3 | 4 | 5 | 6 | 7 | 8 | 9 | 10 |

| Feeling | Then | Now | Feeling | Then | Now |
|---|---|---|---|---|---|
| Afraid | | | Frustrated | | |
| Angry | | | Guilty | | |
| Annoyed | | | Helpless | | |
| Anxious | | | Hurt | | |
| Betrayed | | | Lonely | | |
| Confused | | | Neglected | | |
| Depressed | | | Nervous | | |
| Devastated | | | Paralyzed | | |
| Dirty | | | Rejected | | |
| Disappointed | | | Relieved | | |
| Disgusted | | | Sad | | |
| Disrespected | | | Shameful | | |
| Distrustful | | | Uncomfortable | | |
| Embarrassed | | | Worried | | |
| | | | | | |

Add any other feelings you may have had that are not on here.

## DISCLOSURE QUESTIONNAIRE

1. How long did you keep the trauma a secret?

2. How did the trauma get reported?

3. If you told someone about the trauma, answer the following questions:
   a. Who did you tell?
   b. Why did you tell that person?
   c. Why then, at that time?
   d. How did you feel when you told?
   e. What did you hope would happen when you told?

3. How did your caregiver respond when she/he found out about the trauma?
   a. What did she/he say to you?
   b. What did you want her/him to do or say?
   c. What did your caregiver do that was helpful?
   d. What did she/he do that was not helpful?
   e. Did she/he believe you?
   f. Did you feel she/he supported you?

4. What was your biggest worry when other people found out about what happened?

5. Who knows about what happened? Who else, if anyone, would you like to tell?

6. What would you tell someone if they told you they had been through something similar?

7. If you could do it over, would you tell?

## DISCLOSURE PICTURE: WHEN I FIRST TOLD
## ABOUT THE TRAUMA

Using any art form (e.g., drawing, puppets, instruments), show what happened when you told. Help me understand what your thoughts, feelings, and sensations were when you first told about the trauma (add thought bubbles for your thoughts, feelings, and sensations).

If different, show what you *wished* had happened when you told.

## TRAUMA SELF-STATEMENTS

Using the following scale, write the number you thought *then* (at the time of the trauma) and what you think *now*.

| FALSE | | | | | SO-SO | | | | | TRUE |
|---|---|---|---|---|---|---|---|---|---|---|
| 0 | 1 | 2 | 3 | 4 | 5 | 6 | 7 | 8 | 9 | 10 |

| Self-statements | Then | Now |
|---|---|---|
| There is something wrong with my body. | | |
| I can't control myself. | | |
| I can't control the things around me. | | |
| Anything can happen to me. | | |
| People close to me hurt me. | | |
| Nothing or no one can protect me. | | |
| I can't say no. | | |
| I'm afraid to say what I really think. | | |
| I'll never get over it. | | |
| I think about hurting the person who hurt me. | | |
| I need help. | | |
| I'm an okay person. | | |
| I did the best I could. | | |
| I'm fine now. | | |
| I have learned from what has happened. | | |
| I am stronger than I knew. | | |
| I can face what happened to me. | | |

## REMINDERS OF THE TRAUMA

Trauma is remembered by all our senses: what we see, hear, taste, touch, and smell. We can be reminded of the trauma by things that happen around us. For example, one youth would become very upset when she saw a red car because it reminded her of the person who hurt her. Another child, who witnessed his house on fire, felt scared whenever he would smell smoke. Draw or write the things that remind you of the trauma.

Things I see:

Things I hear:

Things I taste:

Things I touch:

Things I smell:

**PIECES OF MY STORY, PART 1: REMEMBERING**

Write an incident that you remember on each piece of the puzzle. Rate on a scale of 0–10 how upsetting it is to you now, with 10 being most upsetting. Soon, you will create a special safety box or container that will hold these puzzle pieces. Our next steps will be to learn skills to help you feel in charge of your feelings and your body sensations that can increase your courage to work on the hard stuff of the puzzle pieces.

# Appendix F
## Phase Two: Expressive Arts Interventions

### POUCHES, POCKETS, BAGS, AND BOXES

In between our sessions, your puzzle pieces need a safe place to be. We will find the just right container for you puzzle pieces, as there are many kinds of containers you can create. You may have your own idea about what you would like to create to hold the puzzle pieces, or you can choose one of the following ideas:

- Pouches: A pouch is usually made with material and tied with a string to hold things in. You can make them or buy them. If you make your own, you can decorate it however you like.
- Pockets: Having pockets cut out from an old pair of jeans works great. You can decorate the pocket using markers, embroidery thread, buttons, and other materials.
- Paper bags and envelopes: These work well as containers and are easy and fun to decorate. They come in all sizes and shapes.
- Boxes: Your therapist may have a collection of boxes for you to choose from. You can paint and decorate the box. Think about what colors, symbols, or words you would like to put on the box. You can also paint and decorate the inside of the box.

## SETTING MY OWN PACE: STOP, SLOW, GO

When you learn how to ride a bike, you need to know how to steer, move forward, go slow, and stop. It is the same with the hard work you are doing with the trauma. We need to learn to talk about the trauma, feel the feelings and sensations in our bodies, and then learn how to help our bodies feel calm and safe again if we start to feel out of control. This is like learning how to stop or go slower with the brakes on your bike. It would be dangerous to ride your bike without knowing how to brake! Cut out these signs (or make your own) and use them as needed to stop, slow down, or keep the session going.

## LEARNING ABOUT SAFETY

Safety is an important word to know and understand. Together we will explore what it feels like in your body when you are feeling safe or unsafe.

1.  Recall a time when you felt safe. Where were you? Who were you with?

    • Using a body outline, show how safe feels and looks in your body.
    • Add thoughts, feelings, and sensations through color, images, and symbols.

2.  Recall a time when you didn't feel safe. Where were you? Who were you with?

    • Using a body outline, show how unsafe feels and looks in your body.
    • Add thoughts, feelings, and sensations through color, images, and symbols.

3.  Who are the safe people you know? What are safe places you know? What makes these people and places safe?
4.  Who are the unsafe people you know? What are the unsafe places that you know of? What makes these people and places unsafe?
5.  Create a scale from 1 to 10, with 1 meaning the person is unsafe. The higher on the scale, the more safe the person is. Place the people you have identified somewhere on the scale. Create another scale like this for safe and unsafe places. Discuss your thoughts about how you decided to place the people and places where you did.
6.  In our space here, let's create a place that feels safe for you. This means we can use pillows, stuffed animals, or anything that you might want to bring here for the session to help you feel safe. Notice what it is like in your body when you are in your safe space.
7.  At home, create a safe space with your caregiver. When you are feeling sad, scared, or frustrated, practice going to this place and take some time to imagine yourself as something, such as a tree, feeling your deep roots, and reaching up with arms like branches. What are other images you like that help you feel calm and safe?
8.  Let's explore safe versus unsafe feelings and sensations using different art forms. Below are some ideas, or maybe you have your own idea that we can do together.

    • Create a story about a child who was unsafe and how the child became safe again. This story will have a beginning, middle, and end, as well as a title.
    • Using instruments, we can add sound to the story.
    • We can use puppets and props to act this story out.

9.  Draw, paint, or collage an image that represents a safe place for you. A safe place can be made up of all kinds of things that remind you of feeling safe in your body. Using all of your senses, add to this image anything that supports you feeling safe.

    • What do you *see* that reminds you of safety (mountains, grass, trees)?
    • What do you *hear* (birds, wind, music)?
    • What *smells* remind you of being safe (bread baking, scented candle, nature)?
    • What could you *touch* (a pet, fleece blanket, grass)?
    • What *tastes* remind you of safety (chicken soup, warm milk, cookies)?

Let's talk about times when it makes sense to use this image, where it is best to put the image, and how you can use it to support you when you need it most. It is very important that you practice using all these resources when you need them, to remember you have them to assist you, and to take time to connect to your body and your senses to really *feel* the safety in your body.

## CULTIVATING HOPE

What is hope? Let's brainstorm together! Some ideas of hope that other young people have shared with me are:

"Hope is something that keeps you going, even when you don't feel like it."
"Hope keeps you believing that things will turn out okay."

We are going to explore more about hope and find a way to remember there is hope even as we go through the hard stuff together.

### Detectives Searching for Hope

Let's create a story about hope together. First, pretend we are detectives. Detectives are people who search for answers. They look around, ask questions, and find answers. We will go on a search together looking for hope. We will both go away and ask other people what they think hope is, and then we will bring our answers back and either write a story together, create a poem with the ideas, or do another activity.

Use one of the following prompts and keep writing until you have no more ideas.

Hope is . . .
I believe in . . .
My faith tells me . . .

How does hope help you? How does it help you with the hard stuff we are working on?

What does hope look like? Sound like? Feel like?

Can you draw hope? Sound it on the drum?

### Create a Symbol of Hope

A symbol of hope could be a song, a dance, a poem, words, a story, a memory of someone positive in your life, or a memory of something good that happened to you that taught you about hope. It might be an image or symbol, like a butterfly, sun, stars, or tree. Create a symbol of hope and keep it somewhere that you will see it often.

#### Ideas

- On paper or canvas, draw/paint your symbol of hope.
- On nice paper, write out the lyrics to a song or words to a poem that give you hope.
- Create a collage with a photo of someone who gives your hope, or simply create a hope collage with images and words that represent hope to you.
- Find stones, clean them, and write words of hope on them with permanent markers.

When you look at your image or words, where do you sense hope in your body?

## BUILDING RESOURCES 1

### Identifying Inside, Outside, and Body Resources

1. My inside resources

Inside resources are my gifts, talents, personality traits, and beliefs. For example, some inner resources could be your: ability to talk about feelings, confidence, creativity, determination, cleverness, sense of humor, reliability, wisdom, expressiveness, dedication, sensitivity, caring, and intuitiveness. Sometimes it is hard to know if something is a resource. One way to decide if it is a good enough resource is to ask yourself, "Does this resource make me feel alive, content, peaceful, proud, excited, or comforted?" If you can say yes to at least one of these feelings, it is likely a good enough resource.

Make a list of your inside resources. As you speak about each resource, notice how you sense them in your body as you talk about them. For example, you might notice you stand taller when you think about how brave you were to stand up for your friend at school.

Rate each resource from 0–10, with 10 being the strongest, most positive sensation or feeling.

2. My outside resources

Outside resources are people (friends, family, heroes, icons), favorite places, memories, nature, objects (stuffed animals, stones, special gifts), community (church, sports groups), animals, or pets. Anything that makes you feel good inside when you think of them.

Make a list of your outside resources. As you speak about each resource, notice how you sense the resource in your body as you talk about it. For example, when I think about my cat, I feel warm in my heart and a smile comes to my face.

Rate each resource from 0–10, with 10 being the strongest, most positive sensation/feeling.

3. Body resources

Body resources are the things you can do with your body that help you feel more in charge of your feelings, thoughts, and behaviors. Sometimes, you may need to feel more energized and alive, while at other times, you may need to feel calmer and more peaceful. The following are some ideas, though you may have your own:

How to lower your energy:

- Make a big balloon in your belly while slowly breathing in, and make the balloon disappear while slowly breathing out.
- Have your therapist read a relaxing visualization while you find a comfortable position and, if you like, close your eyes.
- Have your therapist teach you progressive relaxation, which is slowly relaxing every part of your body from head to toe.
- Think of images that calm you. We may need to experiment with this to discover the just right images that make your body relax.

How to increase your energy:

- Find a favorite song and dance along.
- Play Thumball.

- Play an imagination game, such as making yourself into something like a tree or car without using any words, just your body movements, and have the therapist guess what you are.
- Make sounds and movements of animals and have your therapist guess which animal you are.
- Play with long, skinny, wooden dowels and see who can balance them the longest.
- Think of things that excite you and notice what happens in your body.

Rate each resource from 0–10, with 10 being the strongest, most positive sensation/feeling.

4.  Inside, outside, or body resources I need and/or want to develop:

5.  How might my life be different with these new resources?

## BUILDING RESOURCES 2

### Strengthening Your Inside, Outside, and Body Resources

1.  Resource cards and pocket

    *   Using recipe cards (or half that size, if desired), create small cards with images of specific resources on them using collage, drawing, and writing and embellishing them with whatever materials are available.
    *   Create a container for the resource cards by using a pocket cut out from an old or pair of blue jeans and embellish the pocket with embroidery thread, fabric markers, or glue-on embellishments.
    *   Practice using the resource cards by thinking of a mildly upsetting event, noticing the experience in your body. Then, look at the resource card and notice the shift in your body that happens naturally as you move to a more pleasant thought or image.

2.  Resource shrine

    *   See examples of shrines in Chapter 7 (Figure 7.5).
    *   Choose any size of card stock to make the shrine.
    *   Fold paper in half from left to right, then unfold.
    *   Fold left side in half to center crease, fold right side in half to center crease.
    *   Fold left to right at the center crease.
    *   On the right side, a third of the way down from the top, cut a curved line to a point to create the shape of the shrine, then unfold.
    *   The shrine naturally has both an outside and inside space that can be used to identify both inside and outside resources.
    *   Embellish the shrine with collage materials that capture your resources.
    *   You may want to add the resources that you are developing, as a reminder of the ones you still need.

3.  Resource flags

    *   Prayer flags have long been used in the Himalayas to send prayers to all people. It is believed that when the flags are strung together and hung outside the wind takes the prayers and spreads them over the countryside.
    *   You can create resource flags with cloth material cut in rectangular pieces and embellish them with meaning related to your resources.
    *   The cloth can be cut from old sheets and painted with acrylic colors that are meaningful to you. (Wet the sheet and add acrylic paint with a paint brush, mixing colors together as desired, let the fabric dry, and cut or rip it into whatever size is wanted.)
    *   Once embellished, the flags can be attached by safety pins or loosely sewn directly on the string and hung where you will see them.

4.  Resource stones and pouch

    *   If time and space permit, going out together to find stones is a wonderful excursion, or it could be homework for you and your caregiver to go and find stones together.
    *   Stones should be washed with soapy water and dried, then painted with acrylics.
    *   Once dry, the resources can be drawn or resource words can be written on the stones.

- Make a pouch by drawing a 6-inch diameter circle on cloth (e.g., old plain colored sheets, muslin, lightweight canvas).
- Decorate your pouch with permanent markers.
- Once the drawing is complete, take embroidery thread and, using a simple stitch 1 inch from the edge of the fabric, create a drawstring for the pouch. Or, simply gather the pouch at the edges and use string to tie it closed.

# EXPLORING AND HEALING BOUNDARIES

The physical space around you is like a protective boundary or bubble around your body and mind. You can usually choose who or what comes close to you and who or what you want to stay away from. However, you don't always have the choice when something traumatic happens.

## Before, After, and Now

Sit on a large piece of paper. You will be drawing boundaries around yourself on the paper. You can use different colors, sizes and shapes of lines, or symbols for lines to help represent your boundary experience. You can also do this exercise with a body outline on a small piece of paper.

- Choose a color and draw a line around you that represents your boundary before the trauma.
- Choose a color and draw another boundary that represents how the trauma affected your boundary.
- Choose a color and show what your boundary looks like now.
- Choose a color and show how you would like your boundary to be in the future.

Pretend that your boundary has a voice. With the same color for each boundary above, write what your boundary would have wanted to say before the trauma, after, and now.

Imagine now that your boundary has healed. On a new piece of paper, draw what it would look like now. What would need to happen in your life for you to feel like your boundary was healed?

## Silent Words

Our boundaries can tell people when to move away or come closer without us even using words. Think of a time when someone you didn't like came and sat beside you. Think of what you sensed in your body. What movement did your body want to make? Now think about someone sitting beside you that you really like. What happens?

## Come Close/Go Away

Let's stand facing each other with as much space between us as we can get. We will take turns inviting the other person to come closer, stop, or go back to the beginning position through hand motions only. Notice what this is like for you. What invitation do you like best (closer, stop, go back)? Least? Is it easier for you to tell others what to do or have them tell you what to do?

## LABYRINTHS, MAZES, AND MANDALAS

Learning to soothe yourself when you are having a hard time is an important skill to learn. Choose a mandala, labyrinth, or maze and make it your own. Think about colors that soothe you or perk you up, whichever is needed. You can add your own symbols and words to create something unique, or you can create your own mandala.

## LEARNING TO BE MY OWN BEST FRIEND

Some people tend to be harder on themselves than they are on other people. Especially when hard things happen, you can start to believe negative things about yourself, such as that you are not good enough, smart enough, or lovable. Learning to be your own best friend is something that children and adults both need to do.

To be your own best friend, you first need to understand the different parts of yourself. It is easy to love yourself when you are kind, caring, and feeling good inside. The tricky part is to love yourself when you do mean things or hurt others or yourself with your words and behaviors. These parts often have negative thoughts and beliefs that are very hard to manage. It is not so easy to love the parts of yourself that do and think these things. Yet, these are parts of yourself that need kind attention too!

We ALL have different parts that express themselves through a range of thoughts, beliefs, and feelings that are both positive and negative. Some are angry, hurt, scared, and abandoned parts that need to be heard. If they don't feel heard they often get LOUDER! For example, if there is a part of me that is feeling frustrated and I just try to ignore it, the frustration seems to grow in me until I finally pay attention and listen to it. All parts need to be listened to. Being our own best friend means doing what best friends do: listen and try to understand what the friend is saying. Sometimes, just by listening to this part, there is a sense of relief. Other times you need to help these parts feel better.

How do you befriend these more difficult parts? This is not just a one-time activity. It is a way of learning how to be with all the parts of yourself throughout life. First, to begin this process, you need the help of a therapist or caregiver who understands. Second, you need to be in a calm place to really listen to these parts. Third, begin to identify, name, and create through art the different parts. It is important that you are aware of the happy, calm part, too. Each part has certain thoughts and beliefs that go with it. The details of how to do this are below.

### Learning About the Different Parts

*Happy and Calm*

We are able to do our best listening when we are in a calm place, so we will start with this part. Of course you have other wonderful parts of you and you can draw them, too, but for now you will start with this part. Spend time really sensing what it is like inside your body when you are calm and happy. Think of words that describe what you are noticing. Some words might be relaxed, open, quiet, still, or peaceful. Draw an image that represents your happy and calm self. What colors and symbols express this part of you? What words, beliefs, thoughts, and feelings go with this part? If you need some help, below are some prompts for possible thoughts and beliefs to get you started and add to your image.

I am . . . (okay, strong, safe, worthy).
I did the best I could . . . (in the situation).
I deserve . . . (to be happy, healthy).
I can . . . (ask for what I need).
I can be. . . .
I will be. . . .

*The Hard Parts*

Go through the same process now and draw an image that best represents the other parts in you. Some of the difficult parts that children tell me about are the angry, hurt, scared, abandoned, and worried parts. You might have other ones too. One little girl described a part of herself that always wanted attention. It just never seemed to get enough. She called it Attention Annie, and she wrote a little booklet about her. You might want to draw the different parts as characters, animals, plants, vehicles, objects, or symbols. Remember to add the different thoughts, feelings, and beliefs these parts have. Below are possible prompts to get you started.

It was my fault that. . . .

I am . . . (unlovable, alone, a bad person, not safe, worthless, alone).

I can't . . . (trust, succeed).

My body is . . . (dirty, unsafe).

No one . . . (understands me, likes me).

I don't . . . (belong).

## Listening Through Art

Now that you have them all drawn out, practice listening to each part. Who needs your attention first? Take the time to listen, like you would a friend. One way of listening is to take the image and write a dialogue between the calm you and the angry you. Another way of doing this is to draw a cartoon strip of the calm, happy you talking to one of the other parts. This helps you really listen to what that part is needing to say and needing you to hear.

## Caregiver Support

It is important that your caregiver learns what he/she can do to help when you are feeling stuck in the difficult parts. Sometimes caregivers are able to help just by listening or by doing things that help you to get unstuck and to feel calm and happy again. Together with your caregiver, go through all the images and discuss the things that can help each part. Add these ideas to the image or on a separate paper. Take them with you, so you and your caregiver can remember to practice taking care of these parts at home.

## Beyond Listening

When you are stuck in those hard parts, listening is the first step to help get unstuck, as described earlier. Sometimes other ideas are needed. Usually these ideas are only helpful *after* the hard parts feel heard and you feel more calm in your body. For example, one idea is identifying exceptions. If this part feels like no one loves or likes it, it may need support in seeing the exceptions and identifying the people who do care for and like it.

Another idea is to offer different points of view. We are not trying to change the angry part's point of view. We are simply offering another perspective. For example, if a part is feeling angry because it thinks no one wants to play with it and it feels unlovable, it might help to first narrow down the trigger. If the trigger was that a friend turned you down to play, there might be MANY other reasons they turned you down. What might they be? The friend might be having a bad day or feeling unfriendly inside himself. So, we look for different points of view rather than agreeing with the part that feels it is unlovable. Again, we are not trying to convince the angry part that it shouldn't feel that way, but just thinking of other possibilities and then noticing what happens to the angry part when it starts to hear different points of view.

You, your caregiver, or your therapist may have many other ideas about how to help these parts. Explore, discuss, and practice different possibilities.

# BUILDING AWARENESS AND RESOURCES THROUGH IMAGERY AND STORIES

With the handout The Inner World of My Body, we learned about tracking our thoughts, feelings, and sensations and we learned about the brain and the fight, flight, and freeze responses. We will now learn how these responses are resources.

C = Child

A = Adolescent

1.  Fight, flight, and freeze are resources (C & A).

As you know by now, when scared, our bodies do some pretty amazing things all on their own. If a person can fight when he is afraid, he will. If he can't fight, he will run away (flight). If he can't do either of these things, he will freeze. These responses are the ways that your body is trying to stay safe.

## Fight Resources

We can learn many things from the animals that live with and around us. When frightened, most animals will attack to protect themselves and their young ones. What animals do you know who would do that (e.g., dogs, cats, moose, coyotes)? To be a strong fighter, we must develop resources such as focus and strength and being grounded and centered.

## Flight Resources

Some animals know they don't stand a chance if they are caught, so they are very skilled at escaping through speed to stay safe. What animals are quick and speedy (e.g., gazelle, deer, cats, rabbits)? These animals are well resourced at being quick, alert, and aware.

## Freeze Resources

If an animal is too small to win the fight and can't run away, what else do animals do to try to protect themselves? They freeze! Freezing is a good thing because it saves lives and protects the animal from harm. Some animals who freeze are opossums, rabbits, or squirrels. Do you know of others?

Humans can also freeze if scared enough. It is a smart defense mechanism, and our bodies are "hard-wired" to do this. That means that it is automatic, and our bodies do it without us thinking or deciding to freeze. When animals come out of the "freeze," their bodies shake and shiver, which helps them feel normal again. Our bodies do that too! It is perfectly normal to shake and shiver after being very scared.

Think of a time when you were really afraid. What did your body do? What do you wish your body did?

Is there one survival resource that you relate to most? Draw images of the resources of fight, flight, and freeze that your own body went through. How do you feel about each?

2.  Research together (C & A)

Do some homework with your caregiver and research what different animals do to protect themselves. What are their survival mechanisms? For example, turtles have protective shells, skunks can spray, and deer have speed and are able to jump.

3.  Create Stories Together (C)

Create a story of the fight, flight, and freeze that fits your situation. You might use the images you drew for number one. What did your body do when it was so scared? What do you wish your body did when it was so scared? Act out spontaneous stories by taking turns being predator and prey, and choose what animals you want to use. Play out the story slowly, being mindful of the feelings and sensations that come up in your body, taking time to experience them fully. Use puppets to help enact the story if you have them. How does the story end?

4.  Visualization (C & A)

Our imaginations are powerful and can be very helpful to us. After all of these discussions about how your body is able to work so hard to protect you, think of the images that make you feel most strong and powerful. Share them out loud. For example, you might find the image of the rabbit very empowering. Now close your eyes and imagine yourself as one of these images. What do you see, hear, smell, feel, and taste? What do you notice in your body as you imagine yourself as this image? Open your eyes and draw yourself as this image.

# GETTING A HANDLE ON TRICKY TRAUMA BEHAVIORS

Do you ever wonder why you do what you do? Do you ever have a reaction that is so big that it feels overwhelming and hard to control? Do you ever have big reactions to small events, even though in the moment the event feels big? You may not notice your reaction was big until the event has passed. Often, when we have had hard things like trauma happen, our brains and bodies react in ways that are challenging to handle and difficult to understand. These reactions are called "tricky trauma behaviors" because we behave in ways that are tricky to manage and they are usually related to the trauma. As examples, some children have angry outbursts, and others try to get their caregivers' attention in inappropriate ways.

To get a handle on the tricky behaviors, we (you, your caregiver, and your therapist) are going to call on our inner detectives, curious cats, and smart scientists. As detectives, we will search for clues to help us learn about the tricky trauma behavior, what it is like, when it happens, and how long it happens for. The curious cat in us can watch and observe what is happening now that makes it feels so big. The curious cat may also wonder if there is something that has happened in your past that it feels similar to. We then need the wisdom of our smart scientist to come up with ideas and strategies to experiment with to help you manage and stand up to the tricky behaviors.

## Questions from the Inner Detective

Name some of the tricky trauma behaviors that perhaps get you in trouble or are just very difficult to manage (e.g., feel angry and throw things, demand attention, isolate self in bedroom)?

What part of you feels most present when this happens (e.g., hurt, angry, scared part)? Can you draw a picture of this part and give it a name? Tell or write the story of this part.

## Questions from the Inner Curious Cat

Check in with your thoughts, feelings, sensations, and behaviors. When did you shift from being your happy and calm self to the other part?

What are the things that triggered this tricky behavior (e.g., loud voice, someone ignoring you)? Check out the Influencers section below to help with this question.

Was there a past need that wasn't met that you may be currently trying to meet now (e.g., to be safe, to be seen, to be understood)?

Create a comic strip that shows exactly what happened, including the trigger, the behavior, and the consequence. Include thought bubbles that show what went on in your mind, so you can share what happened inside. Include feelings and sensations as well.

## Questions from the Inner Scientist

What are some things that have successfully helped you before that could help you now? Which ones can we experiment with now? What goals would you like to set for yourself to improve these behaviors?

What does this part (e.g., angry, scared) need from you? Do you remember your happy and calm part from Learning to Be My Own Best Friend? How can that part help this part? Perhaps the two parts could have a discussion or you could write a story about how the scared part was helped.

Return to the comic strip. Add the ideas from your inner scientist, highlighting the possible outcomes.

**Influencers**

Our thoughts, feelings, sensations, and behaviors are all connected to and influence each other. They can also be influenced by many things, both inside and outside of us. The questions inside the body below may be able to help the detective and curious cat in you understand what caused tricky trauma behaviors.

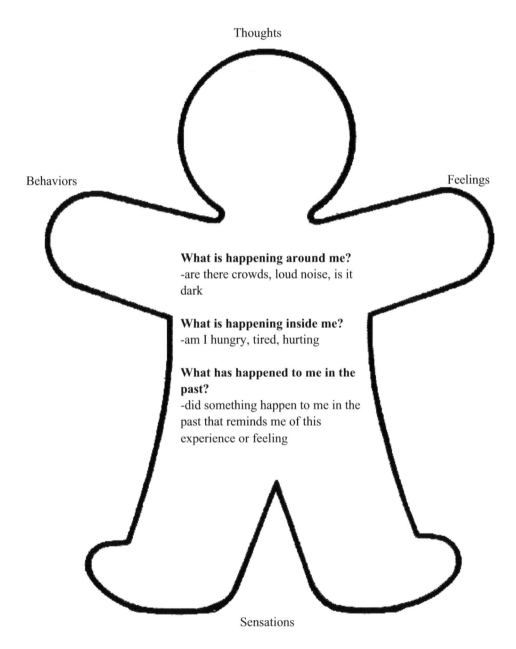

Thoughts

Behaviors

Feelings

**What is happening around me?**
-are there crowds, loud noise, is it dark

**What is happening inside me?**
-am I hungry, tired, hurting

**What has happened to me in the past?**
-did something happen to me in the past that reminds me of this experience or feeling

Sensations

# Appendix G
## Phase Three: Expressive Arts Interventions

### THE WALL

At any time in our work together, you may feel as though you can't talk, do art, or think about the trauma any more. Some say it is like a wall that goes up around them, although it might be different for you. Draw (or use any art material, or build with pillows) what your wall (or whatever word best fits here) looks like. Where do you feel the wall in relation to your body (e.g., outside, inside)? What sensations do you notice in your body when you think about or experience the wall? When have you felt like this before? Give some examples. What makes it change (e.g., get bigger, smaller, go away)? What does it feel like when it disappears/shifts/changes in some way? How has this wall been helpful to you? How has it not been helpful to you?

# SURFING THE WAVES

Our feelings and sensations come and go like waves on the ocean. Sometimes we are in calm water; other times, we experience small, gentle waves; and other times the waves are so big they knock us over. Talking about the scary and hard things that have happened will create some waves. That is okay; the feeling of the waves is just our bodies' way of telling us we need to slow down and notice what our bodies want us to know. At first it might feel like big waves just thinking about what happened. If we don't know how to surf the waves, even the small waves might feel scary and overwhelming. Together we will learn how to surf those big waves, and over time, the waves will become smaller.

Draw a big wave, a middle-sized wave, and a little wave and cut them out. As we prepare to work on the puzzle pieces, we will pay attention to how big the wave (feelings and sensations) feels and write the number on the wave. For example, a 10 is the big wave, which means overwhelmed; 5 is the middle-sized wave, which means manageable; and the little wave might be a 2 or 3. If it is lower than that, it might mean you are feeling numb or frozen. We will have these waves handy as we do our work together. If you feel that the feelings or sensations are too big to handle, point to or hold the biggest wave in the air and we will slow down our work. If you start to feel numb or like you are not really present any more, show the little wave. We want to make sure we are working with the just right size of wave: not too much and not too little. Throughout our work together, we will check in with what size the waves are to ensure that our work is feeling safe enough.

**MY ICEBERG**

What I have already told about the trauma:

Incidents:

Thoughts:

Feelings:

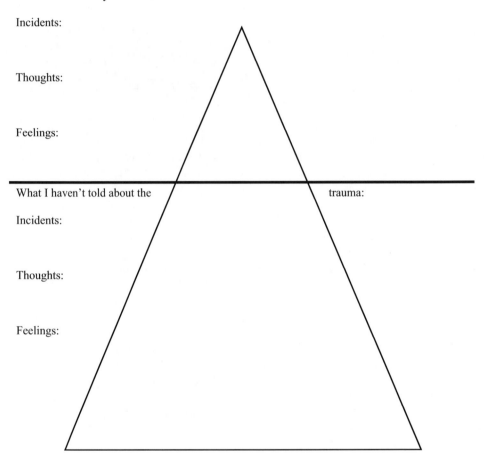

What I haven't told about the                    trauma:

Incidents:

Thoughts:

Feelings:

Icebergs are amazing structures that reveal only a small part of themselves above the water. Below the surface, they can have massive parts of themselves that we can't see. Sometimes, this is what it is like to talk about the hard stuff that has happened. Sometimes young people only tell a little bit of their story, keeping the rest of their story below the surface, untold. Why do you think someone might not share the things below the surface? If this is true for you, what do you need to be able to share what is below the surface? What might be in the way of sharing? If you are ready, use this iceberg image or draw your own iceberg.

## TRACKING TRAUMA PROCESSING

Date:
Memory/incident:


Upset scale (0–10, with 10 being most upset and 0 being not at all upset)
Prior to processing: __/10
After processing: __/10
Outcome:


Date:
Memory/incident:


Upset scale (0–10, with 10 being most upset and 0 being not at all upset)
Prior to processing: __/10
After processing: __/10
Outcome:


Date:
Memory/incident:

Upset scale (0–10, with 10 being most upset and 0 being not at all upset)
Prior to processing: __/10
After processing: __/10
Outcome:


Date:
Memory/incident:


Upset scale (0–10, with 10 being most upset and 0 being not at all upset)
Prior to processing: __/10
After processing: __/10
Outcome:

## PIECES OF MY STORY, PART 2: PUTTING IT ALL TOGETHER

You have done so much work to get to this part. You are strong, brave, and have developed important skills (e.g., using the stop, go, and slow signs and your resource cards, and learning to handle tricky trauma behaviors) that show me you are ready to deal with the hard stuff. It has been some time since you wrote the puzzle pieces. We will first check in to see if there are any new memories, incidents, or themes that you would like to add to the box of puzzle pieces. If so, we will take time for that now. Once finished, you are ready to take out one puzzle piece at a time and start to put your unique puzzle story together.

Here are the steps:

1. Open the box and choose a puzzle piece. Check to see if you would rate it differently on the upset scale from 0–10 than you did when you first wrote it down. If different, write the new number on the puzzle piece.
2. Draw or paint a picture of the hardest part of this puzzle piece.
3. Tell me in as much detail as possible about your picture (including the details of the trauma, even if you only drew how you felt during the trauma). You can let me know if you would like to write it out or if you would like me to.

    - Tell me about your picture.
    - What was the hardest part of this experience?
    - What happened just before this?
    - How did you get there?
    - What were you thinking as it happened?
    - What were you feeling as it happened?
    - What did you notice in your body as it happened?
    - After it was over, what did you think/feel/notice in your body?
    - When did you start feeling safe again?
    - What are you thinking/feeling/noticing now in your body?
    - Map out the thoughts, feelings and sensations on a body outline.
    - Is there anything your body wants to do right now (move, shake, stand)?

4. We know that we can't change what happened, but if you could magically change anything about this picture or incident, what would you change? If you would like, do that now to the image. If you could have anyone or anything that could have helped, protected, nurtured you, who would it be? Add that to your image if you like. What difference does that make now in your thoughts, feelings, and body? Check inside to see if you have any impulse to do something else to this image.
5. What rating would you give this puzzle piece now out of 10 on the upset scale? If less, what helped make it lower? If it is a 3 or higher, what could you do that will help make this one even less upsetting? What helps you feel even a little bit better? Let's experiment by giving something or someone in the image a voice. What would it say? Who needs to hear?
6. Put the piece back in the box and close the lid.
7. Do an art debrief if there is time and if it is needed. This is a chance to do art in response to any leftover yucky feelings or to expand and claim any positive feelings.

## RESOURCE/TRAUMA ART

### Resource Art

Create art that represents your inner resources and strengths that have brought you this far in your therapeutic work. These are the strengths that will get you through the next part of telling about the trauma. Here are some ideas of the strengths or qualities you have that might have helped you:

| | | | | |
|---|---|---|---|---|
| hopeful | curious | creative | determined | kind |
| brave | optimistic | helpful | energetic | positive |
| grateful | confident | good listener | reliable | leader |
| honest | wise | caring | happy | fair |

Once you have your art, tell me about your strength/quality. What do you notice in your body as you share? If there are good sensations, really notice what it is like to feel them and stay with them. What makes the sensations expand? As you notice the sensations in your body, is there anything you would like to change or add to your art?

### Trauma Art

Create art that represents the worse part of the trauma, using your puzzle pieces as a guide. Tell your story in as much detail as possible with your picture, including thoughts, feelings, and sensations. Notice your body as you tell your story (e.g., your breath, any movements in your body, tightening, shifting, or other sensations).

### Combine the Resource and Trauma Art

You are invited to bring these two pieces of art together. Really listen inside to see if this is something that you would like to do. You may not want to do this, and that is fine. If you would like to, you can do whatever you want to either art piece (e.g., rip, tear, cut, add to, take out of, recreate, transform). Is there a name for this new art piece? Is there a story, poem, or dialogue to go with it?

## TIME LINES AND ROAD MAPS

Do you realize just how brave you are and how much work you have completed so far? This intervention helps us to remember that the trauma that happened is in the past, and we have so much to look forward to. You might have your own ideas about how to do this, so please let me know your ideas. Here are two possibilities:

1. Time line

   - Draw one long line.
   - Start on one end of the line and write where you were born.
   - Place your puzzle pieces below the line at the approximate age they happened.
   - Think of positive life events and experiences, and write them above the line at the approximate age they happened.
   - Feel free to use symbols, colors, and images to represent the events and experiences.
   - Imagine your future and all the things you are hoping for, and add those to your time line.

2. Road map

   - Draw a long road.
   - Make the road as interesting as you like, as every road is different (e.g., is it a highway, country road, city road, or pathway).
   - Place your puzzle pieces along the road at the approximate time on your life's journey that they happened.
   - Think of all the resources and skills that you used to deal with these traumas and draw the resources next to the puzzle pieces.
   - Add positive life experiences that happened before and after the trauma.
   - Now, making sure your road is long enough, think of the amazing places that your road might lead you, both in the near future (e.g., saving money for a bicycle) or later in your life (e.g., becoming a dancer).

**Questions for both the time line and road map:**

   - Tell the story that goes with the time line/map in a simple way.
   - As you stand back, what do you notice the most?
   - What gives you hope when you look at your time line/map?
   - What do you notice in your body?
   - What are two things the experiences on your time line/map have taught you?
   - How have you become a stronger person because of them?

Decide if it would be helpful to have your caregiver to assist throughout this intervention, or have him/her come in at the end to see all your hard work. Your caregiver may be able to remember some of the positive experiences before and after the trauma that could be added. He/she may also see the ways you have become stronger because of the trauma.

## HONOR AND TRANSFORMATION

Now is the time to acknowledge and honor how brave you were to tell your story and to close this part of your work. There are two steps. First, you are invited to do something with your puzzle pieces. You can decide, together with your therapist, what it is that you would like to do. Your therapist might have some ideas as well. Some children like to stomp on or rip up the pieces and throw them away. One person ripped them, wet them with water, then rolled them into a small ball and buried it in the garden.

Second, the box that you created has done a great job of taking care of all the pieces of your story throughout this part of our work together. Now is the time to think of how this box might be changed from holding all the hard stuff to holding treasures. You might like to repaint or redecorate the box to change it in some way. Listen inside to what it is you would like to do.

# MY BODY, PART 1: WHAT MY BODY DID AT THE TIME OF THE TRAUMA

Now that you have worked through lots of the hard stuff, these next drawings focus on helping you repair your relationship with your body. Using symbols, words, and colors, show what your body did during the trauma. Include thoughts, feelings, sensations, movements, and behavior.

1

**MY BODY, PART 2: WHAT I WISHED MY BODY DID**

Use symbols, words, and colors to identify what you *wished* your body did or what you *wanted* your body to do during the trauma. Include thoughts, feelings, movements, sensations, and behavior.

1

## MY BODY, PART 3: MY BODY'S VOICE

Show through images, symbols, and words the different hurts your body, mind, and heart experienced during the trauma. Next, give a voice to the body parts that have been hurt. First, write what the body parts might have said at the time of the trauma. Second, write what the body parts might say now.

1

## MY BODY, PART 4: CAREGIVER AND CHILD SESSION

### Child Preparation

1. The child has completed the previous three interventions on the handout sheets or on the large body outline.
2. The child is ready and wanting to share this process with the caregiver. Address any concerns that come up for the child about sharing any parts of the work with the caregiver.

### Caregiver Preparation

1. Invite the caregiver to have the opportunity to have her own body traced in an individual session. Identify through images, color, words, symbols, and collage how she felt when she found out that her child was hurt (include thoughts, feelings, sensations).
2. Identify and add what her body would have wanted to do but didn't get the chance to do at the time of the child's trauma.
3. The caregiver is invited to imagine that her body parts have a voice. What would her body parts have wanted to say at the time, but couldn't because she didn't get the chance, didn't know, or couldn't act?
4. What would her body parts want to say now, if it is different? Use different colored markers for the then and now voices.
5. Debrief any concerns about witnessing her child's therapeutic work and identify the kind of support she will need during the process.

### Caregiver and Child Session

1. Child shares his image with the caregiver, going over all three body interventions. Ensure the process is slow enough to allow the opportunity for meaningful contact between child and caregiver. The caregiver is invited to listen to the child, asking for clarification if needed, using open-ended questions when appropriate. The goal is for the child to feel fully seen, heard, and understood in his experience.
2. Next, ask the child for permission for the caregiver to write on his drawing. Have the caregiver respond compassionately by writing on the child's drawing in response to the body's then and now voices (e.g., for then: I am so sorry you were scared/afraid/hurt; for now: I am happy you are safe now. I am so sorry I couldn't protect you). This process is an opportunity for the caregiver to acknowledge not having protected the child, even if she couldn't have known or stopped it.
3. The caregiver puts actual Band-Aids (or draws bandages) on the child's hurts on the body image.
4. If appropriate, the caregiver shares her image with the child. We pay close to attention to the child's response, slowing or stopping the process if needed to check in with the child as he witnesses his caregiver's image.

## MY EXPRESSIVE ARTS BRAVERY STORY

Now that the hard and brave work of addressing all the pieces of your puzzle is finished, you have the opportunity to close this part of our work together by creating your own original and unique expressive arts story. The theme of your story can be about your bravery. Not only have you lived through the trauma experiences, but you have faced them directly in our work together! Being brave does not mean one is fearless. Being brave means you are likely feeling scared and you still do what needs to be done. You have done just that in all of our work together.

Here are some other words that can relate to bravery:

courage
lionhearted
warrior
champion
determined
luminary
hardiness
spirited
inspiration

Your bravery story can have a title and a beginning, a middle, and an end. It can be done in any way you can imagine! Some young people have expressed their bravery stories in the following ways:

- Created a story book about a caged bird who escaped and found freedom
- Wrote a song about her strength as a girl
- Wrote a poem
- Wrote a six-word bravery story
- Acted out the courage of the hero in a story with hats and dress-up clothes
- Danced to a well-loved song about inner power

There are *so many* ways you could do this. Let's explore together! What ideas do you have?

# Appendix H
## Phase Four: Expressive Arts Interventions

### THERAPY REVIEW: WHAT'S LEFT TO DO

It has been some time since you have completed the handouts and questionnaires at the beginning of our work together. We will go over them together with your caregiver and highlight the progress that you have made and identify what is left for us to do. In particular, we will review the following three handouts:

- Feelings About the Trauma
- Trauma Self-Statements
- Thoughts, Feelings, and Beliefs Checklist

Identify any relationships that need support and what specific issues need to be addressed:

Other areas to be addressed:

## MY HEALING JOURNEY

Healing from the effects of trauma is like being on a journey. It requires that you have special equipment, skills, and people supporting you. You have been learning how to deal with the challenges you faced so far on your journey, including difficult thoughts, feelings, and sensations in your body.

### Healing Scale

Circle the number that represents where you were on your healing journey before you came to therapy. Put a square around the number that represents where you are now.

| Beginning | | | | | Middle | | | | | End |
|---|---|---|---|---|---|---|---|---|---|---|
| 0 | 1 | 2 | 3 | 4 | 5 | 6 | 7 | 8 | 9 | 10 |

### Creative Arts Ideas to Express Your Healing Journey

Create an image that represents your unique healing journey. You may know a special song that could represent your journey. We can listen to the song together. If you have a song, choose a line (or lines) from this song that really captures the meaning of your journey and use that line to write your own song/poem. If you have another idea, let me know.

## SELF-PORTRAITS 2

Way back in Phase One you did self-portraits. You are again invited to do self-portraits, but in a different way.

Self as an animal.
Self as a tree.
Self as a landscape.

After all three are done, create one self-portrait from all three pictures. This means you can, for example, cut out images, create a new image, or use bigger paper. The next step is to do a written response to the final image. The writing can be a dialogue between you and the image; it can give the image a voice; or it can be a story, poem, or song.

**SECRETS**

Secrecy is often a big part of sexual abuse. Sexual abuse usually happens when no one else is around, making sure it is kept a secret. Children can be told directly to keep it a secret through words or threats. For all kinds of reasons, children keep sexual abuse a secret even if not directly told to keep it a secret. On this body outline, show through images, colors, and/or words, you keeping the secret (add any thoughts, feelings, sensations). What was the hardest part about keeping the secret?

On this body outline, show through images, colors, and/or words, you telling your secret for the first time (add any thoughts, feelings, sensations). How is this image different from the one above? What was the hardest part about telling?

On this body outline, show through images, colors, and/or words, you now after telling the secret (add any thoughts, feelings, sensations). How is this image different, if at all, from the first two? If you had the chance to do this over, would you still tell? What was the best thing about telling?

# MY INSIDE/OUTSIDE STORIES

There are two stories that children can experience when they are sexually abused. Before anyone knows about what happened, there is the outside story of survival where everything looks "fine." Yet, there is another story that is often not shared or witnessed; that is the inside story. This is the story of how you managed to live two separate lives by pretending and/or not being able to acknowledge  the abuse and having to have a public relationship with the person who was hurting you while still knowing inside what the truth was.

Use an art form to create your inside story. This story tells about your inner world experience that no one else could see. Next, create your outside story: what you showed the world. The following is a list of ideas about how you could create these two stories.

- Create two masks, one for the inside story and one that represents the face you showed the world, or your outside story.
- Draw/paint images that represent your inside story and your outside story. How are they different? The same? What word best describes the mood of each?
- Give them a voice. Have a dialogue with each one, or between the two or some variation.
- Create a story or poem for each image. Is there a title?
- Using musical instruments, play the mood or sound of each story.
- Act out both stories using masks, puppets, hats, or other available props.

**Written Response**

**My Inside Story: The Truth of My Experience**

1. Where would I go in my mind when it was happening?
2. How did my body feel during the sexual abuse?
3. If parts of it felt good, how do I feel about my body feeling that way?
4. What would I tell myself about why it was happening?
5. How would I know when it would happen? Were there behaviors by the abuser that I came to know and recognize as signs the abuse would happen?

**My Outside Story: The Public Face**

1. How did I manage to face the abuser when the abuse wasn't happening?
2. How did I manage my feelings while we shared meals together or saw each other at gatherings?
3. What would I think/feel/sense when I looked into the abuser's eyes when the abuse was not happening?
4. What did I show the world on the outside?

## BEFORE THERAPY AND NOW

You have done so much work in our time together, and I see you have made many changes! In your favorite art form, create something that represents how you and/or your life were before you began therapy. Next, complete another art form that represents how you and/or your life are now. What are the three main differences between the before and now creations?

Your caregiver and I will also create how we saw you then and how we see you now. Our art is a reflection of our own thoughts and feelings and how we see the changes you have made.

## EVIDENCE OF GROWTH

It takes much courage, bravery, strength, hope, love, trust, and belief in yourself to look at the hard things. What have you learned because of the difficulties you have gone through? What is growing in you as we work on the hard stuff? Is your trust growing? Is your happiness blooming?

Here are some ideas to show evidence of the things you are growing inside:

1. Think of the things you are growing or want to grow inside and where they are in the growth cycle. Are they seeds, sprouts, or full-grown plants? Draw an image of each of them.
2. Decide what kind of seeds you would like to plant and nurture (e.g., flower, fruit, vegetable). Plant seeds in a small pot filled with soil and watch the seeds grow. What lessons do we learn over time as we watch the plants grow? What name could you give the plants? It could be a quality that you have come to know and want to develop in yourself or one that is already sprouting inside you.
3. Pick one of the qualities listed at the end of this handout, or choose your own word, that describes what you have learned from the difficult things you have gone through. Decide what kind of art you would like to create to express this quality. You might do one of the following:

   - Take a drum and find the rhythm that fits best with your words.
   - Draw a picture or create a clay sculpture about your quality.
   - Create a skit about this quality and act it out or use puppets to act out.
   - Create a poem or story about this quality, using the following prompts:

     Brave is. . . .
     I am growing my bravery for/because/to. . . .
     Brave looks like. . . .

   (For teens, you could personify this quality, bringing it alive as though it is human, through writing: "Courage likes to take walks in the safety of others. Courage knows she is strong because she. . . . ")

List of qualities:
balance, compassionate, leader, logical, joyful, practical, powerful, patient, quirky, courageous, helpful, self-reliant, curious, wise, open-hearted, open-minded, sincere, reliable, kind-hearted, trustworthy, honest, focused

What qualities are you growing in yourself?

# VICTIM–SURVIVOR–THRIVER

Victim - Survivor - Thriver Continuum

Process:

1. Identify what kinds of thinking/feeling/behaving/sensation go with each phase.

2. Draw each phase, as you see it, and identify where you are at this time.

3. Tell the story or create a poem about how you have now moved through one or more of these phases in your life.

4. What colors, symbols, or songs go best with each phase? You could create your own song.

5. Together with your therapist, walk around the room thinking about what a person who has been victimized might think, how they might walk, their pace, their body language, and their tone of voice. Walk around the room like that for a minute. Then walk like someone who has survived and is healing from the impact of the trauma. Finally, walk like a thriver. How might a thriver each carry his body, talk, or see the world? Create a gesture or movement that goes with each phase. Really exaggerate this experience. Stay with the sensations in the body that are evoked when you are in each pose. Be curious about the kind of behavior that goes with each phase.

6. Following are images that illustrate how a person in each phase might see the world. Do you agree or disagree? Could you show this in a different way?

## BEYOND THE TRAUMA: ACTION FIGURE AND DOLL MAKING

Sometimes, throughout the healing journey, it can seem as though the trauma will always be part of your life. Some people even say they feel as though the trauma contaminated all parts of their lives. Then there are times when you see evidence of how much you have grown through this experience. You are invited to create a doll that represents the part of you that has never been touched by the trauma. Give yourself permission to imagine this possibility. Begin to imagine moving forward in your life with all the strength and power of a thriver! This might be the part of you that has hopes and dreams, the part that carries your life force and/or your love for life. You can write on the dolls body or add anything you want to the doll. There might be a special note you write and wrap it around the body or stitch it on.

To get started, begin by imagining the possibilities previously described. As you consider this, notice whether any parts of you feel happy, peaceful, content, excited, fulfilled, full, light, or energetic. Invite your creativity to help you find ways to represent these feelings in the body of the doll. Try not to think too much about all the meaning. It is more important to have fun creating and bringing your doll to life.

Write the story of how this doll came to be in the world or simply the story that goes with your doll. As you work on the doll, notice whether you come up with a name for it.

### Options

Some young people prefer to create action figures or superheroes. Imagine which action figure would have meaning for you in your own experience of overcoming the trauma. Perhaps it has special powers to conquer whatever comes its way. It may have particular qualities, similar to you, that helped you get through the tough stuff.

Write the story that goes with this action figure. How did it come into existence? What is its purpose? Does it have a name?

## EXPRESSIVE ARTS REVIEW

We are almost finished with our work together! Today, we will take all your art work and display it around the room. You can decide if you would like your caregiver to witness your art work in this session.

Sit with your work and notice what comes up in your body and mind as you look at all your art work. Whoever is in the session will be invited to do an expressive arts response to your art work. Your caregiver (if present) and I will create art about how we are moved by all the work you have done. You can do whatever kind of art you would like in response to seeing all your art work. You might use some of your old pieces and create a new one, using scissors or ripping parts off that you want to keep or throw away. Follow your own knowing and impulse about what you want to do.

## CELEBRATION OR CEREMONY

Together we will create a celebration or ceremony that honors your healing journey thus far and marks the closing of therapy at this time. In preparation, think about what might be important to include in the celebration.

Songs:


Poems/stories:


Candles/incense/smudge:


Symbols of strength for the center table:


Photos you want to bring:


Photos you want taken:


Art you want to include:


Something you might want to make (e.g., bracelet, clay piece):


What you would like your therapist to do/say/bring:

**Celebration/Ceremony Process**

Opening:


Middle:


Closing:

# Appendix I
## Questions

**Questions That Connect to the Process of Art Making**

Where did you start with the process and what came next?
What materials were you drawn to or not drawn to?
Was there anything that caught your attention in the process?
Did you notice if there were times when you worked faster or slower?
What part of the process was most difficult, emotional, or fun for you?
How did you know you were finished?

**Questions That Connect Directly to the Art**

If this song had a shape, what would it be?
What happens when you stand back a little farther from your image?
What are you most drawn to in your story, in your image, or in the song?
What are you most curious about or most interested in?
If we could step inside the world of your image, what might you hear? See? Touch?
Is there any part of your art that feels incomplete, like there is more to do?

**Questions That Connect to the Body/Sensations**

What are you noticing right now in your body as you look at your image, or as you read your words, or as you play the drum?
Are there any parts of your art that you feel connected to in your body?
As you look at your art, do you notice any sensations in your body? Are there any sensations that have stayed with you over time? (You may offer some words for sensations such as warmth, tingling, flow, tight, prickly.)
Do you notice any parts of you that feel good and strong right now? If yes, where do you notice that? What happens if you stay with it? Does it move up or down?
Do you have any impulse to do something to your image (e.g., add to, rip, cut)?

**Questions That Connect to Feelings**

Is there a feeling that goes with or stands out for you in this (e.g., poem, dance, lyric)?
If yes, tell me more about this feeling.
Do you experience it in your body? If so, where?
Are there other feelings you notice?
Did your feelings shift at different points in the song?
What feelings do you experience when you stand back from the painting?

**Questions That Connect to Relationship**

How is it for you that I am witnessing your dance, your poem, your painting?

Do you need me to be farther away or closer? What happens when I do that?

How would you like me to be with your art? I could join in with creating; just listen, and witness; or I could ask questions of the art. Let me know what feels most needed right now.

Are there parts of the image or song that you feel most connected to? Least?

How would you describe the kind of relationship you have with your art?

Are there any surprises about that relationship?

# Appendix J
## Further Resources

### CHILDREN'S BOOKS

Alderfer, L. (2011). *Mindful monkey, happy panda*. Somerville, MA: Wisdom Publications.
Cave, K., & Maland, N. (2003). *You've got dragons*. Atlanta, GA: Peachtree Publishers.
DiOrio, R. (2010). *What does it mean to be present?* San Francisco, CA: Little Pickle Press.
Kranz, L. (2006). *Only one you*. New York, NY: Cooper Square Publishing.
Nhat Hanh, T. (2008). *Mindful movements: Ten exercises for well-being*. Berkeley, CA: Parallax Press.
Nhat Hanh, T. (2012). *A handful of quiet: Happiness in four pebbles*. Berkeley, CA: Plum Blossom Books.
Reynolds, P. (2004). *Ish*. Cambridge, MA: Candlewick Press.
Roegiers, M. (2010). *Take the time: Mindfulness for kids*. Washington, DC: Magination Press.
Saltzberg, B. (2010). *Beautiful oops*. New York: Workman Publishing.
Snel, E. (2013). *Sitting still like a frog: Mindfulness exercises for kids*. Boston: Shambhala Publishers.

### PDFS

Child and Adolescent Trauma Measures: A Review by The National Child Traumatic Stress Network. This is a review of 35 trauma instruments. Available at www.ncswtraumaed.org/wp-content/uploads/2011/07/Child-and-Adolescent-Trauma-Measures_A- Review-with-Measures.pdf
Keeping the Promise: Expressive Therapy for Working with Abused Children and Youth Mary Manning Centre: Child Abuse Prevention & Counselling Society of Greater Victoria. Available at www.mary-manningcentre.com/sites/default/files/assets/Keeping%20the%20Promise%20Handbook.pdf
Lowensteing, L. (Ed.). (2011). *Favourite therapeutic activities for children, adolescents, and families: Practitioners share their most effective interventions*. Champion Press. This book is available free in PDF form at www.lianalowenstein.com/e-booklet.pdf

### WEBSITES, VIDEOS, AND APPS

The Alert Program: A program to help children with various challenges, develop self-regulation skills. www.alertprogram.com
Canadian Foundation for Trauma Research and Education: A charity created to research and provide education in treating traumatic conditions. Training provided in Self-Regulation Therapy. www.cftre.com
Child Therapy Toys: Provides therapeutic toys, books, and other resources for child therapists. www.childtherapytoys.com/store/index.html
Child Trauma Institute: Training for clinicians and trauma information for clinicians, parents and adolescents. www.childtrauma.com
Focusing Institute: Go to the Children's Corner for articles and information on focusing with children. www.focusing.org
Mindful Kids: A website with resources for teaching mindfulness to children. http://mindfulkids.wordpress.com
Mindsight Institute: Dr. Dan Siegel's website with resources and trainings. www.mindsightinstitute.com

National Child Traumatic Stress Network: An information site that was established in 2000 to improve services for children and adolescents who have experienced or have been exposed to trauma. www.nctsn.org

The National Institute for Trauma and Loss in Children: A training institute that provides professionals with online and in-person training to help trauma-exposed children flourish. The website is replete with resources for clinicians, schools, and parents. www.starr.org/training/tlc

Sensory Awareness Foundation: Sensory awareness is a study and practice that promotes the experience of presence, responsiveness, and authenticity in our day-to-day lives. www.sensoryawareness.org

*Sesame Street* "Belly Breathe": This is a video of a catchy song to help children learn to belly breathe. www.youtube.com/watch?v=_mZbzDOpylA

Sesame Street iPhone App—Breathe, Think, Do with Sesame: Children learn self-regulation skills by helping a Sesame Street monster calm and learn to problem solve. https://itunes.apple.com/ca/app/breathe-think-do-with-sesame/id721853597?mt=8

Trauma Information Pages: A website providing information in the field of traumatic stress for researchers, clinicians, and students. www.trauma-pages.com

Wheel of Awareness by Dr. Dan Siegel. www.drdansiegel.com/resources/wheel_of_awareness/

Zones of Regulation by Leah Kuypers. www.zonesofregulation.com

## RESOURCE LIST

California Paper Goods: Art supplies including blank puzzles of all shapes and sizes. www.CPGbulksales.com

Coloring Castle: Free images to print for coloring, including mandalas. www.coloringcastle.com

Cope Cards: A deck of images that are used by trauma healers to open communication and explore self-expression. A manual comes with the cards offering a variety of interventions and structured uses for the cards. www.oh-cards-na.com/card-decks/cope

Dharma Trading Co: Art supply website where you can buy bendable dolls (muslin pre-stuffed dolls). www.dharmatrading.com

How to Grow a Mandala: A 5 minute YouTube video that illustrates a simple process of creating a mandala. https://www.youtube.com/watch?v=g16B64myG-E

Mazes to Print: A variety of free mazes to print and color. www.MazestoPrint.com

Musical Instruments: A place to buy musical instruments in Canada, the United States, and internationally. www.empire-music.com

OH Cards: Metaphoric associative cards that can be used in a variety of ways in therapeutic settings. www.oh-cards-institute.org

99 Sensory Activities for Any Child. http://mommypoppins.com/ny-kids/99-sensory-activities-for-any-child

100 Art Therapy Exercises for the Mind, Body, and Soul. www.nursingschools.net/blog/2011/01/100-excellent-art-therapy-exercises-for-your-mind-body-and-soul

# Index